my **revisi⏻n** notes

OCR A Level

PE

Keri Moorhouse

HODDER
EDUCATION
AN HACHETTE UK COMPANY

Acknowledgements

The Publishers would like to thank the following for permission to reproduce copyright material.

p.9 © EHStock/ iStock/Thinkstock; **p.10** *t* © Tom Griffiths/ZUMA Wire/ZUMAPRESS.com/ Alamy, *b* © jrroman/iStock/Thinkstock; **p.11** © Bojan656/iStock/Thinkstock; **p.12** © simonkr/ iStock/Thinkstock; **p.13** © Stockbyte/Thinkstock; **p.23** *l* © AntonioGuillem/iStock/Thinkstock, *c* © 36clicks/123RF, *r* © ALAN EDWARDS/Alamy Stock Photo; **p.44** © Crown copyright. Public Health England in association with the Welsh government, the Scottish government and the Food Standards Agency in Northern Ireland; **p.69** © jwyld/iStock/Thinkstock; **p.70** © guruXOOX/iStock/Thinkstock; **p.80** © Bupa UK, PRICE info graphic, http://www.bupa. co.uk/; **p.87** *l* © Aleksandar Kitanovic/123RF, *r* © Shariff Che'Lah/123RF; **p.113** © Ljupco/ iStock/Thinkstock.

Every effort has been made to trace all copyright holders, but if any have been inadvertently overlooked, the Publishers will be pleased to make the necessary arrangements at the first opportunity.

Although every effort has been made to ensure that website addresses are correct at time of going to press, Hodder Education cannot be held responsible for the content of any website mentioned in this book. It is sometimes possible to find a relocated web page by typing in the address of the home page for a website in the URL window of your browser.

Hachette UK's policy is to use papers that are natural, renewable and recyclable products and made from wood grown in sustainable forests. The logging and manufacturing processes are expected to conform to the environmental regulations of the country of origin.

Orders: please contact Bookpoint Ltd, 130 Milton Park, Abingdon, Oxon OX14 4SE. Telephone: +44 (0)1235 827720. Fax: +44 (0)1235 400401. Email education@bookpoint.co.uk Lines are open from 9 a.m. to 5 p.m., Monday to Saturday, with a 24-hour message answering service. You can also order through our website: www.hoddereducation.co.uk

ISBN: 978 1 5104 0521 9

© Keri Moorhouse 2017

First published in 2017 by
Hodder Education,
An Hachette UK Company
Carmelite House
50 Victoria Embankment
London EC4Y 0DZ

www.hoddereducation.co.uk

Impression number   10 9 8 7 6 5 4

Year   2022 2021 2020

Cover photo © Torsak Thammachote/123RF.com

Illustrations by Integra Software Services

Typeset by Integra Software Services Pvt. Ltd., Pondicherry, India

Printed in India

A catalogue record for this title is available from the British Library.

Get the most from this book

Everyone has to decide his or her own revision strategy, but it is essential to review your work, learn it and test your understanding. These Revision Notes will help you to do that in a planned way, topic by topic. Use this book as the cornerstone of your revision and don't hesitate to write in it – personalise your notes and check your progress by ticking off each section as you revise.

Tick to track your progress

Use the revision planner on page 4 to plan your revision, topic by topic. Tick each box when you have:
● revised and understood a topic
● tested yourself
● practised the exam questions, checked your answers and gone online to complete the quick quizzes.

You can also keep track of your revision by ticking off each topic heading in the book. You may find it helpful to add your own notes as you work through each topic.

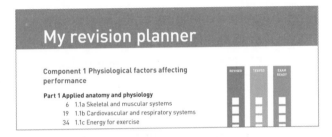

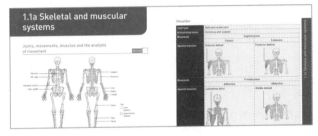

Features to help you succeed

Exam tips

Expert tips are given throughout the book to help you polish your exam technique and maximise your chances in the exam.

Typical mistakes

The author identifies the typical mistakes candidates make and explains how you can avoid them.

Now test yourself

These short, knowledge-based questions provide the first step in testing your learning. Answers are at the back of the book.

Definitions and key words

Clear, concise definitions of essential key terms are provided where they first appear.

Key words from the specification are highlighted in bold throughout the book.

Revision activities

These activities will help you to understand each topic in an interactive way.

Exam practice

Practice exam questions are provided for each topic. Use them to consolidate your revision and practise your exam skills.

Summaries

The summaries provide a quick-check bullet list for each topic.

Online

Go online to try out the extra quick quizzes at **www.hoddereducation.co.uk/myrevisionnotes**

My revision planner

Component 1 Physiological factors affecting performance

Part 1 Applied anatomy and physiology

Part 2 Exercise physiology

Part 3 Biomechanics

Component 2 Psychological factors affecting performance

Component 3 Socio-cultural issues in physical activity and sport

Now test yourself answers

Exam practice answers

REVISED   TESTED   EXAM READY

Countdown to my exams

6–8 weeks to go

- Start by looking at the specification — make sure you know exactly what material you need to revise and the style of the exam. Use the revision planner on page 4 to familiarise yourself with the topics.
- Organise your notes, making sure you have covered everything on the specification. The revision planner will help you to group your notes into topics.
- Work out a realistic revision plan that will allow you time for relaxation. Set aside days and times for all the subjects that you need to study, and stick to your timetable.
- Set yourself sensible targets. Break your revision down into focused sessions of around 40 minutes, divided by breaks. These Revision Notes organise the basic facts into short, memorable sections to make revising easier.

REVISED ☐

2–6 weeks to go

- Read through the relevant sections of this book and refer to the exam tips, exam summaries, typical mistakes and key terms. Tick off the topics as you feel confident about them. Highlight those topics you find difficult and look at them again in detail.
- Test your understanding of each topic by working through the 'Now test yourself' questions in the book. Look up the answers at the back of the book.
- Make a note of any problem areas as you revise, and ask your teacher to go over these in class.
- Look at past papers. They are one of the best ways to revise and practise your exam skills. Write or prepare planned answers to the exam practice questions provided in this book. Check your answers at the back of the book and try out the extra quick quizzes at **www.hoddereducation.co.uk/myrevisionnotes**
- Use the revision activities provided in this book to try out different revision methods. For example, you can make notes using mind maps, spider diagrams or flash cards.
- Track your progress using the revision planner and give yourself a reward when you have achieved your target.

REVISED ☐

One week to go

- Try to fit in at least one more timed practice of an entire past paper and seek feedback from your teacher, comparing your work closely with the mark scheme.
- Check the revision planner to make sure you haven't missed out any topics. Brush up on any areas of difficulty by talking them over with a friend or getting help from your teacher.
- Attend any revision classes put on by your teacher. Remember, he or she is an expert at preparing people for exam.

REVISED ☐

The day before the exam

- Flick through these Revision Notes for useful reminders, for example the exam tips, exam summaries, typical mistakes and key terms.
- Check the time and place of your exam.
- Make sure you have everything you need — extra pens and pencils, tissues, a watch, bottled water, sweets.
- Allow some time to relax and have an early night to ensure you are fresh and alert for the exam.

REVISED ☐

My exams

A Level PE Paper 1: Physiological factors affecting performance (2 hours)

Date:..

Time:..

Location:..

A Level PE Paper 2: Psychological factors affecting performance (1 hour)

Date:..

Time:..

Location:..

A Level PE Paper 3: Socio-cultural issues in physical activity and sport (1 hour)

Date:..

Time:..

Location:..

1.1a Skeletal and muscular systems

Joints, movements, muscles and the analysis of movement

REVISED

The diagram below shows the major bones of the skeleton.

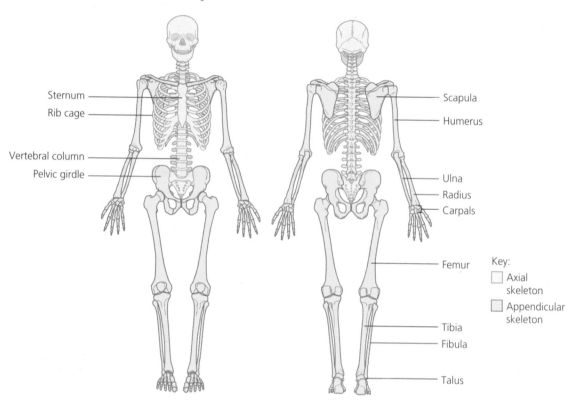

Figure 1.1.1 The bones of the axial and appendicular skeleton

The following table outlines the structure and function of a synovial **joint**.

> **Joint**: an area of the body where two or more bones articulate to create human movement.

Common features of a synovial joint	Structure	Function
Ligament	A tough band of slightly elastic connective tissue	Connects bone to bone and stabilises joints during movement
Synovial fluid	Lubricating liquid contained within the joint cavity	Reduces friction and nourishes articular cartilage
Articular cartilage	Smooth tissue which covers the surface of articulating bones	Absorbs shock and allows friction-free movement
Joint capsule	A fibrous sac with an inner synovial membrane	Encloses and strengthens the joint secreting synovial fluid
Bursa	A closed, fluid-filled sac found where tendons rub over bones	Reduces friction between tendons and bones

Planes of movement

If a person stands in an anatomical position, we describe their movement in three dimensions, based on three planes:

- sagittal plane (vertical – divides the body into left/right)
- frontal plane (vertical – divides the body into anterior/posterior)
- transverse plane (horizontal – divides the body into upper/lower).

Plane of movement: the description of three dimensional movements at a joint.

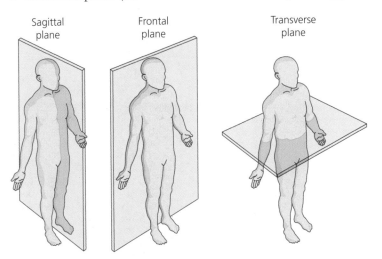

Figure 1.1.2 The three planes of movement

Movement patterns

The table below describes the three types of plane and their movements.

Plane	Movement pattern	Example
Sagittal plane	Flexion	Bending arm at elbow
	Extension	Straightening arm at elbow
	Dorsi-flexion	Pointing toes up
	Plantar flexion	Pointing toes down
Frontal plane	Abduction	Moving arm at shoulder away from midline
	Adduction	Moving arm at shoulder towards midline
Transverse plane	Horizontal extension	Moving arm at shoulder away from midline parallel to ground
	Horizontal flexion	Moving arm at shoulder towards midline parallel to ground
	Rotation	Movement whereby articulating bones turn about their longitudinal axis in a screwdriver action

The following table provides an overview of joint types and **movement patterns** possible.

Movement pattern: a description of the action taking place at a joint.

Joint type	Description	Plane of movement	Movement patterns possible
Ball and socket	Shoulder and hip	Sagittal plane	Flexion and extension
		Frontal plane	Abduction and adduction
		Transverse plane	Horizontal flexion, horizontal extension, medial and lateral rotation
Hinge	Elbow, knee and ankle	Sagittal plane	Flexion, extension, dorsi-flexion and plantar flexion
Condyloid	Wrist	Sagittal plane	Flexion and extension
		Frontal plane	Abduction and adduction

Shoulder

Joint type	Ball and socket joint	
Articulating bones	Humerus and scapula	
Movement	Sagittal plane	
	Flexion	Extension
Agonist muscles	Anterior deltoid	Posterior deltoid
Movement	Frontal plane	
	Adduction	Abduction
Agonist muscles	Latissimus dorsi	Middle deltoid
Movement	Transverse plane	
	Horizontal flexion	Horizontal extension
Agonist muscles	Pectoralis major	Posterior deltoid and teres minor

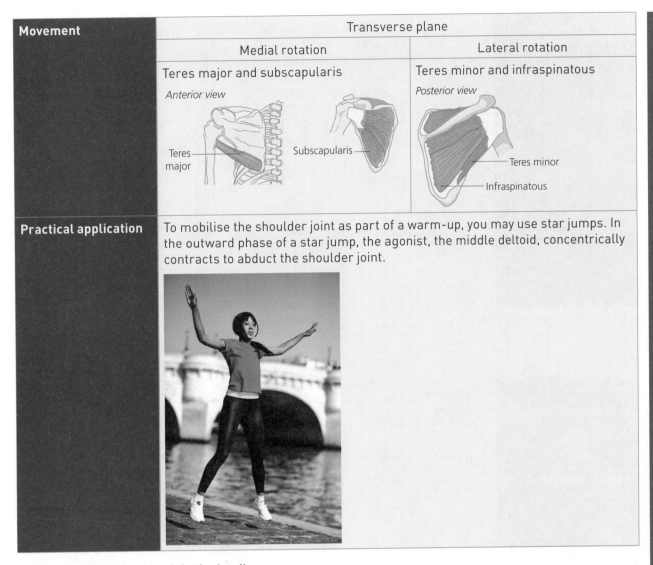

Movement	Transverse plane	
	Medial rotation	Lateral rotation
	Teres major and subscapularis *Anterior view* Teres major Subscapularis	Teres minor and infraspinatous *Posterior view* Teres minor Infraspinatous
Practical application	To mobilise the shoulder joint as part of a warm-up, you may use star jumps. In the outward phase of a star jump, the agonist, the middle deltoid, concentrically contracts to abduct the shoulder joint.	

Figure 1.1.3 The shoulder joint in detail

Elbow

Joint type	Hinge joint	
Articulating bones	Humerus, radius and ulna	
Movement	Sagittal plane	
	Flexion	Extension
Agonist muscles	Biceps brachii *Anterior view* Clavicle Scapula	Triceps brachii *Posterior view* Clavicle Scapula — Humerus Ulna

Practical application	The elbow joint is essential for creating power in a netball shot. In the preparation phase, the biceps brachii will concentrically contract to flex the elbow, lowering the ball. In the execution phase, the triceps brachii concentrically contracts to extend the elbow joint through a large range of motion to generate a large force to apply to the ball. 

Figure 1.1.4 The elbow joint in detail

Wrist

Joint type	Condyloid joint	
Articulating bones	Radius, ulna and carpals	
Movement	Sagittal plane	
	Flexion	Extension
Agonist muscles	Wrist flexors	Wrist extensors
Practical application	Basketball players concentrically contract the agonist, the wrist flexors, to flex the wrist as the ball is released in a jump shot. This enables backspin to be put on the ball, causing the ball to 'pop up' from the back board rather than roll off.	

Figure 1.1.5 The wrist joint in detail

Hip

Joint type	Ball and socket joint	
Articulating bones	Pelvic girdle and femur	
Movement	Sagittal plane	
	Flexion	Extension
Agonist muscles	Iliopsoas 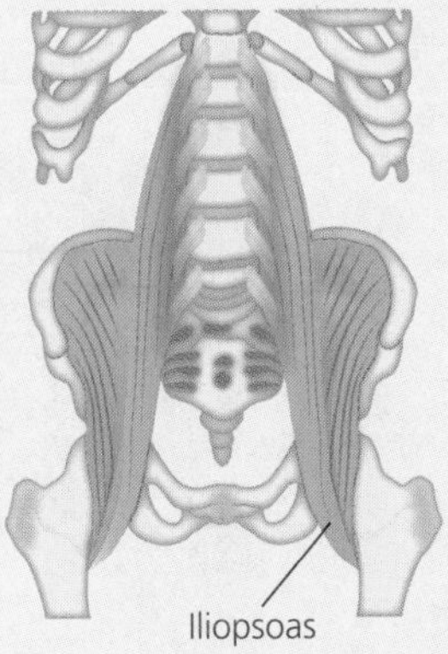 Iliopsoas	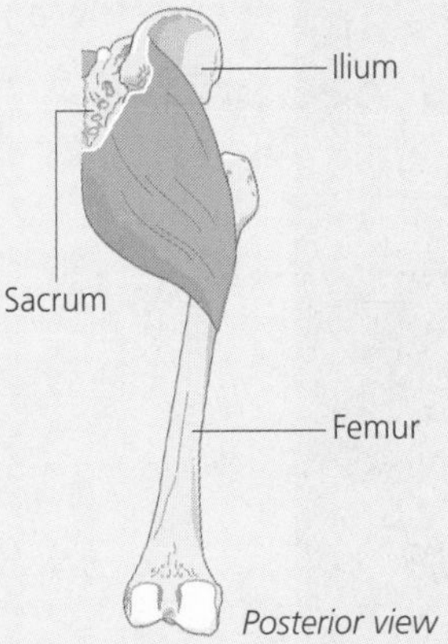 Gluteus maximus Ilium / Sacrum / Femur / *Posterior view*
Movement	Frontal plane	
	Adduction	Abduction
Agonist muscles	Adductor brevis, adductor longus and adductor magnus 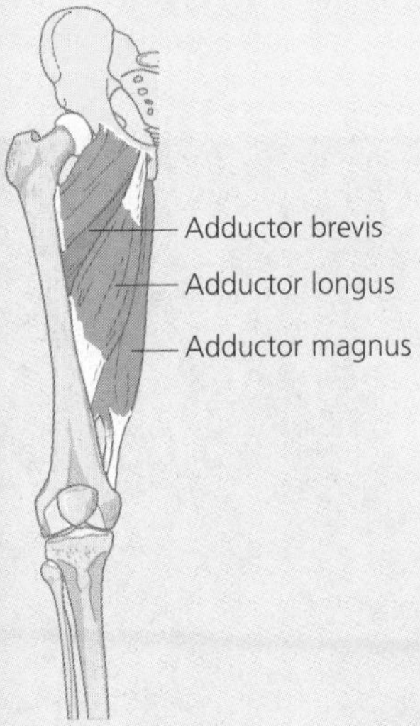 Adductor brevis / Adductor longus / Adductor magnus	Gluteus medius and gluteus minimus *Posterior view* / Gluteus medius / Gluteus minimus 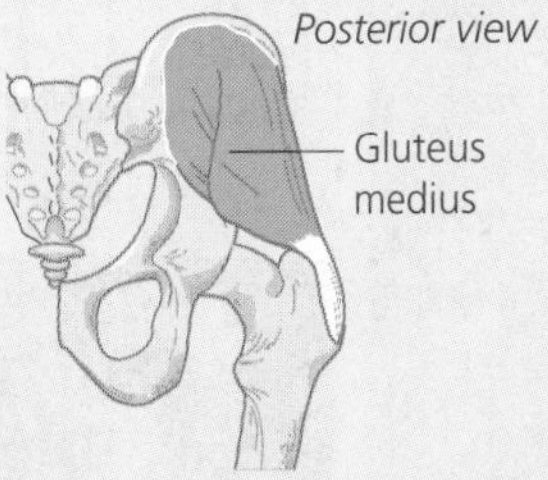 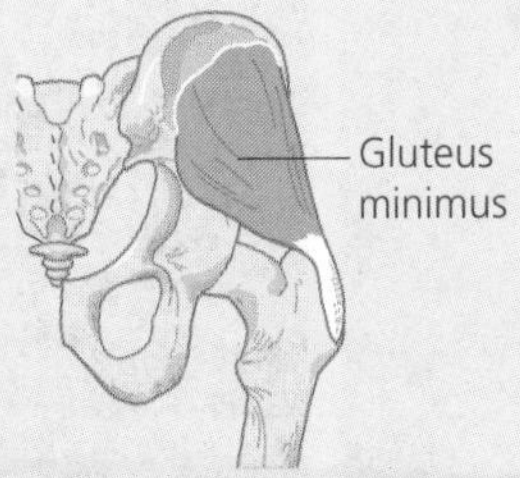
Movement	Transverse plane	
	Medial rotation	Lateral rotation
Agonist muscles	Gluteus medius and gluteus minimus (as above)	Gluteus maximus (as above)
Practical application	When Olympic weightlifting in the upward phase, the agonist, the gluteus maximus, will concentrically contract to create hip extension while the antagonist, the iliopsoas, co-ordinates the action. 	

Figure 1.1.6 The hip joint in detail

Knee

Joint type	Hinge joint	
Articulating bones	Femur and tibia	
Movement	Sagittal plane	
	Flexion	Extension
Agonist muscles	Biceps femoris, semitendinosus and semimembranosus (hamstring group)	Rectus femoris, vastus lateralis, vastus intermedius and vastus medialis (quadriceps group)
	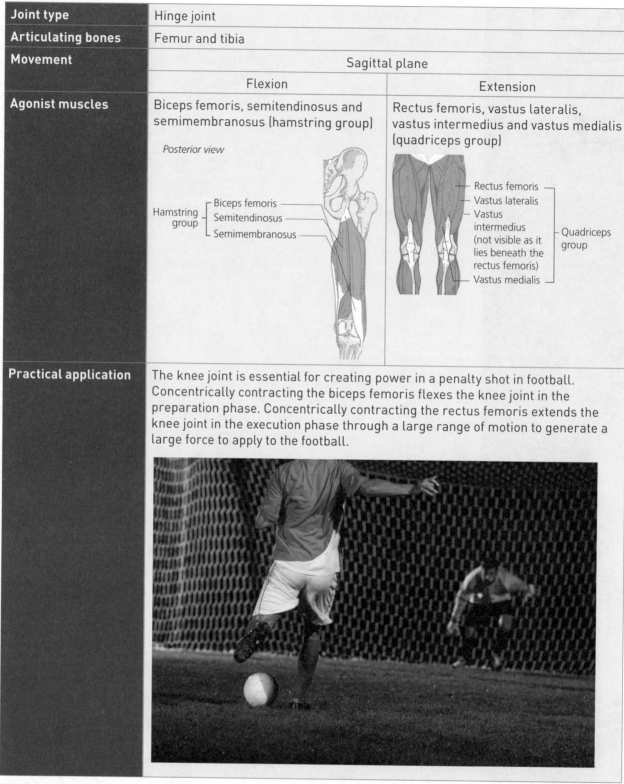	
Practical application	The knee joint is essential for creating power in a penalty shot in football. Concentrically contracting the biceps femoris flexes the knee joint in the preparation phase. Concentrically contracting the rectus femoris extends the knee joint in the execution phase through a large range of motion to generate a large force to apply to the football.	

Figure 1.1.7 The knee joint in detail

Ankle

Joint type	Hinge joint	
Articulating bones	Tibia, fibula and talus	
Movement	Sagittal plane	
	Dorsi-flexion	Plantar flexion
Agonist muscles	Tibialis anterior	Gastrocnemius and soleus
	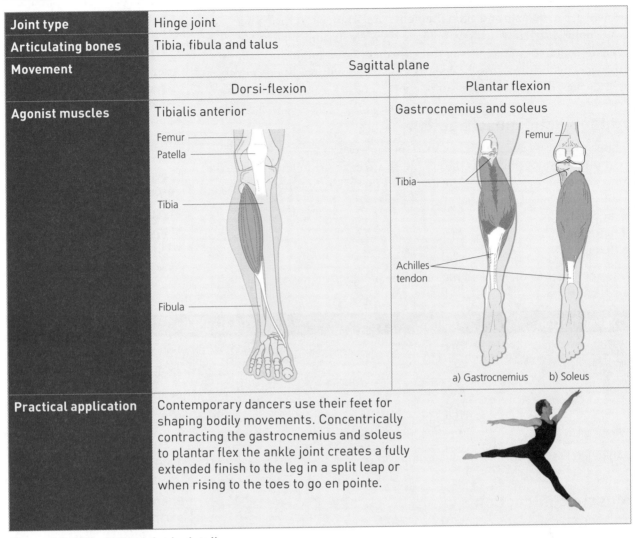	
Practical application	Contemporary dancers use their feet for shaping bodily movements. Concentrically contracting the gastrocnemius and soleus to plantar flex the ankle joint creates a fully extended finish to the leg in a split leap or when rising to the toes to go en pointe.	

Figure 1.1.8 The ankle joint in detail

Functional roles of muscles and types of contraction

REVISED

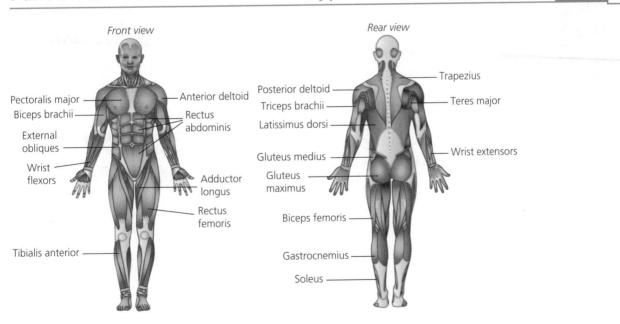

Figure 1.1.9 Major skeletal muscles

Muscles are made of up fibres which contain filaments. Thick filaments are made of the protein myosin and thin filaments are made of the protein actin. **Myosin and actin filaments** are arranged to form and overlapping pattern which gives muscle tissue its striated appearance. During contraction, the myosin thick filaments grab on to the actin thin filaments by forming cross bridges. An increased number of cross bridges will increased overall force of contraction.

Antagonistic muscle action

Muscles never work alone. They work in pairs or groups to produce co-ordinated movement. As the agonist shortens to create movement, the antagonist lengthens to co-ordinate the action. There are three main roles a muscle can adopt:

- **agonist**
- **antagonist**
- **fixator**

It is important to understand the common antagonistic muscle pairings for flexion.

> **Myosin and actin filaments**: proteins which form the contractile units of skeletal muscles.
>
> **Agonist**: a muscle responsible for creating movement at a joint. Also known as the prime mover.
>
> **Antagonist**: A muscle that opposes the agonist, providing a resistance for co-ordinated movement.
>
> **Fixator**: a muscle that stabilises one part of a body while another part moves.

Type of flexion	Agonist	Antagonist
Wrist	Wrist flexors	Wrist extensors
Elbow	Biceps brachii	Triceps brachii
Shoulder	Anterior deltoid	Posterior deltoid
Hip	Iliopsoas	Gluteus maximus
Knee	Biceps femoris (hamstring group)	Rectus femoris (quadriceps group)
Ankle (dorsi-flexion)	Tibialis anterior	Gastrocnemius and soleus

Muscle contraction

A muscle uses **energy** to create force by contracting. Muscles can contract in the different ways shown in the following table.

> **Energy**: the ability to perform work (measured in joules or calories).

Isotonic (changes length)	Concentric	Muscle shortens to produce tension, e.g. during the upward phase of a biceps curl, the biceps brachii concentrically contracts to lift weight
	Eccentric	Muscle lengthens to produce tension, e.g. during the downward phase of a biceps curl, the biceps brachii eccentrically contracts to lower weight
Isometric (does not change length)		Muscle contracts but does not change length and no movement is created, e.g. holding the press-up position still with arms and elbows extended

Exam tip

You will need to be able to put together all the information discussed so far to analyse different movements from sport. Always identify joint type, articulating bones, movement pattern, agonist muscle, antagonist muscle and contraction type.

Typical mistake

Always refer to a joint when identifying movement patterns, such as flexion at the shoulder. Arm flexion is too vague!

Revision activity

Choose a picture of an athlete playing sport. Complete a movement analysis of the knee, shoulder, hip, ankle, wrist and elbow. Refer to all the key points: joint type, articulating bones, movement pattern, agonist muscle, antagonist muscle and contraction type.

Skeletal muscle contraction

Skeletal muscle can only contract when stimulated by an electrical impulse sent from the central nervous system.

- Motor neurons are specialised cells which transmit nerve impulses rapidly to a group of muscle fibres. They have a cell body in the brain or spinal cord with an extending axon which branches to connect motor end plates to a group of muscle fibres.
- The motor neuron and its muscle fibres are termed the 'motor unit'.
- Sending the nerve impulse to the muscle fibres is an electrochemical process which relies on a nerve **action potential** to conduct the nerve impulse as a wave of electrical charge down the axon to the end plates.
- The point where the axon's motor end plates meet the muscle fibre is called the neuromuscular junction.
- There is a small gap between the motor end plates and muscle fibre called the synaptic cleft. An action potential cannot cross a synaptic cleft without the neurotransmitter acetylcholine (ACh).
- The neurotransmitter is secreted into the synaptic cleft to help the nerve impulse cross the gap.
- If enough of the neurotransmitter is secreted and the electrical charge is above threshold, a muscle action potential is created. This results in a wave of contraction down the muscle fibres.

> **Action potential**: positive electrical charge inside the nerves and muscles cells which conducts the nerve impulse down the motor neuron and into the muscle fibres.

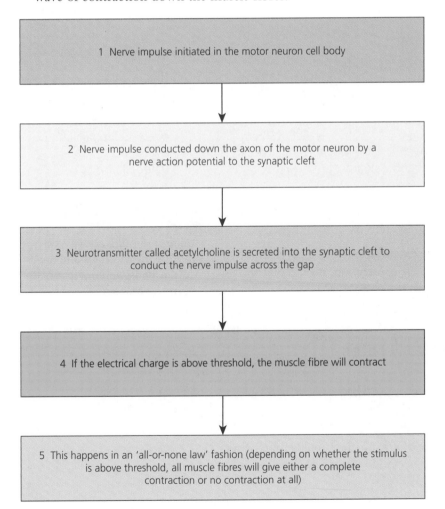

Figure 1.1.10 **Flow diagram summarising the role of a motor unit**

The flow diagram contains the following steps:

1. Nerve impulse initiated in the motor neuron cell body

2. Nerve impulse conducted down the axon of the motor neuron by a nerve action potential to the synaptic cleft

3. Neurotransmitter called acetylcholine is secreted into the synaptic cleft to conduct the nerve impulse across the gap

4. If the electrical charge is above threshold, the muscle fibre will contract

5. This happens in an 'all-or-none law' fashion (depending on whether the stimulus is above threshold, all muscle fibres will give either a complete contraction or no contraction at all)

Muscle fibre type and exercise intensity

The strength of muscular contraction is dependent on the number of motor units recruited by the brain. The greater the number of motor units, the greater the force. As shown in the following table, any one muscle contains three fibre types; the percentage of each fibre is dependent on genetics. The table outlines the structural and functional characteristics of the three muscle fibre types.

Fibre type	Slow oxidative	Fast oxidative glycolytic	Fast glycolytic
Structural characteristics			
Neuron size	Small	Large	Large
Fibres per neuron	Few	Many	Many
Capillary density	High	High	Low
Mitochondria density	High	Moderate	Low
Myoglobin density	High	Moderate	Low
Phosphocreatine store	Low	High	High
Functional characteristics			
Speed of contraction	Slow	Fast	Fast
Force of contraction	Low	High	High
Fatigue resistance	High	Moderate	Low
Aerobic capacity	High	Moderate	Low
Anaerobic capacity	Low	Moderate	High
Sporting application			
Highest percentage of fibres	Endurance athletes: ● marathon ● triathlon ● cross-country skiing	High-intensity athletes: ● 800–1500 m ● 200 m freestyle	Explosive athletes: ● 60–100 m sprinting ● javelin ● long jump

Combining motor units and muscle fibre type indicates how the nervous system can produce movement for different activity requirements.

Small motor neurons stimulate relatively few muscle fibres. This is important for activities which require sustained muscle contraction, such as posture.

Large motor neurons stimulate many large muscle fibres. This is important for brief exertions of large force, such as jumping and throwing.

Revision activity

Using the table above, copy out the information and colour code/add diagrams to help you learn it.

Muscle fibre type and recovery rates

Slow oxidative (SO) fibres

Key points
- These are recruited and provide energy for sub-maximal aerobic work.
- They contract intermittently to give overall low force of contraction.
- Individual fibres will recover very quickly.

Application for training and recovery

- 1:1 or 1:0.5 work:relief ratio, for example 3 minutes moderate-intensity running with relief of 90 seconds.
- Training can be performed on a daily basis, as fibre damage is not associated with low-intensity training.
- Low-intensity use of SO fibres is advised between heavy weight training sessions to increase blood flow and enhance the healing process.

Fast oxidative glycolytic (FOG) fibres

Key points

- These are designed to produce a large amount of force quickly.
- They have capacity to resist fatigue.

Application for training and recovery

- They are more likely to be used in high-intensity activities lasting a few minutes, for example the 800 m.

Fast glycolytic (FG) fibres

Key points

- These are recruited in the last 2–10 seconds of contraction, when maximal efforts are needed quickly.
- This will be accompanied by eccentric muscle fibre damage, which causes **DOMS** (delayed onset muscle soreness) felt 24–48 hours after exercise.

> **Delayed onset muscle soreness (DOMS):** pain and stiffness felt in the muscles, which peaks 24–72 hours after exercise, associated with eccentric muscle contraction.

Application for training and recovery

- If fast glycolytic fibres have been used to exhaustion, they take 4–10 days to recover.
- Maximal weight training sessions should leave 48 hours before using the same muscle group again.

Now test yourself

TESTED

1 Identify the agonist and antagonistic pairings for flexion in the:
   a) wrist
   b) elbow
   c) shoulder
   d) hip
   e) knee
   f) ankle (dorsi-flexion)
2 What are the three planes of movement and how do they divide the body?
3 What are the roles of the agonist, antagonist and fixator?
4 What is the difference between concentric and eccentric muscle contraction?
5 What makes a motor unit?
6 Name the three types of muscle fibre.

Answers on page 167

Exam practice

1 State the movement at the ankle joint, of the striking foot, at the point of contact and name the agonist muscle responsible for creating the movement. [2]
2 An athlete performs an upright row. Complete the table (A, B, C, D) for the athlete's shoulder joint while the bar is being raised. [4]

Joint	Joint type	Movement	Agonist	Antagonist	Type of muscular contraction
Shoulder	A	Abduction	B	C	D

3 Explain the role of the triceps brachii in both the upward and downward phases of a press-up. [4]
4 Explain how a performer's mix of muscle fibre types might influence their reasons for choosing to take part in particular types of physical activity. [4]

Answers on page 174

Summary

You should now have an understanding of:
- joints, movements and muscles – including analysis of movement with reference to: joint type, movement produced, agonist and antagonist muscles involved, and type of muscle contraction taking place, at the:
  - shoulder
  - elbow
  - wrist
  - hip
  - knee
  - ankle
- planes of movement: sagittal, frontal, transverse
- roles of muscles: agonist, antagonist, fixator
- types of contraction: isotonic, concentric, eccentric, isometric
- the structure and role of motor units in skeletal muscle contraction
- nervous stimulation of the motor unit: motor neuron, action potential, neurotransmitter, 'all-or-none' law
- muscle fibre types: slow oxidative, fast oxidative glycolytic, fast glycolytic
- recruitment of different fibre types during exercise of differing intensities and during recovery.

1.1b Cardiovascular and respiratory systems

The cardiovascular system at rest

REVISED

The cardiovascular system refers to the heart, blood and blood vessels. At the core is the heart, a dual pump moving blood through two separate circuits: the **pulmonary circuit** and the **systemic circuit**.

> **Pulmonary circuit**: circulation of blood through the pulmonary arteries to the lungs and pulmonary veins back to the heart.
>
> **Systemic circuit**: circulation of blood through the aorta to the body and vena cavae back to the heart.

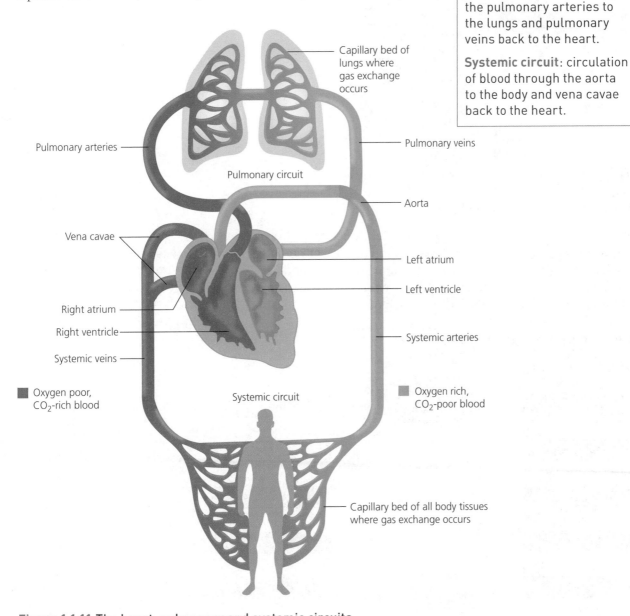

Capillary bed of lungs where gas exchange occurs

Pulmonary arteries

Pulmonary veins

Pulmonary circuit

Aorta

Vena cavae

Left atrium

Left ventricle

Right atrium

Right ventricle

Systemic arteries

Systemic veins

■ Oxygen poor, CO_2-rich blood

Systemic circuit

■ Oxygen rich, CO_2-poor blood

Capillary bed of all body tissues where gas exchange occurs

Figure 1.1.11 The heart: pulmonary and systemic circuits

The structure of the heart

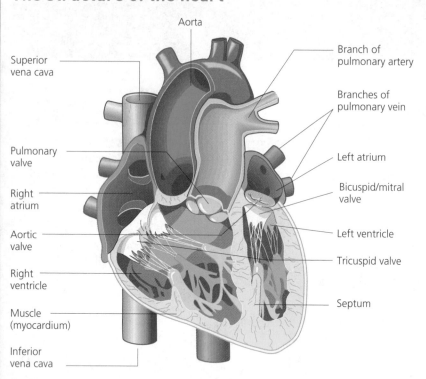

Figure 1.1.12 The structure of the heart

The left side of the cardiac muscle has a thicker muscular wall than the right side, allowing it to forcefully contract to circulate **oxygenated blood** through the systemic system to the muscles and organs. The atrioventricular (bicuspid and tricuspid) valves and semilunar (aortic and pulmonary) valves prevent the backflow of blood.

> **Oxygenated blood**: blood saturated with oxygen and nutrients, such as glucose.

The path of blood through the heart

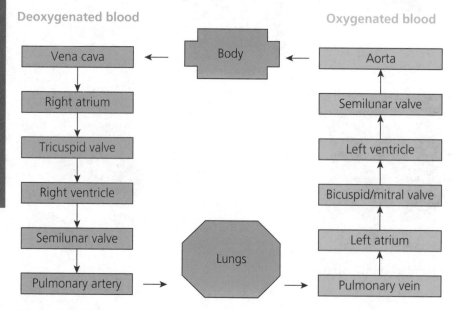

Figure 1.1.13 The pathway of blood

The conduction system

The cardiac muscle is **myogenic**. The **conduction system** is a set of five structures which pass the electrical impulse through the cardiac muscle:

1 SA node – this generates electrical impulses, causing atria walls to contract. It is known as the 'pacemaker' and determines heart rate.
2 AV node – this collects the impulse and delays it by 0.1 seconds to allow the atria to finish contracting.
3 Bundle of His – located in the septum, this splits the impulse in two, ready to be distributed to the ventricles.
4 Bundle branches – these carry the impulse to the base of each ventricle.
5 Purkinje fibres – these distribute the impulse through the ventricle walls, causing them to contract.

> **Revision activity**
>
> Draw a flow diagram to help you learn the conduction system. Add small illustrations to each structure to create a visual learning medium or create a mnemonic to help you remember the order – SABBP.

The cardiac cycle

The cardiac cycle refers to cardiac muscle contraction and the movement of blood through its chambers. One complete cardiac cycle is a single heartbeat. At rest, a complete cycle takes approximately 0.8 seconds. It has two phases: **diastole** and **systole** as described in the table below.

Diastole (relaxation)	• Relaxation of the atria and ventricles means lower pressure within the heart. • Blood then passively flows through the atria and into the ventricles. • AV valves are open, allowing blood to move freely from the atria to the ventricles. • Semilunar valves are closed at this time.
Systole (contraction)	**Atrial systole** • Atria contract, forcing blood into the ventricles. **Ventricular systole** • Ventricles contract. • AV valves close. • Semilunar valves open. • Blood is pushed out of the ventricles and into the large arteries leaving the heart.

Myogenic: the capacity of the heart to generate its own electrical impulse, which causes the cardiac muscle to contract.

Conduction system: a set of structures in the cardiac muscle which create and transmit an electrical impulse, forcing the atria and ventricles to contract.

Diastole: the relaxation phase of cardiac muscle where chambers fill with blood.

Systole: the contraction phase of cardiac muscle where blood is forcibly ejected into the aorta and pulmonary artery.

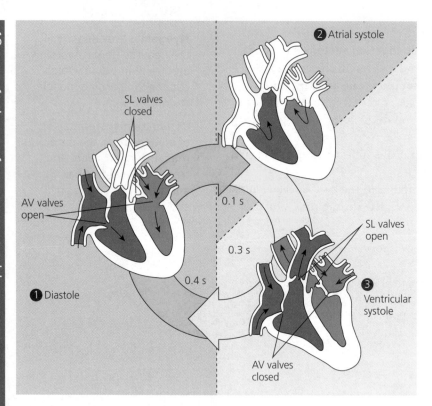

Figure 1.1.14 The stages of the cardiac cycle

Heart rate, stroke volume and cardiac output

Key term	Definition	Typical resting value
Heart rate (HR)	The number of times the heart beats per minute	72 bpm
Stroke volume (SV)	The amount of blood ejected from the left ventricle per beat	70 ml
Cardiac output (CO)	The amount of blood ejected from the left ventricle per minute: HR × SV = CO	5 l/min
Bradycardia	A resting heart rate below 60 bpm	< 60 bpm
Maximum heart rate	Calculated by subtracting your age from 220	220 – age = HRmax (bpm)

The following table compares HR, SV and CO of an untrained and a trained individual at rest.

	HR	SV	Q
Untrained	70–72 bpm	70 ml	5 l/min
Trained	50 bpm	100 ml	5 l/min

Cardiovascular system during exercise and recovery

As we start to exercise, the demand for oxygen of the muscles increases rapidly. It is the role of the cardiovascular system to increase oxygenated blood flow to the muscles.

Heart rate response to exercise

HR increases in proportion to the intensity of exercise until we reach HRmax, as shown in Figure 1.1.15.

> **Exam tip**
>
> It can be helpful to include a sketch of a graph in an answer. Always label axes and take care to plot the resting value (not at zero).

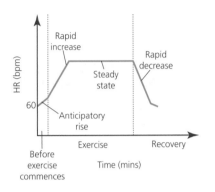

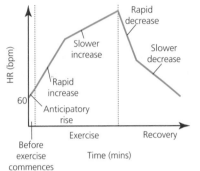

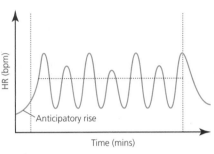

a) HR response to sub-maximal (aerobic) exercise

b) HR response to maximal (anaerobic) exercise

c) HR response to fluctuating intensities of exercise

Figure 1.1.15 HR response to exercise of different intensities

Stroke volume response to exercise

SV increases in proportion to exercise intensity until a plateau is reached at approximately 40–60 per cent of working capacity. This corresponds to **sub-maximal** intensity exercise.

SV is able to increase due to:
- increased **venous return** (due to skeletal muscle pump)
- the **Frank-Starling mechanism** (Starling's law).

SV reaches a plateau during sub-maximal intensity because increased HR towards **maximal** intensities does not allow enough time for the ventricles to fill completely in the diastolic phase, limiting the Frank-Starling mechanism.

> **Sub-maximal**: a low-to-moderate intensity of exercise within a performer's aerobic capacity.
>
> **Venous return**: the return of the blood to the right atria through the veins.
>
> **Frank-Starling mechanism**: increased venous return leads to increased SV, due to an increased stretch of the ventricular walls and therefore force of contraction.
>
> **Maximal**: a high intensity of exercise above a performer's aerobic capacity that will induce fatigue.

Cardiac output response to exercise

CO increases in line with exercise intensity and plateaus during maximal exercise.

This table shows average HR, SV and CO at rest and during sub-maximal and maximal intensity exercise for an untrained performer.

Untrained performer	Rest	Sub-maximal intensity	Maximal intensity
Heart rate	70–72 bpm	100–130 bpm	220 – age
Stroke volume	70 ml	100–120 ml	100–120 ml
Cardiac output	5 l/min	10–15 l/min	20–30 l/min

By comparison, this table shows HR, SV and CO at rest and during sub-maximal and maximal intensity exercise for a trained athlete.

Trained athlete	Rest	Sub-maximal intensity	Maximal intensity
Heart rate	50 bpm	95–120 bpm	220 – age
Stroke volume	100 ml	160–200 ml	160–200 ml
Cardiac output	5 l/min	15–20 l/min	30–40 l/min

Heart rate, stroke volume and cardiac output in recovery

- SV is maintained during the early stages of recovery, as HR rapidly reduces. This will maintain blood flow and the removal of waste products while lowering the stress and workload on the cardiac muscle.
- CO – in recovery, there is a rapid decrease followed by a slower decrease to resting levels.

Regulation of heart rate during exercise

When a situation arises where the heart rate needs to increase or decrease, the brain gets involved. This is known as cardiac control. The **cardiac control centre (CCC)** is:

- controlled by the autonomic nervous system (ANS) and determines the firing of the SA node
- located in the medulla oblongata of the brain
- responsible for regulating the heart via motor nerves; the **sympathetic nervous system** increases HR via the accelerator nerve, while the **parasympathetic nervous system** decreases HR via the vagus nerve.

There are three factors which control the activity of the CCC: neural, intrinsic and hormonal, as shown in the following table (page 25).

Cardiac control centre (CCC): a control centre in the medulla oblongata responsible for HR regulation.

Sympathetic nervous system: part of the autonomic nervous system responsible for increasing HR, specifically during exercise.

Parasympathetic nervous system: part of the autonomic nervous system responsible for decreasing HR, specifically during recovery.

Neural control	Proprioceptors	In muscles, tendons and joints, these inform the CCC that movement has increased.
	Chemoreceptors	Located in the aorta and carotid arteries, these detect a decrease in blood pH due to an increase of lactic acid and CO_2.
	Baroreceptors	Located in blood vessel walls, these inform the CCC of increased blood pressure.
Intrinsic control	Temperature	Changes will affect blood viscosity and the speed of nerve impulse transmission.
	Venous return	Changes will affect the stretch in ventricle walls, force of contraction and therefore SV.
Hormonal control	Adrenaline and noradrenaline	These are released from the adrenal glands and increase SV and HR.

The vascular system

The dense network of blood vessels and the blood they carry form the vascular system. Blood is approximately 45 per cent cells and 55 per cent plasma.

Blood vessels

Arteries and arterioles	Capillaries	Veins and venules
• These carry oxygenated blood from the heart to muscles and organs. • They contain blood under high pressure. • They have a large layer of smooth muscle and elastic tissue. • Smooth muscle can **vasodilate** and **vasoconstrict**, regulating blood flow and pressure. • Arterioles have a ring of smooth muscle surrounding the capillary bed, called pre-capillary sphincters. These dilate and constrict to control blood flow.	• Capillary walls are one cell thick. • This is where gas exchange takes place. Oxygen passes through the capillary wall and into the tissues; carbon dioxide passes from the tissues into the blood through the capillary wall.	• These carry **deoxygenated blood** from the muscles and organs back to the heart. They have thin walls. • They have a smaller layer of smooth muscle allowing them to **venodilate** and **venoconstrict**. • They contain blood under low pressure. • They have one-way pocket valves to prevent blood flowing backwards against gravity.

Venous return mechanisms

At rest, blood pressure and the structure of the veins maintain venous return. However, during exercise more oxygenated blood is needed, therefore a far greater venous return is required in order to increase SV and CO. During exercise, there are additional mechanisms that aid venous return:
• Pocket valves – these are located within the veins and prevent the backflow of blood.
• Smooth muscle – the wall of each vein contains smooth muscle which venoconstricts, helping push the blood back towards the heart.
• Gravity – blood from the upper body, above the heart, is aided by gravity in its return to the heart.
• Muscle pump – many veins are situated between skeletal muscles; during exercise, these muscles squeeze on the veins and help push the blood back towards the heart.
• Respiratory pump – this helps return blood in the thoracic cavity and abdomen back to the heart. While exercising, we inspire and expire faster and more deeply; this rapidly changes the pressure within the thorax between high and low to help to squeeze the blood in the area back to the heart.

Vasodilation: widening of arteries, arterioles and pre-capillary sphincters.

Vasoconstriction: narrowing of arteries, arterioles and pre-capillary sphincters.

Deoxygenated blood: blood depleted of oxygen and saturated with carbon dioxide and waste products.

Venodilation: widening of the veins and venules.

Venoconstriction: narrowing of the veins and venules.

Redistribution of cardiac output during exercise and recovery

Vascular shunt mechanism

As we start to exercise, our muscles demand more oxygen. As a result, blood flow is diverted to working muscles and away from non-essential organs. This is called the **vascular shunt mechanism**.

At rest:
- **arterioles** to organs vasodilate, increasing blood flow; arterioles to muscles vasoconstrict to limit blood flow
- **pre-capillary sphincters** vasodilate, opening up the capillary beds to allow more blood flow to the organ cells; pre-capillary sphincters of capillary beds of muscle vasoconstrict.

During exercise:
- arterioles to organs vasoconstrict, decreasing blood flow; arterioles to muscles vasodilate to increase blood flow
- pre-capillary sphincters vasoconstrict, closing up the capillary beds to decrease blood flow to the organ cells; pre-capillary sphincters of capillary beds of muscle vasodilate.

Vasomotor control

- The **vasomotor control centre (VCC)** is located in the medulla oblongata of the brain.
- The smooth muscle in the walls of arterial blood vessels is always in a slight state of constriction, known as **vasomotor tone**.
- The VCC alters the level of stimulation sent to the arterioles and pre-capillary sphincters at different sites in the body, thus allowing the vascular shunt mechanism.

The VCC receives information from:
- chemoreceptors – chemical changes such as CO_2 and lactic acid
- baroreceptors – pressure changes on arterial walls.

In receipt of this information, sympathetic stimulation is either increased or decreased:
- Increased sympathetic stimulation limits blood flow to an area.
- Decreased sympathetic stimulation increases blood flow to an area.

Vascular shunt mechanism: the redistribution of cardiac output around the body from rest to exercise which increases the percentage of blood flow to the skeletal muscles.

Arterioles: blood vessels carrying oxygenated blood from the arteries to the capillary beds, which can vasodilate and vasoconstrict to regulate blood flow.

Pre-capillary sphincters: rings of smooth muscle at the junction between arterioles and capillaries, which can dilate or constrict to control blood flow through the capillary bed.

Vasomotor control centre (VCC): the control centre in the medulla oblongata responsible for cardiac output distribution.

Vasomotor tone: the partial state of smooth muscle constriction in the arterial walls.

Now test yourself

TESTED ☐

1 Define heart rate, stroke volume and cardiac output.
2 Name the two phases of the cardiac cycle.
3 Name, in order, the features through which the electrical impulse in the heart travels.
4 Sketch a graph showing the heart rate response to sub-maximal exercise.
5 Sketch a graph showing heart rate response to maximal exercise.
6 Where are the CCC and VCC located?
7 Name the five mechanisms of venous return.
8 Which factors affect the activity of the CCC?

Answers on page 167

The respiratory system at rest

The respiratory system has two main functions:

1 pulmonary ventilation – breathing of air into (inspiration) and out of (expiration) the lungs.

2 **gaseous exchange**
   a) external respiration – exchange O_2 and CO_2 between the lungs and blood
   b) internal respiration – exchange of O_2 and CO_2 between blood and the muscle tissues (cells).

> **Gaseous exchange**: the movement of oxygen from the alveoli into the blood stream and carbon dioxide from the blood stream into the alveoli.
>
> **Alveoli**: clusters of tiny air sacs covered in a dense network of capillaries which together serve as the external site for gaseous exchange.

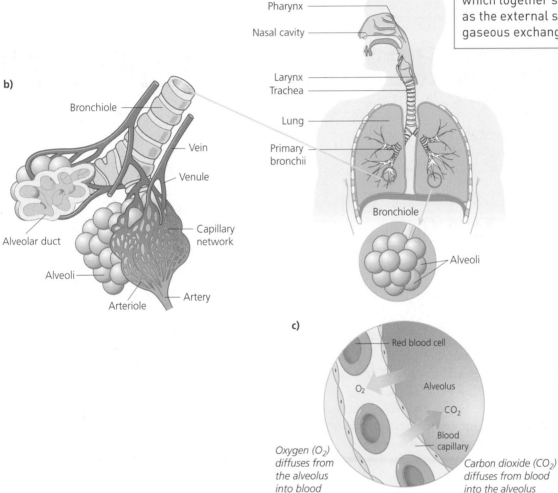

Figure 1.1.16 The respiratory system: a) the pathway of air through the respiratory organs, b) the dense capillary network on the surface of the alveoli, and c) gaseous exchange at the alveolar–capillary site

Gas transport

The following table outlines how O_2 and CO_2 are transported in the body.

Gas	How is it transported?
O_2	97% within haemoglobin (HbO_2)
	3% within blood plasma
CO_2	70% dissolved in water carried as carbonic acid
	23% within haemoglobin ($HbCO_2$)
	7% dissolved in blood plasma

Breathing rate, tidal volume and minute ventilation

Key term	Definition	Resting value (untrained)	Maximal value (untrained)	Resting value (trained)	Maximal value (trained)
Breathing rate (f)	The number of inspirations or expirations per minute	12–15 breaths/min	40–50 breaths/min	11–12 breaths/min	50–60 breaths/min
Tidal volume (TV)	The volume of air inspired or expired per breath	500 ml	2.5–3 litres	500 ml	3–3.5 litres
Minute ventilation (VE)	The volume of air inspired or expired per minute: TV × f = VE (tidal volume × breathing rate = minute ventilation)	6–7.5 l/min	100–150 l/min	5.5–6 l/min	160–210 l/min

During exercise

- Breathing rate increases in proportion to exercise intensity up to a maximum of 50–60 breaths per minute.
- Tidal volume increases initially in proportion to exercise intensity at sub-maximal intensities up to approximately 3 litres.
- Minute ventilation increases in line with exercise intensity. During sustained sub-maximal intensity exercise, minute ventilation can plateau as we reach a comfortable steady state.

Mechanics of breathing at rest and during exercise

	At rest	During exercise

Inspiration	**Active process**
	● External intercostal muscles between the ribs contract, pulling the chest walls up and out.
	● The diaphragm muscle below the lungs contracts and flattens, increasing the size of the chest.
		Active process
		● In addition to the external intercostal muscles and diaphragm:
		  ○ the sternocleidomastoid lifts the sternum
		  ○ the scalene and pectoralis minor contract and lift the ribs more.
		● Effect – the volume of the thoracic cavity increases, creating a larger concentration gradient between inside the lungs and outside the body, therefore more air enters the lungs more quickly.

Expiration	**Passive process**
	● External intercostal muscles between the ribs relax so that the chest walls move in and down.
	● The diaphragm muscle below the lungs relaxes and bulges up, reducing the size of the chest.
		Active process
		● In addition to the external intercostal muscles and diaphragm:
		  ○ internal intercostal muscles contract and pull the ribs down and in
		  ○ the rectus abdominus contracts and pushes the diaphragm up.
		● Effect – a decrease in volume of the thoracic cavity increases pressure in the lungs, therefore air is forced out quickly because of the larger concentration gradient.

Respiratory regulation

Breathing rate and depth is continually adjusted to maintain the appropriate levels of O_2 and CO_2. The respiratory control centre (RCC) located in the medulla oblongata is responsible for respiratory regulation. There are two centres within the RCC: the inspiratory centre (IC) and the expiratory centre (EC):

● The IC stimulates inspiratory muscles to contract at rest and during exercise.
● The EC is inactive at rest, but will stimulate additional expiratory muscles to contract during exercise.

Respiratory regulation at rest

At rest, the IC is responsible for the rhythmic cycle of breathing. Nerve impulses are generated and stimulate the inspiratory muscles, causing them to contract, via the:

● intercostal nerve to the external intercostal
● phrenic nerve to the diaphragm.

Respiratory regulation during exercise

Sensory nerves relay information to the RCC where a response is initiated by the IC and EC. The RCC receives information as shown in the following table.

> **Exam tip**
>
> Intercostals are not an acceptable answer. You have to be more specific: external intercostals for inspiration and internal intercostals for expiration.

> **Typical mistake**
>
> Candidates tend to forget to state whether inspiration is a passive or an active process. This is often worth a mark in the exam.

Chemical control	Chemoreceptors	Located in the aorta and carotid arteries, detect changes in blood acidity, increases in CO_2 and decreases in O_2
Neural control	Thermoreceptors	Inform of increases in blood temperature
	Proprioceptors	Inform of motor activity in the muscles and joints
	Baroreceptors	Located in the lung tissue and bronchioles, inform of the state of lung inflation

Gaseous exchange

Gaseous exchange is the exchange of oxygen and carbon dioxide by the process of diffusion:

- Diffusion is the movement of gas from an area of high pressure to an area of low pressure.
- The difference between the high and low pressure is called the diffusion gradient.
- The larger the gradient, the larger the diffusion/gaseous exchange that takes place.

Partial pressure (pp) is the pressure a gas exerts within a mixture of gases. Gas always moves from areas of high partial pressure to areas of low partial pressure.

pO_2 = partial pressure of oxygen

pCO_2 = partial pressure of carbon dioxide

Gaseous exchange at rest

External respiration

External respiration is the exchange of gases at the lungs between the deoxygenated blood that arrives in capillaries and the oxygen-rich atmospheric air held in the alveoli:

- Oxygen moves from high pp in the alveoli to low pp in capillary blood down the diffusion gradient (alveoli pO_2 105 – capillary pO_2 40 = 65mmHg).
- Carbon dioxide moves from high pp in capillary blood to low pp in the alveoli down the diffusion gradient (capillary pCO_2 46 – alveoli pCO_2 40 = 6mmHg).

Internal respiration

Internal respiration is the exchange of gases at the muscle cells between the oxygenated blood that arrives in the capillaries and the carbon dioxide-producing muscle cells. Haemoglobin molecules dissociate (release) the O_2 as they pass the muscle cells:

- Oxygen moves from high pp in capillary blood to low pp of the muscle cell down the diffusion gradient (capillary pO_2 100 – muscle cell pO_2 40 = 60mmHg).
- Carbon dioxide moves from high pp in the muscle cell to low pp in capillary blood down the diffusion gradient (muscle cell pCO_2 46 – capillary pCO_2 40 = 6mmHg).

Gaseous exchange during exercise

External respiration

During exercise, muscle tissues use a greater volume of O_2 and produce a greater volume of CO_2. This means the deoxygenated blood that returns to the lungs has a lower pO_2 and a higher CO_2 than at rest:

- The O_2 diffusion gradient steepens and O_2 diffuses from high pO_2 in the alveoli to lower pO_2 in capillary blood.
- The CO_2 diffusion gradient steepens and CO_2 diffuses from high pCO_2 in capillary blood to lower pCO_2 in the alveoli.

Internal respiration

The more intense the exercise, the more the muscle tissue's demand for oxygen will increase. Therefore, the more intense the exercise, the lower the pO_2 and the higher the pCO_2 in the muscle tissue:

- The O_2 diffusion gradient steepens and O_2 diffuses from high pO_2 in capillary blood to lower pO_2 in the muscle cell.
- The CO_2 diffusion gradient steepens and CO_2 diffuses from high pCO_2 in the muscle cell to lower pCO_2 in capillary blood.

Dissociation of oxygen from haemoglobin

- The **oxyhaemoglobin dissociation curve** informs us of the amount of haemoglobin saturated with oxygen.
- Oxygen unloading from haemoglobin is termed **dissociation**.
- Haemoglobin fully loaded with oxygen is referred to as being **saturated**.

> **Oxyhaemoglobin dissociation curve**: a graph showing the relationship between pO_2 and percentage saturation of haemoglobin.
>
> **Dissociation**: the release of oxygen from haemoglobin for gaseous exchange.

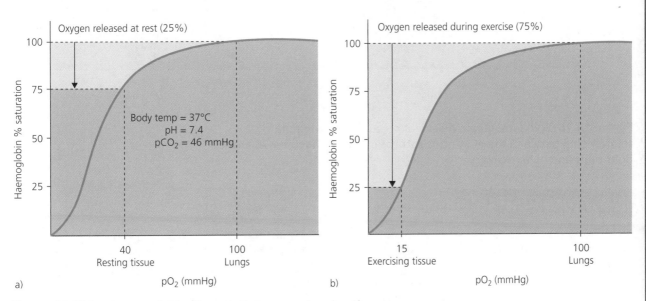

Figure 1.1.17 Oxyhaemoglobin dissociation curve showing the relationship between the pO_2 and % saturation of haemoglobin a) at rest and b) during exercise

The Bohr shift

In addition to the pO_2 lowering, there are three other effects of exercise which increase the dissociation of O_2 from haemoglobin. These effects move the oxyhaemoglobin dissociation curve to the right. This is known as the **Bohr shift**.

The effects are:
1 increase in blood and muscle temperature
2 increase in pp of carbon dioxide (raising pCO_2)
3 increase in production of lactic acid and carbonic acid (lowers pH).

> **Bohr shift**: a move in the oxyhaemoglobin dissociation curve to the right caused by increased acidity in the blood stream.

Impact on performance

- At any given pO_2 for exercising muscle tissue, the percentage saturation of oxyhaemoglobin is far lower and therefore dissociation of O_2 to respiring tissues is greater.
- This enhances the volume of O_2 available for diffusion and therefore aerobic energy production for exercise.

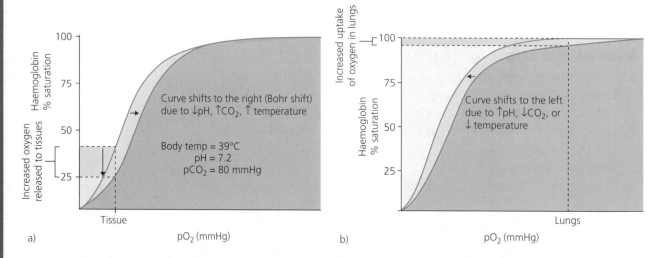

Figure 1.1.18 Oxyhaemoglobin dissociation curve showing the relationship between the pO_2 and % saturation of haemoglobin a) at the Bohr shift and b) in recovery

Now test yourself

TESTED

9 Define breathing rate, tidal volume and minute ventilation.
10 Describe the differences between the mechanics of breathing at rest and during exercise for inspiration.
11 Describe the differences between the mechanics of breathing at rest and during exercise for expiration.
12 How does the RCC receive information?
13 What is dissociation?
14 What is partial pressure?
15 What is the diffusion gradient?

Answers on page 167

Exam practice

1 Explain how intrinsic control mechanisms cause cardiac output to increase during exercise. [5]
2 Describe how the heart's conduction system controls the contraction and relaxation phases of the cardiac cycle. [5]
3 Outline how oxygen is transported in the blood. [2]
4 Describe the process of oxygen diffusion at the alveoli during exercise. [3]
5 Describe the mechanics of expiration during exercise. [4]

Answers on page 174

Summary

You should now have an understanding of the:
- cardiovascular system at rest
- relationship between and resting values for: heart rate, stroke volume, cardiac output; methods of calculating the above
- cardiac cycle: diastole, systole
- conduction system of the heart linked to the cardiac cycle
- cardiovascular system during exercise of differing intensities and during recovery
- effects of different exercise intensities and recovery on: heart rate, stroke volume, cardiac output; methods of calculating the above
- redistribution of cardiac output during exercise of differing intensities and during recovery:
  - vascular shunt mechanism,
  - role of the vasomotor centre
  - role of arterioles
  - role of pre-capillary sphincters.
- mechanisms of venous return during exercise of differing intensities and during recovery.
- regulation of heart rate during exercise: neural factors, hormonal factors and intrinsic factors

- respiratory system at rest
- relationship between resting values for: breathing frequency, tidal volume, minute ventilation; methods of calculating the above
- mechanics of breathing at rest and the muscles involved: diaphragm, external intercostals, at the alveoli, at the muscles
- respiratory system during exercise of differing intensities and during recovery
- effects of differing intensities of exercise and recovery on: breathing frequency, tidal volume and minute ventilation
- mechanics of breathing during exercise of differing intensities and during recovery, including additional muscles involved
- regulation of breathing during exercise of different intensities and during recovery; neural control, chemical control
- effect of differing intensities of exercise and recovery on gas exchange at the alveoli and at the muscles
- changes in pressure gradient
- changes in dissociation of oxyhaemoglobin.

1.1c Energy for exercise

Adenosine triphosphate (ATP)

- ATP is made up of one adenosine molecule and three phosphate groups held together by bonds of chemical energy. This compound is the only immediately usable form of energy stored in our bodies.
- ATP is readily available as it is stored in the muscle cell.
- The energy is stored in the bond between the last two phosphate groups. When this bond is broken down by the enzyme ATPase, energy is released that can be used to make the muscle cell contract and cause movement:

  ATP → ADP (adenosine diphosphate) + P (phosphate) + energy
- This is a **coupled reaction** – it can be broken down then resynthesised, then broken down and resynthesised, etc.:
  - breakdown of ATP:

    ATP → ADP + P + energy
  - resynthesis of ATP:

    ADP + P + energy → ATP
- The only problem is our body can only store a very small amount of ATP (85 g) – enough to last about 2 seconds.
- To maintain exercise beyond 2 seconds, ATP has to be resynthesised.

> **Coupled reaction**: where products of one reaction are used in another reaction.

ATP resynthesis

- Depending on the intensity of the exercise, this is achieved by three energy systems: ATP/PC, glycolytic or aerobic.
- Energy systems do not work in isolation (separately).
- The amount of ATP resynthesised by each system will depend purely on the intensity of the exercise and two systems can be working at the same time.

Energy systems

The table below gives the key descriptors, strengths and weaknesses of each energy system.

	ATP/PC system	Glycolytic system	Aerobic system
Type of reaction (anaerobic/aerobic)	Anaerobic	Anaerobic	Aerobic
Chemical or food fuel used	Phosphocreatine (PC)	Glycogen/glucose	Glycogen/glucose or fat
Site of reaction	Sarcoplasm	Sarcoplasm	Stage 1 = Sarcoplasm Stage 2 = Krebs cycle – matrix Stage 3 = Cristae

→

Quick quizzes at **www.hoddereducation.co.uk/myrevisionnotes**

	ATP/PC system	Glycolytic system	Aerobic system
Controlling enzymes	Creatine kinase	• Glycogen phosphorylase (GPP) • Phosphofructokinase (PFK) • Lactate dehydrogenase (LDH)	• Phosphofructokinase • Acetyl-CoA
Energy yield	1 mole of ATP	2 moles of ATP	38 moles of ATP
Specific stages of system	• PC → P + C + energy (exothermic) • energy + ADP + P → ATP (endothermic)	• Glucose undergoes anaerobic glycolysis • Pyruvic acid/without O_2 → lactic acid	• Aerobic glycolysis • Krebs cycle • Electron transport chain
Energy equations	• PC → P + C + energy • energy + ADP + P → ATP	$C_6H_{12}O_6 \rightarrow 2C_3H_6O_6$	$C_6H_{12}O_6 + 6O_2 \rightarrow 6CO_2 + 6H_2O + energy$
By-products formed	None	Lactic acid	$CO_2 + H_2O$
Intensity of activity	Very high intensity	High intensity	Low-moderate/sub-maximal intensity
Duration of system	2–10 seconds	Up to 3 minutes	3 minutes onwards
Strengths	• No delay for O_2 • PC readily available in muscle cell • Simple and rapid breakdown • Provides energy quickly • No fatiguing by-products	• No delay for O_2 • Large fuel stores in liver, muscles and blood stream • Provides energy for high-intensity activities for up to 3 minutes • Lactic acid can be recycled into fuel for further energy production	• Large fuels: triglycerides, free fatty acids (FFAs), glycogen and glucose • High ATP yield and long duration of energy production • No fatiguing by-products
Weaknesses	Low ATP yield and small PC stores lead to rapid fatigue after 8–10 seconds	• Fatiguing by-product lactic acid reduces pH and enzyme activity • Relatively low ATP yield and recovery can be lengthy	• Delay for oxygen delivery and complex series of reactions • Slow energy production limits activity to sub-maximal intensity FFAs demand 15% more O_2 for breakdown

Energy continuum

Intensity and duration of exercise

The energy continuum is the relative contribution of each energy system to overall energy production, depending on intensity and duration of the activity.

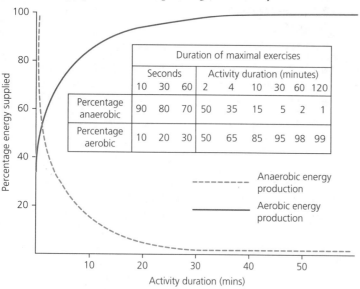

	Duration of maximal exercises								
	Seconds			Activity duration (minutes)					
	10	30	60	2	4	10	30	60	120
Percentage anaerobic	90	80	70	50	35	15	5	2	1
Percentage aerobic	10	20	30	50	65	85	95	98	99

Figure 1.1.19 The relative contribution of aerobic and anaerobic energy production over time

Intermittent exercise

An example of **intermittent exercise** is a rugby player who is required to alternate between various modes of activity, such as standing, walking, running, sprinting, tackling and jumping. Research has shown this type of exercise to have varying physiological demands as they switch from one energy system predominance to the other.

The threshold of any energy system is the point at which it is unable to provide energy and therefore switches to another system. For example, the threshold of the PC system is the point at which PC can no longer provide energy to the working muscles. This threshold is about 10 seconds.

Intermittent exercise: activity where the intensity alternates, either during interval training between work and relief intervals or during a game with breaks of play and changes of intensity.

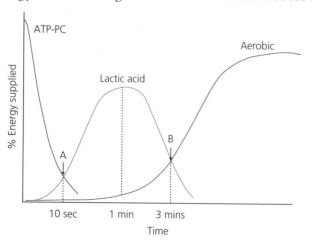

A = ATP-PC LA threshold
The point at which the ATP-PC energy system is exhausted and the lactic acid system prevails

B = LA O$_2$ threshold
The point at which the lactic acid system is exhausted and the aerobic system takes over

Figure 1.1.20 The percentage of energy supplied by each energy system over time

Revision activity

Note down the relative contributions of the various energy systems for your practical activity.

Recovery periods

Predominantly anaerobic activities, such as basketball and netball, rely heavily on ATP-PC and glycolytic energy systems. Although PC stores deplete quickly, they are also replenished quickly: 50 per cent in 30 seconds, 100 per cent in 3 minutes. Equally, oxygen stored in **myoglobin** can be fully replenished in 3 minutes.

Blood lactate levels can rise dramatically with prolonged high intensity activity. With the correct work:relief ratios and sufficient oxygen supply, lactic acid can be broken down and removed.
● Time-outs and quarter- and half-time breaks aid recovery.
● Recovery periods also allow for rehydration and glycogen replacement.

Fitness level

Once blood lactate values go above 4 mmol, the onset of blood lactate accumulation (OBLA) has been reached.

This point will vary depending on the aerobic fitness of the performer. In untrained individuals, this may occur at about 50 per cent of their **VO_2max**, whereas in highly trained individuals this may occur at about 85 per cent of VO_2max. This is due to their increased ability to tolerate lactic acid and to remove waste products and supply oxygen to working muscles (buffering capacity).

Other factors that may contribute to the relative contribution of the energy systems include:
● position of the player
● tactics and strategies used
● level of competition
● structure of the game.

Myoglobin: a protein molecule that, similar to haemoglobin, helps with the transport of oxygen.

VO_2max: maximum volume of oxygen inspired, transported and utilised per minute during exhaustive exercise.

Now test yourself

TESTED

1 What is ATP?
2 Name the three energy systems that provide energy for the resynthesis of ATP.
3 Name the three stages of the aerobic energy system.
4 What is the energy continuum?

Answers on page 168

The recovery process

To help the body return to its pre-exercise state, energy is required. Continued aerobic energy production fulfils this additional energy requirement. This is termed **excess post-exercise oxygen consumption (EPOC)**. Recovery (EPOC) takes place in two stages:

1 fast (alactacid) component of recovery
2 slow (lactacid) component of recovery.

The two tables that follow detail what happens during the two stages of the recovery process.

> **Excess post-exercise oxygen consumption (EPOC)**: the volume of oxygen consumed post-exercise to return the body to a pre-exercise state.

Fast alactacid component	(First stage of recovery – up to 3 minutes after exercise)
Phosphocreatine (PC) stores restored	• 3 minutes – PC stores to fully recover • 30 seconds for 50% of the recovery, 75% in 60 seconds • Process requires approximately 3–4 litres of oxygen
Replenishment of blood and muscle oxygen	Within the first minute, oxygen resaturates the blood stream, associating with haemoglobin, and within 3 minutes restores the oxymyoglobin link in the muscle cells.

Slow lactacid component	(Second stage of recovery – from 3 minutes up to 24 hours after exercise)
Elevated ventilation and circulation	Post-exercise respiratory rate, depth and HR remain elevated. These gradually decrease to resting levels to maximise the delivery of O_2 and the removal of by-products.
Elevated body temperature	Post-exercise elevated temperature increases metabolic rate, accounting for 60–70% of the slow lactacid component of EPOC.
Removal of lactic acid	Lactic acid is removed from the body in four ways: • 50–75% is converted back to pyruvic acid and enters the Krebs cycle; it is used in aerobic metabolism. • Approximately 10–25% can be converted back to glucose and glycogen (a process known an gluconeogenesis and glyconeogenesis). • It can be converted into proteins by the Cori cycle. • It can be removed via sweating and in urine. Lactate removal takes on average an hour, although it can be up to 24 hours.

Implications of recovery on training

At an elite level, each athlete's recovery is individually designed following these general principles:

1 Warm-up – this will minimise time spent using anaerobic energy systems, thereby reducing oxygen deficit.
2 Active recovery – this maintains respiratory rate and HR, speeding up removal of lactic acid.
3 Cooling aids – these can be used post-event to speed up lactic acid removal and reduce muscle soreness and DOMS.
4 Intensity of training – high-intensity training will: a) increase muscle mass, ATP and PC storage, boosting efficiency of the fast component; b) increase tolerance to lactic acid, increasing buffering capacity and c) delay OBLA, reducing demand of the slow component. Low-moderate intensity will increase aerobic capacity, delaying OBLA, and maximise oxygen delivery during EPOC.

> **Typical mistake**
> Do not get the two components of recovery the wrong way round. Fast stage deals with restoring the body; slow stage deals with removing waste products and getting the body back to normal.

5 Work:relief ratios – based on the predominant energy system required in a physical activity, training intensity and the correct work:relief ratio can maximise recovery: a) speed/explosive strength 1:3+; b) lactate tolerance and high intensity muscular endurance 1:2; c) aerobic capacity and endurance 1:0.5.

6 Strategies and tactics – time-outs and substitutions should be used. Lower intensity set plays can delay OBLA and fatigue.

7 Nutrition – correct pre-, during and post-event nutrition can help maximise fuel stores, delay fatigue, reduce lactic acid accumulation and speed up recovery.

Now test yourself

TESTED ☐

5 State the two stages of recovery.
6 What seven things should an athlete consider to maximise recovery?

Answers on page 168

Exam practice

1 Explain the role of ATP. [3]
2 The recovery process returns the body to its pre-exercise state. Describe the main processes involved in the alactacid component of recovery. [5]
3 Critically evaluate the use of anaerobic energy systems to resynthesise ATP. [10]

Answers on page 175

Summary

You should now have an understanding of:
- ATP as 'energy currency'
- the principle of energetically coupled reactions: breakdown of ATP to ADP (adenosine diphosphate) + P (phosphate)
- resynthesis of ATP from ADP + P
- energy systems: ATP-PC (phosphocreatine) system, glycolytic system, aerobic system; for each system: type of reaction (aerobic or anaerobic), chemical or food fuel used, specific site of the reaction, controlling enzyme, ATP yield, specific stages within the system and by-products

- how the energy continuum is the predominant energy system used during exercise
- interplay of energy systems during intermittent exercise and factors that affect this interplay, intensity of exercise, duration of exercise, recovery periods and fitness levels
- the recovery process
- excess post-exercise oxygen consumption (EPOC); fast components of EPOC, the processes that occur and the duration; slow components of EPOC
- the effect of exercise intensity on EPOC and implications of the recovery process for planning exercise or training sessions.

1.1d Environmental effects on body systems

Exercise at altitude

Differing environmental conditions affect the efficiency of the cardiovascular and respiratory systems and can dramatically affect the performance and even health of athletes and spectators. Athletes and coaches must prepare for these conditions and alter strategies to ensure peak performance.

Effect of altitude on the cardiovascular and respiratory systems

As **altitude** increases, **barometric pressure** decreases. Even though the composition of air stays the same, the partial pressure of oxygen (pO_2) decreases, which has a severe impact on performance. The greater the diffusion gradient, the faster oxygen will move from one area to another.

The greater the altitude, the greater the negative impact on the diffusion gradient.

The table below details partial pressures of oxygen at different diffusion gradients and altitudes.

> **Altitude**: the height or elevation of an area above sea level.
>
> **Barometric pressure**: the pressure exerted by the Earth's atmosphere at any given point.

Sea level pO_2 = 159mmHg	Diffusion gradient of 119 to capillary blood
3600 m above sea level pO_2 = 105mmHg	Diffusion gradient of 65 to capillary blood (45% reduction)
8800 m above sea level pO_2 = 43mmHg	Diffusion gradient of 3 to capillary blood

If an athlete competes at high altitude, the rate of oxygen diffusion decreases, reducing haemoglobin saturation and resulting in poor transport of O_2. As a consequence:
- blood volume decreases – plasma volume decreases by 25 per cent to allow increase in density of RBCs
- stroke volume decreases, which increases heart rate
- maximal cardiac output, stroke volume and heart rate decrease during maximum-intensity exercise.

> **Typical mistake**
>
> When referring to partial pressures, remember to include units (mmHg – millimetres of mercury).

The above combine to reduce aerobic capacity and VO_2max, impacting on the intensity and duration of an athlete's performance.

Acclimatisation

Altitude starts to have an effect around 1500m, and although different people **acclimatise** at different speeds, guidelines allow:
- 3–5 days for low-altitude performance (1000–2000m)
- 1–2 weeks for moderate-altitude performance (2000–3000m)

> **Acclimatisation**: a process of gradual adaption to a change in environment (for example lower pO_2 at altitude).

- 2+ weeks for high altitude (3000 m+); athletes going above 3000 m should sleep no more than 300 m higher each day and have regular rest days to prevent altitude sickness
- 4+ weeks for extreme altitude (5000–5500 m), for example a climber will spend one month at base camp before making a summit attempt at Everest.

Acclimatisation benefits for the cardiovascular and respiratory systems are:
- increase in red blood cell production, due to increased release of **erythropoietin**
- breathing rate and ventilation stabilise, although remain elevated at rest, compared to sea levels
- SV and CO reduce as O_2 extraction becomes more efficient
- reduced incidences of altitude sickness, headaches, breathlessness, poor sleep and lack of appetite.

> **Erythropoietin**: a naturally produced hormone responsible for the production of red blood cells.

Revision activity

Create a revision card detailing how to acclimatise for different altitudes. Use colours and diagrams.

Exercise in the heat

REVISED

Thermoregulation is the process of maintaining internal core temperature. **Thermoreceptors** deep in the core sense a change in body temperature. If core temperature rises, metabolic heat is transported by the circulating blood to the surface of the body and released mostly by convection and evaporation (sweat).

An athlete exercising in the heat can lose around 2–3 litres of sweat per hour, which if not replaced decreases blood volume and causes **dehydration**. The rate of heat loss through sweating is affected by **humidity**.

Hyperthermia is cause by:
1 high and prolonged exercise intensities
2 high air temperatures
3 high relative humidity.

> **Thermoreceptors**: sensory receptors which sense a change in temperature and relay information to the brain.
>
> **Dehydration**: loss of water in body tissues, largely caused by sweating.
>
> **Humidity**: the amount of water vapour in the atmospheric air.
>
> **Hyperthermia**: significantly raised core body temperature.

Cardiovascular drift

During prolonged exercise in the heat, a rise in core body temperature can cause cardiovascular drift: an upward drift in heart rate associated with a rise in body temperature (1 °C increases heart rate by 10 bpm).

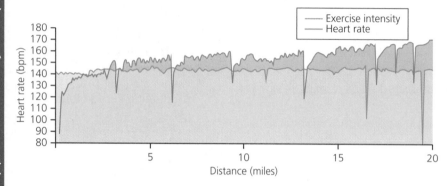

Figure 1.1.21 Cardiovascular drift

The effects of heat and humidity and the body's thermoregulatory response

The following table summarises the effects of heat and humidity on the cardiovascular and respiratory systems.

Cardiovascular system	
Effect	**Implication**
Dilation of arterioles and capillaries to the skin	• Increased blood flow and blood pooling in the limbs
Decreased blood volume, venous return, SV, CO, and BP	• Increased HR to compensate • Increased strain on the cardiovascular system • Reduced O_2 transport to the working muscles
Respiratory system	
Effect	**Implication**
Dehydration and drying of the airways in temperatures above 32°C makes breathing difficult	• Increased mucus production • Constriction of the airways • Decreased volume of air for gaseous exchange
Increased breathing frequency to maintain oxygen consumption	• Increased oxygen 'cost' of exercise
High levels of sunlight increase the effects of pollutants in the air	• Increased irritation of airways, leading to coughing, wheezing or asthma symptoms

Strategies to maximise performance in heat and humidity

The table below summarises strategies to maximise performance in heat and humidity.

Pre-competition	• 7–14 days of acclimatisation in the same conditions to increase the body's tolerance to heat • Using cooling aids such as ice vests to reduce core temperature and delay effects of dehydration
During competition	• Pacing strategies to reduce the feelings of exertion at low-exercise intensities • Wearing suitable clothing to maximise heat loss • Rehydrating as often and as much as possible with a hypotonic or isotonic solution
Post-competition	• Use cooling aids such as cold fans • Rehydrating using isotonic solutions to replace lost fluids, glucose and electrolytes

Now test yourself

TESTED ☐

1 What is altitude?
2 Describe how the diffusion gradient is affected as altitude increases.
3 How does altitude affect an athlete's cardiovascular system?
4 How does altitude affect an athlete's respiratory system?
5 What is acclimatisation?
6 What is the cardiovascular drift?
7 State one pre-competition, one during competition and one post-competition strategy to maximise performance in heat and humidity.

Answers on page 168

Exam practice

Explain the effects of altitude on the respiratory system and how these effects impact on the overall performance of an endurance athlete performing at altitude.   [5]

Answers on page 175

Summary

You should now have an understanding of:
• the effect of altitude on the cardiovascular and respiratory systems
• acclimatisation, including the importance of timing arrival, at altitude
• the effect of heat on the cardiovascular and respiratory systems, including temperature regulation and cardiovascular drift.

1.2a Diet and nutrition and their effect on physical performance

Diet and nutrition

A well-planned diet and nutritional strategy will aid any performer or athlete. Diet and nutrition can support fitness or performance gains, assist recovery or reduce the risks posed by overtraining.

Healthy, balanced diet

For 19–50 year olds, the government recommends the following calorie guidelines:

- men – 2,500 calories per day
- women – 1,940 calories per day
- for both – 55 per cent CHO (carbohydrate), 15 per cent protein, no more than 30 per cent fats, a variety of foods including five portions of fruit and vegetables per day.

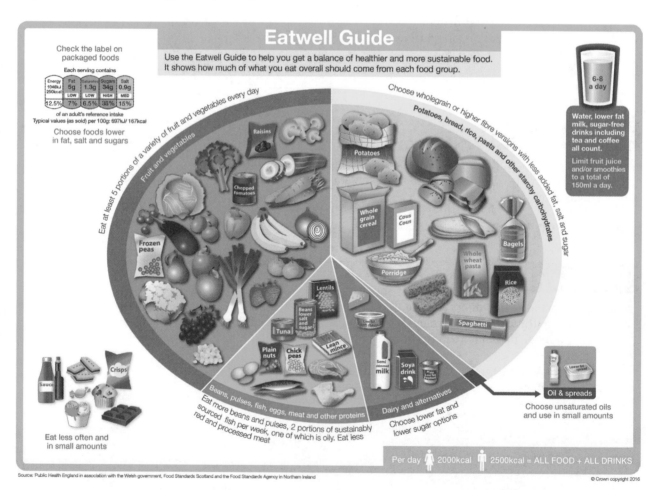

Figure 1.2.1 **Public Health England guidelines on the composition of a healthy balanced diet**

Carbohydrates (CHOs)

CHOs are vital for energy production. They are the preferred fuel for exercise, accounting for approximately 75 per cent of energy requirements. CHOs can be consumed (eaten/drunk) in several forms, as shown in the table below.

CHO	Food example	Where are they stored in the body?
Starches	Rice, potatoes	Stored as glycogen in liver and muscles
Sugars	Fruit, honey	Circulate in blood stream as glucose

Glycogen and glucose provide energy for aerobic and anaerobic performers. Surplus glucose, for example a high sugar diet, will be converted into triglycerides (the main constituents of body fat in humans) and stored in the body as fat.

Proteins

Proteins (found in milk, eggs, meat and soya) are essential for:
- growth and repair of tissues and cells
- making muscle proteins (increasing muscle size)
- making haemoglobin
- making **enzymes**, antibodies and collagen.

They can also be used as a fuel (when CHOs and **fats** are depleted).

Fats

Role of fats:
- insulate nerves, form cell membranes and cushion organs
- provide an energy store – they can be broken down for aerobic energy production and have twice the yield of CHOs.

Fat type	Example	Consideration
Unsaturated fatty acids	Avocado and soya beans Omega 3s (fish oil), olive oil	Can boost the delivery of oxygen, improve endurance recovery and reduce joint inflammation
Saturated fatty acids	Butter, bacon	Limit intake to reduce the risk of cardiovascular disease

Carbohydrates (CHOs): sugars and starches stored in the body as glycogen and converted to glucose in order to fuel energy production.

Proteins: amino acids essential for the growth and repair of cells and tissues.

Enzymes: biological catalysts which increase the speed of chemical reactions.

Fats: triglycerides which provide the body with fatty acids for energy production.

Saturated fatty acids: a type of fat molecule, typically solid at room temperature and mainly found in animal products. When consumed excessively they can be associated with heart disease.

Unsaturated fatty acids: a type of fat molecule that is typically liquid at room temperature and found in sunflower, olive and fish oils. They can help lower cholesterol.

Exam tip

Ensure you are able to apply food fuels (CHOs, fats and proteins) to the relevant energy systems.

Vitamins and minerals

Vitamins and minerals are essential to maintain healthy body functions. They can be consumed in adequate quantities through a balanced diet.

The following table summarises the different vitamins and minerals and their uses in the body.

> **Vitamins and minerals**: essential organic and inorganic nutrients required for healthy body function.

Name of vitamin/mineral	Essential for
Calcium	Bone health, muscle contraction, nerve transmission and blood clotting
Iron	Formation of haemoglobin, enzyme ration and the immune system
Phosphorus	Bone health and energy production
Vitamin A	Antioxidant properties, eye health
Vitamin D	Bone health, protection against cancer and heart disease
Vitamin E	Antioxidant properties, skin and eye health
Vitamin K	Blood clotting and bone health
Vitamin C	Skin, blood vessels and soft tissues
Vitamin B	Breakdown of food, haemoglobin formation, skin and eye health

Fibre and water

Fibre is essential for the function of the large intestine. It is found in cereals, bread, beans, lentils, fruit and vegetables. Adequate fluid intake allows fibre to work properly and to provide bulk in the bowel.

Water is essential for hydration before, during and after exercise. Two-thirds of the body weight is water. Dehydration can result in decreased plasma volume, decreased stroke volume and increased temperature and heart rate.

> **Revision activity**
>
> Create a table which has three columns: component of a healthy diet; importance and function; example of source. Complete the table by adding information for the seven components of a healthy diet.

Now test yourself

TESTED ☐

1 What are the seven components of a balanced diet?
2 What is the difference between saturated and unsaturated fatty acids?

Answers on page 168

Energy intake, expenditure and balance in physical activity and performance

An athlete's diet may differ from that of an inactive (sedentary) individual. Each performer has unique nutritional needs. Failure to consume sufficient calories will have a negative impact on training and performance, such as:
- muscle loss (atrophy)
- decreased intensity and duration of performance
- increased risk of fatigue, injury and illness.

Energy expenditure

Having accurate knowledge of an individual's **energy expenditure** allows the accurate planning of the correct diet to facilitate training and performance.

Physical activity expenditure

This is the total number of calories required to perform daily tasks (often around 30 per cent of total energy expenditure, but can be higher for a training athlete). Metabolic equivalent (MET) values are used to give a precise picture of expenditure. For example:
- sitting quietly = 1 MET (1kcal/kg/hr)
- running at 11.5 minute/mile pace = 9 METs.

To calculate the total amount of energy an individual expends, we must add together **basal metabolic rate (BMR)**, the **thermal effect of food (TEF)** and physical activity expenditure.

> **Typical mistake**
>
> When calculating or describing energy expenditure, always include units (joules or calories): failure to do so will mean no marks!

Energy intake and energy balance

Energy intake is the total amount of energy from food and drinks, measured in joules or calories. As mentioned earlier, an average individual should intake approximately 55 per cent CHO, 15 per cent protein and no more than 30 per cent fat. An athlete's diet may differ significantly depending on the intensity and duration of their activity.

Energy balance is the relationship between energy intake and energy expenditure:
- energy in > energy expenditure = weight gain
- energy in < energy expenditure = weight loss
- energy in = energy expenditure = weight stays the same.

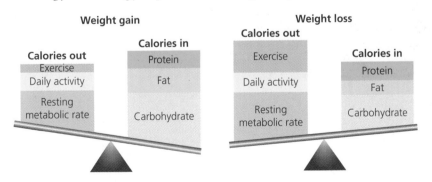

Figure 1.2.2 The energy balance scales

Energy expenditure: the sum of basal metabolic rate, the thermic effect of food and the energy expended through physical activity.

Basal metabolic rate (BMR): the minimum amount of energy required to sustain essential physiological function at rest which can account for as much as 75 per cent of total energy expenditure.

Thermic effect of food (TEF): the energy required to eat, digest, absorb and use food taken in.

Energy intake: the total amount of energy from food and drinks consumed, measured in joules or calories.

Energy balance: the relationship between energy intake and energy expenditure.

Now test yourself

3 Define energy.
4 Explain how an athlete would calculate their overall energy expenditure and why this information is important for them.

Answers on page 168

TESTED

Ergogenic aids

An ergogenic aid is a substance, object or method used to improve or enhance performance. A pharmacological aid is a group of ergogenic aids taken to increase the levels of hormones or neural transmitters. A physiological aid is a group of ergogenic aids used to increase the rate of adaptation of the body to increase performance.

Pharmacological aids

The following table outlines the benefits, drawbacks and practical applications of pharmacological aids.

Pharmacological aid	Legal or illegal	+ Benefits	– Drawbacks	Practical application
Anabolic steroids Synthetic derivatives of testosterone; tablets, capsules, cream, injected	Illegal	+ Increased muscle mass and strength + Increased recovery + Increased intensity and duration of training	– Irritability – Mood swings – Liver damage – Heart failure – Acne – Hormonal disturbances	● Can be used for rehabilitation and muscle wastage diseases ● Used by weightlifters, body builders, sprinters and power athletes
Erythropoietin/EPO A hormone made naturally in the body, secreted by the kidneys; RhEPO is the artificial version	Illegal	+ Increased RBCs and haemoglobin count + Increased O_2 transport and aerobic capacity + Increased intensity and duration of performance	– Increased blood viscosity – Decreased cardiac output – Increased risk of blood clots and heart disease – Decreased natural production of EPO	● Difficult to detect as some athletes have high concentration of RBCs ● Used by endurance athletes, e.g. Tour de France cyclists
Human growth hormone (HGH) Synthetically produced HGH, used by some athletes in place of anabolic steroids	Illegal	+ Increased muscle mass and strength + Increased fat metabolism and decreased fat mass + Increased blood glucose + Increased recovery + Increased intensity and duration of training	– abnormal bone and muscle development – enlargement of vital organs – increased risk of cancer and diabetes	Used by any type of athlete

Revision activity

Create a revision card for each pharmacological aid. Use colours to highlight benefits and drawbacks, and use diagrams to illustrate the application to a practical example.

Physiological aids

The table below outlines the benefits, drawbacks and practical applications of physiological aids.

Physiological aid	Legal or illegal	+ Benefits	– Drawbacks	Practical application
Blood doping ● Red blood cell volume is increased ● Remove blood 4–6 weeks before ● Body then compensates, replenishing lost RBCs	Illegal	+ Increased RBC therefore more haemoglobin + Increased O_2 transportation and aerobic capacity + Increased intensity and duration of performance	– Increased blood viscosity – Decreased cardiac output – Increased risk of blood clots and heart disease – Risk of transfusion infections (HIV/AIDS)	Used by endurance athletes
Intermittent hypoxic training (IHT) Athletes live at sea level but train under hypoxic conditions (low pO_2)	Legal	+ Allows acclimatisation for events at altitude + Increased RBC therefore more haemoglobin + Increased intensity and duration before fatigue + Increased mitochondria and buffering capacity therefore delay OBLA	– Benefits lost when IHT stops – May disrupt training patterns = loss of motivation – Hard to reach normal work rates – Decreased immune function and increased risk of infection – Dehydration	Used by endurance athletes
Cooling aids ● Pre-event: ice vests, cold towel wraps – used 10–30 minutes before to reduce core body temperature ● Injury: ice packs, sprays, PRICE (protect, rest, ice, compression, elevate) ● Post-event: ice baths	Legal	+ Reduce core body temperature + Decreased sweating, dehydration and early fatigue + Decreased injury pain and swelling + Increased speed of recovery and repair + Decreased DOMS	– Difficult to perceive exercise intensity – Ice burns and pain – May mask or worsen injuries – Chest pain and decreased efficiency in elderly – Dangerous for those with heart and blood pressure problems	● All athletes use post-event ● Used to speed up recovery – vessels constrict, capillaries dilate and 'new' blood flows back to the muscles, bringing fresh oxygen

Nutritional aids: dietary manipulation

The table below outlines the benefits, drawbacks and practical applications of dietary manipulation.

Dietary manipulation	Legal or illegal	+ Benefits	– Drawbacks	Practical application
Glycogen/ carbohydrate loading (pre- competition) CHO loading starts one week before competition: ● Day 1: intense exercise (deplete glycogen stores) ● Days 2–3: high-protein/high-fat diet ● Day 4: intense exercise (deplete glycogen stores further) ● Days 5–7: high-CHO diet and tapering training or rest This super-compensates, and muscles store more CHO than usual	Legal	+ Increased glycogen stores + Increased endurance capacity + Increased time to exhaustion (up to 30%) + Delays fatigue	– Hypoglycaemia and poor recovery rates in depletion phase – Lethargy and irritability – Gastrointestinal problems – Increased risk of injury – Affects mental preparation	● Used for endurance events, e.g. marathon running, or all-day events, e.g. hockey tournament over a weekend ● Used to ensure body has enough glycogen for aerobic glycolysis
Pre-event meal CHO meal 3 hours before event – low–GI food, e.g. porridge 1–2 hours before event, a high-GI food (maintains blood glucose levels) **Pre-training meal** A small meal 30–60 minutes before an event	Legal	+ Tops up liver glycogen + Maintains blood glucose levels	– Avoid CHOs immediately prior to an event, as the body may try to counteract raised glucose levels – the athlete may become dizzy/fatigued	● A CHO meal before event within timescale ● Used by all athletes
During event meal/ food Vital to eat small amounts in activity lasting longer than 1 hour	Legal	+ Tops up liver glycogen + Maintains blood glucose levels	– Can be difficult to eat during activity – Must be pre-planned to have best effects	● E.g. energy gels in marathon ● Banana at change of ends in tennis

→

Dietary manipulation	Legal or illegal	+ Benefits	– Drawbacks	Practical application
Post-event meal Consume CHOs ASAP, within the first 30 minutes of finishing an event, and repeat at 2–hour intervals up to 6 hours post-event **Post-training meal** ASAP after, but within 2 hours of an event	Legal	+ Promotes faster recovery rate of glycogen	– Not always practical or possible within 30 minutes of finishing	● Consume moderate and fast-digesting CHOs for faster recovery e.g. white bread or rice ● Used by all athletes

Revision activity

Using the information about nutritional aids, create ten revision questions about dietary manipulation. Write answers to the questions, then ask someone else to test you.

Hydration

An athlete should be well hydrated prior to training/performance and replace all lost fluids throughout performance. Electrolytes lost through sweat must be replaced.

All dehydration decreases performance due to:
● decreased heat regulation and increased temp.
● increased blood viscosity
● increased HR
● increased fatigue
● decreased cognitive function and skill level

There are 3 types of sports drinks which contain glucose & electrolytes

Type of sports drink	Description	Practical application
Hypotonic	**Lower** concentration of glucose than blood	Vital during prolonged exercise
Isotonic	**Equal** concentration of glucose to blood	Used for events of over 1 hour
Hypertonic	**Higher** concentration of glucose than blood	Used during recovery. **Do not** use during as can increase dehydration

1.2a Diet and nutrition and their effect on physical performance

OCR A Level PE   51

Supplementation

The following table outlines the benefits, drawbacks and practical applications of dietary supplements.

Dietary supplement	Legal or illegal	+ Benefits	– Drawbacks	Practical application
Creatine Taking supplement in the form of powder/tablet to increase phosphocreatine (PC) stores in muscle; used for very high intensity energy production	Legal	+ Increased PC stores = more fuel for high intensity training (ATP-PC system) + Increased intensity and duration of training + Increased maximum and explosive strength	– Increased weight gain – Increased water retention – Muscle cramps and gastrointestinal problems – Long-term effects unclear	Used by power athletes – weightlifters/sprinters
Caffeine Stimulates CNS and increases breakdown of FFAs for aerobic energy production	Legal	+ Increased nervous stimulation + Increased focus/concentration + Increased metabolism of fats + Preservation of muscle glycogen + Increased endurance performance	– Diuretic effect = dehydration – Insomnia and anxiety – Gastrointestinal problems	Found in tea/coffee, energy drinks or tablet form
Bicarbonate Alkaline which acts as a buffer to neutralise a rise in acidity in the blood stream	Legal	+ Increased buffering capacity + Increased tolerance to LA = delay OBLA + Increased intensity and duration of performance	– Gastrointestinal problems – Unpleasant taste causing nausea	Soda loading (ingesting large amounts of bicarbonate in advance of an event to make blood more alkaline, therefore increasing anaerobic endurance by limiting lactic acid build-up)
Nitrates Inorganic compounds which dilate blood vessels and reduce blood pressure	Legal	+ Decreased BP + Increased blood flow + Increased intensity and duration of performance + Delays fatigue	– Headaches, dizziness, light headedness – Long-term effects unclear – Possible carcinogenic risk	Consumed by eating root vegetables, beetroot and greens

---

Revision activity

Create a mindmap for each dietary supplement. Use green to highlight benefits and red to highlight drawbacks. Use diagrams where possible.

Exam tip

When analysing the effect or use of an ergogenic aid, always give a brief description, practical example and discuss benefits and drawbacks.

Now test yourself

TESTED ☐

5 Describe the possible benefits and drawbacks of EPO, glycogen loading and creatine supplements.

Answers on page 168

Exam practice

1 How would you increase the muscle glycogen stores of an endurance athlete? [4]
2 For some endurance athletes, the pressure to perform at the highest level means the temptation to gain unfair aerobic training benefits from ergogenic aids, despite the dangers, becomes too great. Outline how a named pharmacological aid would benefit such an athlete and identify the possible risks associated with it. [4]
3 Explain how cooling aids are used to help athletes post-competition. [3]

Answers on page 176

Summary

You should now have an understanding of:
- components and functions of a balanced diet
- how to relate diet, hydration and dietary supplements to performance in physical activities and sports
- ergogenic aids and how they are used to improve sports performance.

1.2b Preparations and training methods

Training

Training programme design

It is important to include the following in any training programme:
1 evaluation test
2 warm-up
3 cool-down.

The basic building blocks of training programme design are called the **principles of training**. Correct use of the principles of training will result in desirable **adaptation** of the body.

Specificity

- To get the best results from training, it must be geared towards the demands of the activity.
- These demands could be the energy system that is predominantly used, the muscle groups involved or the fitness components that are crucial, for example maximum strength for a weightlifter.
- Training also has to be specific to who is doing it: age, ability, current fitness level, etc.
- Specificity is applied in two ways:
  1 the individual
  2 the sport/activity.

Progression

- Our bodies adapt to the stresses and loads put on them, so training should gradually increase over time.
- After a while, the body will have adapted fully and no other changes occur unless the training is made harder.

Overload

- To make the body adapt, it must be made to work harder than it normally does. This is known as overload.
- The body can be overloaded by manipulating training in terms of:
  - frequency
  - intensity
  - time
  - type.

Variance

- To make the body adapt, a long period of training must take place. Boredom can become an issue.
- A variety of different training sessions are vital to avoid repetition and keep up concentration and commitment.

Moderation

- Although overload is vital for the body to adapt, caution must be taken not to overload too much.
- Overuse injuries will occur and in younger performers burnout is possible.

> **Principles of training**: the rules that underpin training programme design to ensure safe and effective fitness adaptation.
>
> **Adaptation**: a physiological change in response to training, e.g. increased RBC production.

> **Exam tip**
>
> Always give relevant practical examples when referring to the principles of training, e.g. 'the athlete must take into account specificity, for example an 800 m swimmer would conduct most of their training in the pool, focusing on aerobic training, as this targets the muscle movements and the specific energy system used in their event'.

Reversibility

- Fitness levels quickly drop when periods of inactivity occur.
- It is vital that training programmes avoid any long periods of inactivity, even during off-season time.
- The loss of fitness will be reduced if steady progression has been made throughout the training.

Periodisation

REVISED

Periodisation is the organised division of training into blocks, each with a goal and time frame. The aims are:

1 Reaching physiological peak at the correct time
2 Avoiding injury and burnout
3 Structured training to give realistic and achievable goals

Cycles

Olympic Games are held every four years; most athletes and coaches plan training on a yearly basis.

1 A **macro-cycle** is the whole training programme, typically over the course of a calendar year. For an Olympic athlete, it may be 4 years. This is broken down into meso-cycles and is a long-term training plan.
2 A **meso-cycle** is a phase of training, often about a month or 6 weeks long. The length of each meso-cycle will depend on its aim. Many performers will use six meso-cycles or phases. This is broken down into micro-cycles and is a mid-term training plan.
3 A **micro-cycle** can be a typical week that is broken down into training units. Any training sessions may contain one or more units. This is a short-term training plan.

> **Macro-cycle**: a long-term training plan, typically over a year, to achieve a long-term goal.
>
> **Meso-cycle**: a mid-term training plan, typically 6 weeks, to achieve a mid-term goal.
>
> **Micro-cycle**: a short-term training plan, typically 1 week, to achieve a short-term goal.
>
> **Tapering**: maintaining the intensity but decreasing the volume of training by one-third to prepare for competition.

Phases of training

There are three main training phases in a periodised year, as shown in the table below.

Phase	When	What happens
Preparatory 1	Off-season	General conditioning; aerobic and mobility training, strength conditioning
Preparatory 2	Pre-season, approaching competition	Training intensity increases; sport-specific fitness is central, e.g. anaerobic training for a 400m runner
		Training volume reduces; more competition-specific training, e.g. practice games
Competitive 3	During the season	Training load reduces, allowing adequate rest; strategy, tactics and game–play is focus; endurance performers still need high-intensity training
Competitive 4	2–3 weeks before the main event	**Tapering** – maintaining intensity but decreasing volume by a third
Transition	After the season, before the start of the new season	Active rest or low-intensity aerobic work, e.g. swimming/cycling

Now test yourself

TESTED

1 What are the six principles of training?
2 What are the three cycles commonly used in periodisation?

Answers on page 168

Revision activity

Divide up your own practical activity into a periodisation programme of training.

Annual periodised training programme

	January	February	March	April	May	June	July	August	September	October	November	December
Month												
Meso cycle	8	9	10	11	12	1	2	3	4	5	6	7
Comp phase	Competitive league season – international fixtures occur in this time phase					Off-season	Pre-season			Season begins mid-september		
Training phase	Maintenance					General prep		Specific prep (includes technical, aerobic and tactical training)		Maintenance		
	Maintenance of technical and tactical training – decrease in strength training					Hypertrophy	Max strength development	Strength endurance development / Convert strength to power		Maintenance of strength and endurance training – decreased aerobic training volume – increased technical and tactical training		
Peaking		Key international period e.g Six Nations	Attempt to maintain performance levels – training levels adjusted 1–2 days before game so as not to affect physiological performance		HC final peak	No specific peaking during non-competitive season – training levels adjusted 1–2 days before game so as not to affect physiological performance			Start of season	Attempt to maintain performance levels – secondary weekly targets for matches		
Testing	Mid-season testing					Baseline tests and injury screening	Pre-season strength tests		Pre-season re-test			
Goals	Peak in physical condition for key international period		Maintenance of physical conditioning for season run-in, no specific peaking but aim for weekly preparation for matches			Hypertrophy	Development of optimum strength	Conversion of strength to rugby–related power		Maintain power and strength without causing performance–inhibiting fatigue due to training		

Figure 1.2.3 Complex and detailed periodised training programme for an elite rugby player

Aerobic training

Aerobic capacity is a key fitness component that underpins all endurance-based work, such as long-distance running, triathlon, open-water swimming and cross-country running. It is also an important contributor to many other sporting situations, such as football, hockey and rowing.

It is reliant on the efficiency of the respiratory, cardiovascular and muscular systems. A key component of aerobic capacity is VO_2 max.

> **Aerobic capacity:** the ability of the body to inspire, transport and utilise oxygen to perform sustained periods of aerobic activity.

VO_2max

VO_2max is measured in millilitres per kilogram per minute (ml/kg/min):
- untrained individual = 40–50 ml/kg/min
- highly trained athlete = 90 ml/kg/min.

Factors that affect VO_2max

The following table outlines the factors which can affect the VO_2max of an individual.

Factor	Effect on VO_2max	Explanation
Physiological make-up	The greater the efficiency of body systems to transport and utilise O_2 = higher VO_2max; can be determined by genetics	Stronger respiratory muscles, larger heart, SV, CO, increased number of RBCs, capillaries, SO fibres = higher VO_2max
Age	From age 20, VO_2max drops 1% each year	Efficiency is lost in elasticity of the heart, blood vessels and lung tissue = lower VO_2max
Gender	Females lower than males	Females have higher body fat, smaller lung volumes, lower haemoglobin levels = lower VO_2max
Training	Aerobic training increases VO_2max up to 20%	Aerobic training causes long-term adaptions to the heart, lungs and blood = higher VO_2max

Evaluation

The table below identifies the methods of evaluating VO_2max, including advantages and disadvantages of each method.

Method	Advantages	Disadvantages
Direct gas analysis Expired air captured, results graphed and a calculation used	+ Direct measurement + Accurate and reliable + Uses different exercises, e.g. running, cycling, rowing	– Maximal test to exhaustion – Not suitable for elderly/those with health problems – Specialist equipment required
Cooper 12-minute run Run as far as possible in 12 minutes – calculation used	+ Good for large groups + Can test yourself + Simple/cheap	– Only a prediction – Result affected by subject motivation – Not suitable for elderly/those with health problems – Not sport-specific
NCF multi-stage fitness test 20 m progressive shuttle run; results compared to standardised tables	+ Good for large groups + Simple/cheap + Published table of VO_2max equivalents	– Only a prediction – Result affected by subject motivation – Not suitable for elderly/those with health problems – Not sport-specific
Queens College step test Stepping on and off box for 3 minutes; HR recovery used to predict results	+ Sub-maximal test + Simple/cheap + HR easily monitored + Published table of data and simple VO_2max calculations	– Only a prediction – HR recovery affected by lots of factors – food, fluid, prior exercise – Not sport-specific – Shorter subjects may be at a disadvantage

Revision activity

Create a fact card for each method of evaluating VO_2max. Give the card to a friend and get them to ask you questions.

Training zones

Training at the correct intensity is essential. If intensity is too high, performers will experience fatigue quickly and adapt anaerobically. If intensity is too low, no adaptations will take place.

Heart rate is often used as a prediction of training intensity. This can be done in two ways:

1 Heart rate training zones:

Heart rate (bpm)	200	190	180	170	160		Physiological benefit
5 Maximum 90–100%	180	171	162	153	144	0–2 mins	Max performance capacity
4 Hard 80–90%	160	152	144	136	128	2–10 mins	Lactate threshold
3 Moderate 70–80%	140	133	126	119	112	10–40 mins	Aerobic zone
2 Light 60–70%	120	114	108	102	96	40–80 mins	Targets fat burning
1 Very light 50–60%	100	95	90	85	80	20–40 mins	Basic endurance
Age	20	30	40	50	60		

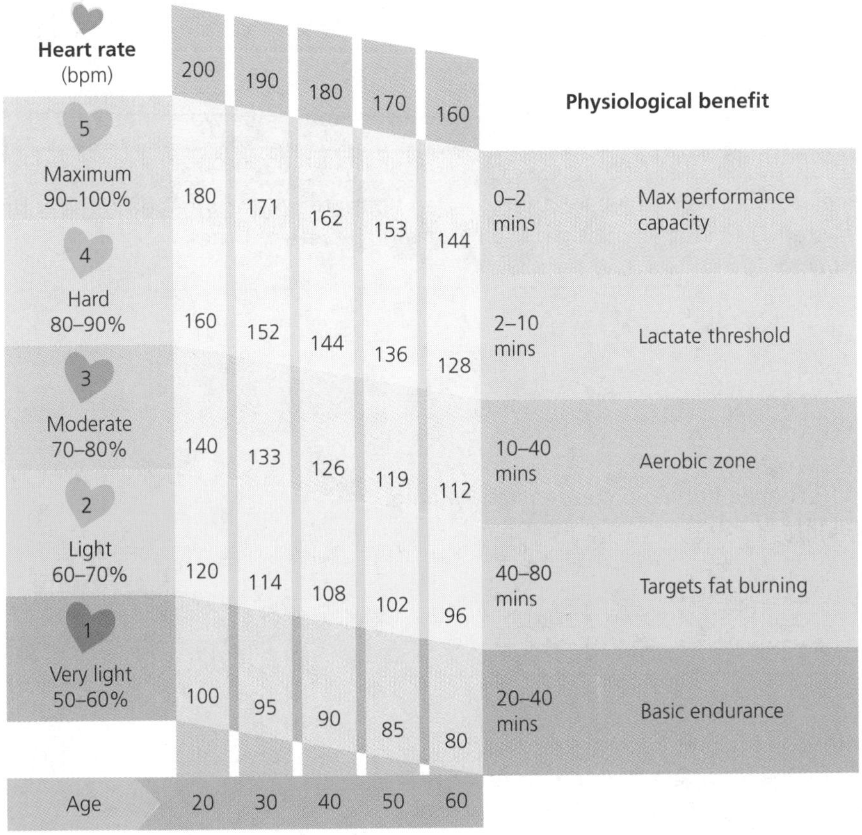

Figure 1.2.4 Heart rate training zones

2 Karvonen's principle:
   ○ HR max = (220 − age)
   ○ training HR = resting HR + % (HR max − resting HR)

For example, for a 60 per cent HR for a 17-year-old with a resting HR of 72:

Training HR = 72 + (0.60 × (203 − 72))

= 72 + 78.6

= 150.6 bpm

Training methods: aerobic capacity

The table below identifies the key features of continuous and HIIT training

Key feature	Continuous training	HIIT training
Intensity of work	Low–moderate, 60% to 80% max HR	High, 80% to 95% max HR
Duration of work	20–80 minutes	5 seconds to 8 minutes, repeated bouts of high intensity work with varied recovery time – overall 20–60 minutes
Intensity of recovery	No recovery, non-stop activity	40% to 50% of max HR
Duration of recovery	No recovery, non-stop activity	Recovery interval = work interval (1:1)
Practical example	Jogging, swimming, cycling	Cycling, running, cross-training
Type of athlete suited to	Endurance athletes as it stresses the aerobic system and slow-oxidative muscle fibres	Can be modified for most athletes with varying levels of fitness

Now test yourself

TESTED

3 Define aerobic capacity and VO_2max.
4 Name four methods to evaluate VO_2max.
5 Outline the similarities and differences between continuous training and high intensity interval training.

Answers on page 168

Exam tip

If you are asked to compare methods of training, compare carefully point by point. Marks are only awarded for a direct comparison of similar points, e.g. work intervals of both, activities of both, practical example of both.

Adaptations: aerobic capacity

After a prolonged period of aerobic training (12 weeks, 3–5 times a week),
a large number of long-term responses or adaptations will take place.

Respiratory system

The table below outlines the long-term adaptations in the respiratory
system after 12 weeks of aerobic training.

Adaptation	Functional effects
Respiratory muscles become stronger	• Increased efficiency of mechanics of breathing • Increased maximum-exercise lung volumes • Decreased respiratory fatigue
Increased surface area of alveoli	• Increased external gaseous exchange
	Overall effects
	• Increased volume of O_2 diffused into blood • Decreased breathing rate at rest and sub-maximal exercise • Easier to perform exercise • Reduced onset of fatigue • Delayed OBLA • Increased intensity and duration of performance • Alleviates symptoms of asthma

Cardiovascular system

The table below outlines the long-term adaptations in the cardiovascular
system after 12 weeks of aerobic training.

Adaptation	Functional effects

Cardiac hypertrophy	• Increased SV at rest and during exercise and increased CO (at rest), due to:
	  ○ increased filling capacity and force of ventricular contraction
	  ○ decreased resting and sub-maximal HR (←60 bradycardia)
	  ○ decreased HR and recovery after exercise

Increased elasticity of arterial walls	• Increased vascular shunt efficiency • Decreased resting BP
Increased number of RBC/haemoglobin volume	• Increase in O_2-carrying capacity • Increased gaseous exchange
Increased blood plasma volume	• Lower blood viscosity aids blood flow and venous return
Increased capillarisation of alveoli and SO muscle tissue fibres	• Increased surface area for blood flow • Increased gaseous exchange • Decreased distance for diffusion
	Overall effects
	• Increased blood flow and O_2 transport to muscles • Decreased BP • Easier to perform exercise • Reduced onset of fatigue • Delayed OBLA • Increased intensity and duration of performance • Lower risk of CHD, hypertension and stroke

Musculo-skeletal system

The following table outlines the long-term adaptations in the musculo-skeletal system after 12 weeks of aerobic training.

Adaptation	Functional effects
SO muscle fibre hypertrophy	• Increased potential for aerobic energy production • Increased strength, decreased energy cost, which delays fatigue
Increased size and density of mitochondria	• Increased utilisation of O_2 • Increased aerobic energy production • Increased metabolism of fats
Increased stores of myoglobin	• Increased storage and transport of O_2 to mitochondria
Increased stores of glycogen and fats	• Increased aerobic energy fuels • Increased duration of performance
FOG fibres become more aerobic	• Increased aerobic energy production, fuel and O_2 utilisation
Increased strength of connective tissue	• Tendons and ligaments strengthen • Increased joint stability • Decreased risk of injury
Increased thickness of articular cartilage	• Increased synovial fluid production
Increased bone mineral density	• Increased calcium absorption • Increased bone strength • Decreased risk of injury
	Overall effects
	• Increased capacity of aerobic energy production • Increased joint stability • Increased metabolic rate • Decreased risk of injury, osteoarthritis and osteoporosis • Easier to perform exercise • Reduced onset of fatigue • Delayed OBLA • Increased intensity and duration of performance

Metabolic function

The table below outlines the long-term adaptations to metabolic function after 12 weeks of aerobic training.

Adaptation	Functional effects
Increased activity of aerobic enzymes	● Increased metabolism of fats and glycogen
Decreased fat mass	● Increased lean mass ● Increased metabolic rate ● Increased breakdown of fats
Decreased insulin resistance	● Increased glucose tolerance ● Treatment and prevention of type 2 diabetes
	Overall effects
	● Increased use of fuel and O_2 to provide energy ● Improved body composition ● Easier to perform exercise ● Reduced onset of fatigue ● Delayed OBLA ● Increased intensity and duration of performance ● Increased metabolic rate, increased energy expenditure and better management of body weight

Now test yourself

TESTED ☐

6 Describe the adaptations that would occur in the heart after a sustained period of aerobic training. How would these impact health and performance?

Answers on page 169

Strength training

REVISED ☐

The following table identifies and defines the different types of strength.

Type of strength	Definition	Practical example
Static	Force is applied against a resistance without movement occurring (isometric contraction)	Gymnastics – arabesque on the beam, handstand on the floor, crucifix position
Dynamic	Force is applied against a resistance with movement occurring; also known as **power output**	Hop, step and jump phases of triple jump
Maximum	The ability to produce a maximal amount of force in a single muscular contraction, e.g. 1 RM (repetition maximum)	Olympic weightlifter performing a deadlift, a throw in judo, a push in a rugby scrum, a throw in shot putt
Explosive (elastic)	The ability to produce a maximal amount of force in one or a series of rapid muscular contractions	Long jump or high jump run up (sprint) and take off, sprinting down the wing in rugby or hockey, driving for an interception in netball
Strength endurance	The ability to sustain repeated muscular contractions over a period of time	Swimming, rowing and wrestling, where muscles perform the same movement repeatedly

> **Power output**: the amount of work performed per unit of time, measured in watts (W).

Factors that affect strength

The table below identifies the factors that affect strength.

Factor	Effect on strength	Explanation
Cross-sectional area of muscle	Greater cross-sectional area of muscle = greater strength	Maximum of 16–30 Newtons per cm²
Fibre type	Greater % FG + FOG = greater strength over a short period of time	Fast-twitch fibres contract with higher force = greater force of contraction
Gender	Males have greater strength than females	Males have higher muscle mass and cross-sectional area due to higher testosterone levels
Age	Peak strength: ● females – 16–25 years ● males – 18–30 years Thereafter strength decreases with age	Age-related decline due to decrease in efficiency of neuromuscular system, elasticity, testosterone and reduction in muscle mass

Figure 1.2.5 shows how the type of muscle fibre affects the amount of force produced over a period of time.

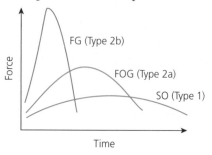

Figure 1.2.5 Effect of fibre type on force production

Evaluation

The following table identifies the different methods of evaluating strength, highlighting advantages and disadvantages of each method.

Test	Advantages	Disadvantages
Maximum strength One repetition maximum test (1RM) (lifting a high weight for one repetition only)	+ Direct measurement + Easy procedure + Most muscle groups can be tested	– Difficult to isolate individual muscles – Trial and error may induce fatigue – Potential for injury
Maximum strength Grip strength dynamometer	+ Simple and objective measure + Inexpensive equipment + High reliability	– Only the forearm muscles are assessed – Test is not sport-specific
Strength endurance UK abdominal curl test – continuous sit-ups at progressive intensities to exhaustion (press-up or sit-up test)	+ Good for large groups + Simple/cheap + Abdominal muscles can be isolated + Valid and reliable	– Good technique needed – Safety concern over strain on lower back – Result affected by subject motivation as test to exhaustion – Not sport-specific
Explosive strength Vertical jump test – compared to standardised tables	+ Data can be converted to calculate a power output + Easy test/minimal equipment + Can test yourself	– Measure not isolated to one muscle group – Only estimates explosive strength in legs

Quick quizzes at **www.hoddereducation.co.uk/myrevisionnotes**

7 Name three types of strength and state how you would evaluate them.
8 Identify four factors that can affect an athlete's strength.

Answers on page 169

Training methods to develop strength

There are many methods of training to improve strength, and design of these programmes will depend on the type of strength desired. All training programmes will manipulate several factors:

● resistance (weight – measure as a percentage of 1RM)
● repetitions (the number of times an exercise is repeated)
● number of sets (series of repetitions and relief period)
● work to relief ratio (e.g. 1:1 – so you work for the same amount of time as you rest).

Below are the strength training guidelines for maximum, explosive and endurance strength.

Type of strength	Intensity: % of one rep max	Repetitions	Sets	Work:relief ratio	Recovery between sets
Maximum	85–95%	1–5	2–6	1:3+	4–5 minutes
Explosive	75–85%	6–10	4–6	1:3	3–5 minutes
Endurance (advanced)	50–75%	15–20	3–5	1:2	30–45 seconds
Endurance (basic)	25–50%	15–20	4–6	1:2	60 seconds

Weight training and plyometric training

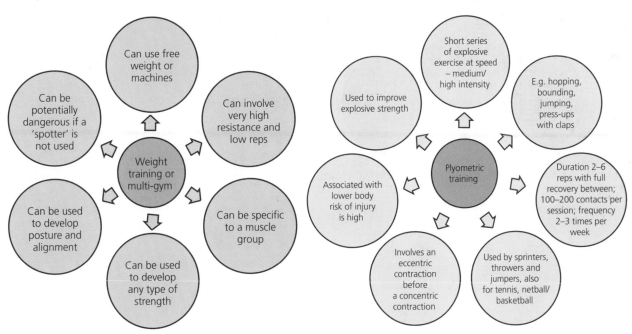

Figure 1.2.6 Key features of weight training and plyometric training

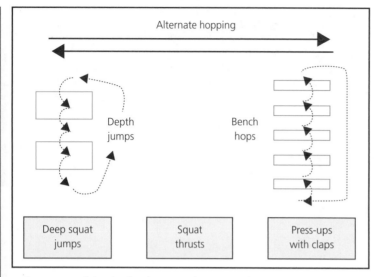

Rotate around the circuit twice, one minute on each exercise, stretch off during rest intervals

Figure 1.2.7 **A plyometric circuit**

Circuit and interval training

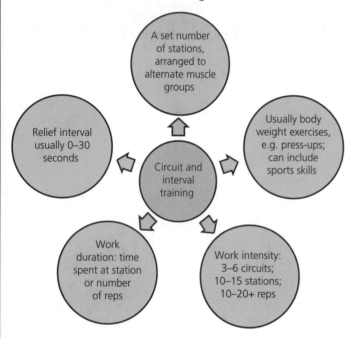

Figure 1.2.8 **Key features of circuit and interval training**

Quick quizzes at **www.hoddereducation.co.uk/myrevisionnotes**

Adaptations: strength

By following a specific strength training programme at the correct intensity and duration, two to five times a week, for at least 12 weeks, significant changes and adaptations will take place. Strength can increase 25–100 per cent in 6 months due to improvements in neural pathways and muscle physiology.

> **Muscle hypertrophy:** increased muscle cell size.
>
> **Muscle hyperplasia:** increased number of muscle fibres.

Muscle and connective tissues adaptations

The table below outlines adaptations of the muscle and connective tissues after 12 weeks of strength training.

Adaptation	Functional effects
Muscle hypertrophy **Muscle hyperplasia**	• Increased force of contraction • Maximum and explosive training = increased size of FG fibres • Strength endurance training = increased size of FOG fibres
Increase in number/size of contractile protein and myofibrils	• Increased force of contraction • Increased actin/myosin filaments and cross bridges • Myofibrils become thicker due to increased protein synthesis
Increased strength of tendons and ligaments	• Increased joint stability • Decreased risk of injury
Increased bone density and mass	• Increased absorption of calcium • Decreased risk of osteoporosis
	Overall effects
	• Increased muscle mass • Increased speed, strength and power output • Increased intensity of performance • Hypertrophic physique–may increase self-esteem

Metabolic adaptations

The following table outlines metabolic adaptations after 12 weeks of strength training.

Adaptation	Functional effects
ATP, PC and glycogen stores within the muscle increase	• Increased capacity for alactic (very high intensity) energy production • Increased energy for speed- and power-based activities
Increased enzyme activity	• Increased efficiency of anaerobic energy production • Increased activity of ATPase, creatine kinase and glycolytic enzyme • Delaying of OBLA/fatigue
Increased buffering capacity	• Increased tolerance and removal of lactic acid • Delaying of OBLA/fatigue • Increased anaerobic threshold
Increased muscle mass	• Improved body composition • Increased metabolic rate
	Overall effects
	• Increased aerobic fuel stores • Increased intensity/duration of performance and delaying of OBLA/fatigue • Increased metabolic rate, increasing energy expenditure and helping manage weight

Neural adaptations

The table below outlines neural adaptations after 12 weeks of strength training.

Adaptation	Functional effects
Increased recruitment of motor units and FG and FOG fibre types	• Increased force of contraction • Improved co-ordination and simultaneous stimulation of motor units
Decreased inhibition of the stretch reflex	• Increased force of contraction from the agonist muscle, allowing the antagonist to stretch further and the agonist to contract with more force
	Overall effects
	• Increased speed, strength and power output

Now test yourself

TESTED

9 Design two strength training programmes, one for a rower and one for a shot putter. Refer to types of strength to develop, frequency, intensity, duration, type and work:relief ratio.

Answers on page 169

Flexibility

There are two main types of flexibility:
1 **static flexibility**, for example holding a hamstring stretch:
   ○ static active flexibility – performer completes a voluntary contraction to move a joint just beyond its range of movement
   ○ static passive flexibility – assistance from a partner to move the joint just beyond its range of movement
2 **dynamic flexibility**, for example a gymnast performing a straddle vault.

Static flexibility: the range of motion about a joint without reference to speed of movement.

Dynamic flexibility: the range of motion about a joint with reference to speed of movement.

Factors that affect flexibility

Factor	Effect on flexibility	Explanation
Type of joint	Ball and socket joint has a greater range of movement (ROM) than a condyloid joint	The size and shape of joints and their articulating bones can aid and limit ROM; the presence of bony features such as processes will limit movement
Length and elasticity of surrounding connective tissue	The greater the length and elasticity of surrounding muscles, tendons and ligaments, the greater the ROM	The greater the length, the greater the distance before the stretch reflex is inhibited, preventing further ROM; the greater the elasticity, the greater the ROM possible
Gender	Females are generally more flexible than males	Females have higher levels of the hormones oestrogen and relaxin
Age	Flexibility is greatest in childhood and declines with age	Age-related decline is due to loss of elasticity in connective tissues

Typical mistake

Flexibility is a very specific component of fitness. If a performer is flexible around the hip joint, this does not mean they are flexible around the shoulder joint.

Evaluation of flexibility

The table below identifies the methods of evaluating flexibility, highlighting advantages and disadvantages of each method.

Test	Advantages	Disadvantages
Goniometry 360-degree protractor; difference in starting angle and full range of motion calculated	+ Objective + Valid/accurate + Any joint can be measured + Can be sport-specific	– Difficult to locate axis of rotation – Training required for accurate measure
Sit and reach test Test box placed against wall, straight legs at full stretch, best score is recorded	+ Easy + Cheap, accessible equipment + Standardised data score	– Measures flexibility in lower back and hamstrings only – Not joint-specific – Need to warm up and hold position for 2 seconds

Training used to develop flexibility

There are two main types of stretching routine, based on whether a performer wants to maintain or improve flexibility:

1 maintenance stretching – performed as part of a warm-up to maintain current ROM and prepare for exercise
2 developmental stretching – designed to improve the ROM at a joint.

There are a number of stretching techniques that can be used to improve flexibility. These are **static active stretching, static passive stretching**, isometric, PNF and ballistic.

Figure 1.2.9 Static passive stretching technique

Static active stretching: a performer moves the joint into its fully stretched position without any assistance and holds for 10–30 seconds.

Static passive stretching: a performer moves the joint just beyond its point of resistance with assistance and holds for 10–30 seconds.

Static and isometric stretching

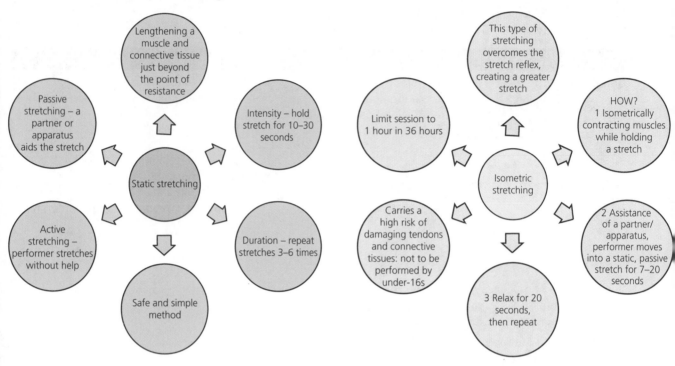

Figure 1.2.10 Static stretching

Figure 1.2.11 Isometric stretching

PNF, dynamic and ballistic stretching

Proprioceptive neuromuscular facilitation (PNF) is a stretching technique to desensitise the stretch reflex, whereby a performer completes a static passive stretch, isometrically contracts against the agonist, relaxes, then stretches further.

Figure 1.2.12 A PNF chest stretch

Figure 1.2.13 Ballistic high leg kick exercises

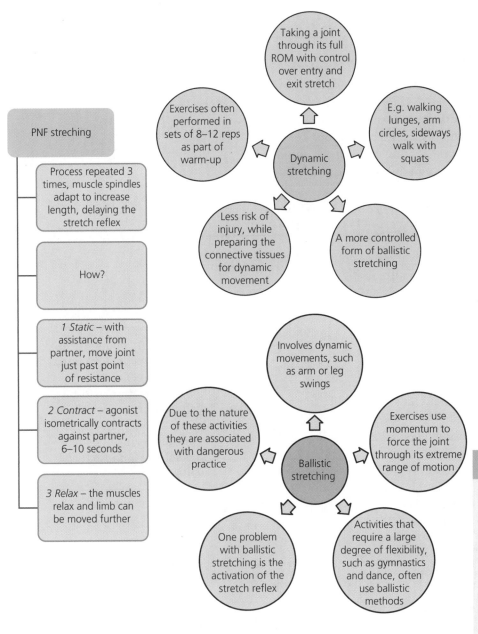

Figure 1.2.14 PNF, dynamic and ballistic stretching

Now test yourself

10 Provide a definition of static flexibility and dynamic flexibility.
11 State the factors that affect an individual's flexibility.
12 Identify and briefly describe two methods of evaluating flexibility.
13 Identify the different types of training to develop flexibility.

Answers on page 169

TESTED

Adaptations

By following a specific flexibility training programme three to six times a week, for at least 6 weeks, significant structural changes will take place. The table below summarises the effects for the following adaptations.

Adaptation	Functional effects
Increased resting length	● Increased ROM about a joint ● Muscle spindles adapt to increased length, reducing stretch reflex stimulus
Increased elasticity	● Increased potential for static and dynamic flexibility ● Decreased inhibition from the antagonist ● Increased stretch of the antagonist
	Overall effects
	● Increased ROM about a joint ● Increased distance and efficiency for muscles to create force at speed ● Decreased risk of injury ● Increased posture and alignment

Impact of training on lifestyle diseases

Cardiovascular disease

Cardiovascular disease (CVD) is a term for all diseases of the heart. Specific diseases include:

- atherosclerosis – a build-up of fatty deposits on arterial walls, leading eventually to chronic high blood pressure (hypertension)
- coronary heart disease (results from atherosclerosis of the coronary arteries); the reduction in blood flow and O_2 to the cardiac muscle can ultimately lead to angina (pain) or heart attack
- heart attack – a blockage or clot in the coronary artery cuts off O_2 supply to the cardiac muscle, causing the death of cells or permanent damage
- stroke – caused by a blockage in a cerebral artery cutting off blood supply to the brain, or a blood vessel bursting in the brain.

The effects of training

Exercise can reduce the overall risk of developing CVD by 30 per cent. Regular training can:

- reduce blood lipids (fats) and cholesterol and increase the proportion of **HDL to LDL cholesterol**
- prevent hardening and loss of elasticity in arterial walls, slowing onset of atherosclerosis and hypertension
- decrease blood viscosity, preventing blood clots and reducing BP
- increase coronary circulation
- lead to cardiac hypertrophy, increased SV and lowered resting HR
- decrease body fat, reducing strain on the heart
- increase blood flow and O_2 transport, reducing strain on the heart
- reduce the risk of a stroke by 27 per cent by lowering BP.

> **HDL and LDL cholesterol**: high-density lipoproteins (HDL) actively remove cholesterol from arterial walls and transport it to the liver, whereas low-density lipoproteins (LDL) deposit cholesterol in the arterial walls.

Respiratory disease

Respiratory disease is characterised by one or several diseases of the airways:

- asthma – the constriction of the bronchial airways and inflammation of the mucus membranes, which limit breathing; can also be exercise-induced (EIA)
- chronic obstructive pulmonary disease (COPD) – condition of the lungs where airways become inflamed and narrowed; over time the inflammation causes permanent changes and can lead to an inability to exercise and a reduced quality of life.

Smoking is the biggest risk factor for respiratory disease.

The effects of training

Exercise can reduce the risk of developing respiratory disease. Regular exercise and training can:

- increase respiratory muscle strength, alleviating symptoms of asthma
- decrease resting and sub-maximal breathing rate
- increase airflow
- maintain full use of lung tissue and elasticity, decreasing the risk of infection
- increase the surface area of the alveoli, maximising gaseous exchange.

Exam practice

1 Identify and explain three physiological adaptations that take place after a strength training programme. [3]

2 A performer carries out a number of fitness tests. The table below gives the results of two of these tests.

Component of fitness	Test	Result	Evaluation by comparison norm tables
Aerobic capacity	**Test A**	Predicted VO$_2$max = 50ml/kg/min	High
Fitness component B	UK abdominal curl test	Stage 6	Very good

   a) Identify test A and fitness component B. [2]
   b) Explain three physiological factors related to the heart and skeletal muscle that enable the performer to score so highly on test A. [3]

3 Describe proprioceptive neuromuscular facilitation (PNF) flexibility training and explain why PNF is considered to be such an effective method of stretching. [6]

Answers on page 176

Summary

You should now have an understanding of:
- periodisation of training:
  - macro-cycle
  - meso-cycle
  - micro-cycle
- phases of training
- aerobic capacity and maximal oxygen uptake (VO$_2$max)
- how VO$_2$max is affected by:
  - the individual
  - physiological make-up
  - training
  - age
  - gender
- methods of evaluating aerobic capacity
- how intensity and duration of training is used to develop aerobic capacity:
  - continuous training
  - high intensity interval training (HIIT)
- the use of target heart rates as an intensity guide
- physiological adaptations from aerobic training:
  - cardiovascular
  - respiratory
  - muscular
  - metabolic

- sports in which aerobic capacity is a key fitness component
- types of strength
- factors that affect strength
- methods of evaluating each type of strength
- training to develop strength, referring to repetitions, sets, resistance, work intensity, work duration and relief interval
- physiological adaptations from strength training
- activities and sports in which strength is a key fitness component
- types of flexibility
- factors that affect flexibility
- methods of evaluating flexibility
- training used to develop flexibility
- Physiological adaptations from flexibility training
- sports in which flexibility is a key fitness component
- how to plan personal health and fitness programmes for aerobic, strength and flexibility training
- the impact of training on lifestyle diseases of the cardiovascular and respiratory systems.

1.2c Injury prevention and the rehabilitation of injury

Acute and chronic injuries

Acute injuries

Acute injuries happen suddenly after a stress to the body, such as a fractured eye socket after being hit with a ball in hockey.

A hard tissue injury involves damage to the bone, joint or cartilage, including fractures and dislocations.

> **Acute injury**: a sudden injury associated with a traumatic event.

Hard tissue injuries: fracture

Fractures are a partial or complete break in the bone. In simple (closed) fractures, the skin remains unbroken. Compound (open) fractures are where the bone breaks through the skin.

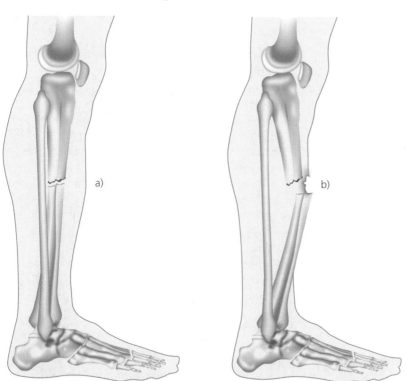

a) b)

Figure 1.2.15 Simple (a) and compound (b) fractures

Signs of a fracture	Symptoms of a fracture
● Deformity ● Swelling ● Discolouration	● Pain ● Inability to move the injured area

> **Signs of an injury**: things you can see.
>
> **Symptoms of an injury**: things a performer may feel.

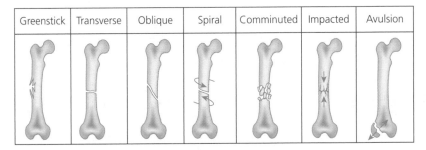

Greenstick	Transverse	Oblique	Spiral	Comminuted	Impacted	Avulsion

Figure 1.2.16 Additional types of possible fracture

Hard tissue injuries: dislocation

- A **dislocation** occurs from a direct force (collision or object) or an indirect force (a fall) pushing the joint past its extreme range of motion.
- A **subluxation** often causes damage to ligaments and increases the likelihood of recurrent dislocations. This may compromise an athlete's career.

Signs of a dislocation	Symptoms of a dislocation
• Deformity • Swelling and discolouration	• May feel a 'pop' • Severe pain • Loss of movement

Dislocation: the displacement of one bone from another out of their original position.

Subluxation: an incomplete or partial dislocation.

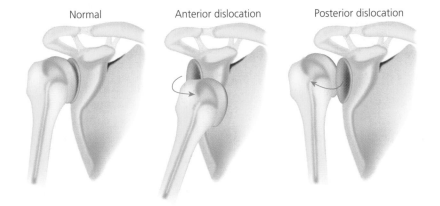

Figure 1.2.17 Anterior and posterior dislocation of the humerus from the shoulder joint

A soft tissue injury involves damage to the skin, muscle, tendon or ligament, including tears, strains and sprains.

Soft tissue injuries: contusion and haematoma

- A contusion (bruise) is an area of skin or tissue where the blood vessels have become damaged. While it is usually a minor injury, severe contusion can cause deep tissue damage and ultimately a **haematoma**.
- Haematoma is internal bleeding, ranging from minor bruises under the skin to deep tissue bleeding.

Haematoma: localised congealed bleeding from ruptured blood vessels.

Signs of contusion/haematoma	Symptoms of contusion/ haematoma
Swelling and discolouration	Pain (at touch in a minor case)

Soft tissue injuries: sprain

Sprains are caused by a sudden twist, impact or fall that forces the joint beyond its extreme range of motion. They are common at the ankle joint of games players.

Signs of a sprain	Symptoms of a sprain
● Swelling ● Bruising	● Inability to bear weight ● Pain

Soft tissue injuries: strain

Strains result from overstretching a muscle. They are common in dynamic lunging movements, For example lunging to return a drop shot in badminton. A very serious sprain or strain can result in a **rupture**.

Signs of a strain	Symptoms of a strain
● Swelling/discolouration ● Bruising	● Pain on movement

Soft tissue injuries: abrasion

Abrasions are caused by falling or slipping, or by clothing rubbing on the body. If an abrasion causes an open wound it will need to be cleaned; severe abrasions may need stitching.

Most sports have blood rules; players have to leave the game until the bleeding stops or is covered.

Soft tissue injuries: blister

Blisters occur due to friction on the skin. They can be painful but may not stop participation. They are preventable with the correct footwear, equipment and training load.

Concussion

Concussion occurs after a trauma to the head, resulting in headaches, dizziness, balance problems, nausea and sometimes a loss of consciousness.

A blow to the head can cause swelling and possibly a disruption in the electrical processes of the brain.

Signs of concussion	Symptoms of concussion
● Possible post-traumatic seizure ● Loss of consciousness ● Balance problems ● Disorientation/confusion	● Lying motionless/slow to get up ● Headache/dizziness ● Visual problems/light sensitivity ● Nausea/vomiting

Sprain: overstretch or tear in the ligament that connects bone to bone.

Strain: overstretch or tear in the muscle or tendon that connects muscle to bone.

Rupture: a complete tear of muscle, tendon or ligament.

Typical mistake

Be clear on the difference between a strain and a sprain. Strain = muscle, sprain = ligaments.

Abrasion: superficial damage to the skin caused by scraping against a surface.

Blister: separation of layers of skin where a pocket of fluid forms, caused by friction.

Concussion: a traumatic brain injury resulting in a disturbance of brain function.

Exam tip

Always give a relevant sporting example to describe how an injury may have occurred, for example 'a hockey player may suffer a concussion after being hit in the head by a hockey ball'.

Chronic injuries

Chronic injuries develop by repeated continued stress on the body over a period of time, for example pain in a runner's knees or heels.

Hard tissue injuries: stress fracture

Stress fractures are common in distance running events, tennis, gymnastics and basketball, where the repetitive stress of the foot on the ground can cause a trauma.

Overtraining can cause stress fractures. Pain will usually stop with rest.

Soft tissue injuries: shin splints

Through excessive use, the tendons connecting the muscles to the tibia via the periosteum become inflamed, leading to pain in a specific area of the shin bone.

Also known as **MTSS**, this type of injury is common in distance runners, dancers and football players. Being overweight, wearing inadequate footwear or poor leg biomechanics can be a cause.

Soft tissue injuries: tendinosis

Tendons are tough fibrous connective tissues designed to transmit force. Repetitive strain causes small injuries that are not given time to heal, resulting in a chronic injury, for example tennis elbow or Achilles **tendinosis**.

Signs of tendinosis	Symptoms of tendinosis
Limited movement/stiffness	Burning/stinging/aching

Chronic injury: a slowly developed injury associated with overuse.

Stress fracture: a tiny crack in the surface of a bone caused by overuse.

Shin splints/medial tibia stress syndrome (MTSS): chronic shin pain due to the inflammation of muscles and stress on the tendon attachments to the surface of the tibia.

Tendinosis: the deterioration of a tendon in response to chronic overuse and repetitive strain.

Now test yourself

TESTED

1 What is the difference between an acute and a chronic injury?
2 State two acute hard tissue injuries.
3 State two acute soft tissue injuries.
4 What is the difference between a stress fracture and shin splints?
5 What are the signs and symptoms of concussion?

Answers on page 169

Injury prevention

Risk factors must be identified in order to prevent injuries. Risk factors have two classifications, which are outlined in the table below. An intrinsic risk factor is an injury risk or force from inside the body. An extrinsic risk factor is an injury risk or force from outside the body.

Intrinsic risk factors	Extrinsic risk factors
● Previous injury ● Posture and alignment issues ● Age ● Nutrition ● Poor preparation ● Inadequate fitness level ● Inappropriate flexibility level	● Poor technique and training ● Incorrect equipment and clothing ● Inappropriate intensity duration or frequency of activity ● Warm-up and cool-down ineffectiveness

Warm-up and cool-down effectiveness

Warm-up

Warm-ups are used for:

1 raising body temperature – a rise of 2–3 degrees increases enzyme activity, diffusion gradients and metabolic activity, improving efficiency of muscular contraction
2 preparing the body physiologically – the elasticity of muscles, tendons and ligaments improves, antagonistic co-ordination improves
3 preparing the body psychologically – mentally performers are ready for the task ahead
4 minimising the risk of injury – for example the performer is less likely to suffer strains/sprains.

Key features

- Lasts 20–45 minutes
- Gradually increases in intensity
- Has three stages – pulse raising, stretching and mobility, sport-specific drills
- Stretching and mobility should be dynamic in sport-specific patterns
- Static stretching should be avoided

Cool-down

Cool-downs are used for:

1 maintaining heart rate – to maintain blood flow and metabolic activity, flushing muscle tissue with oxygenated blood
2 aiding the removal of lactic acid – enhancing future performances, delaying fatigue and injuries
3 aiding the healing process.

Key features

- Lasts 20–30 minutes
- Gradually decreases in intensity
- Has several stages – moderate intensity activity, to maintain HR, aid venous return and remove waste; and stretching exercise to reduce muscle tension and lower temperature.

Debates about warm-up and cool-down

Historically, static stretches have been a large part of a warm-up. However, research suggests static stretching:

- has no effect on injury prevention
- may reduce the peak force produced in the Achilles tendon by 8 per cent
- deteriorates antagonistic co-ordination, hampering explosive movements
- reduces eccentric strength by 9 per cent, decreasing the ability to change direction at speed
- reduces the muscles' ability to consume O_2 by 50 per cent.

As a result, static stretching should be avoided in a warm-up routine unless advised by a physiotherapist. Injury prevention researchers believe that dynamic stretching exercises such as high knee skips and walking lunges should be used as part of a warm-up instead.

Historically, an active cool-down has been thought to benefit all athletes. However, during low-intensity activity, such as jogging for an aerobically fit athlete, a passive recovery period (such as sitting on a bench) has been shown to be more beneficial.

Equally, there is little evidence to suggest an active cool-down can prevent or limit DOMS.

Now test yourself

TESTED

6 Identify two intrinsic risk factors of injury.
7 Identify two extrinsic risk factors of injury.
8 Give three reasons why is it important to warm up.
9 Give three reasons why is it important to cool down.

Answers on page 169

Responding to injuries and medical conditions in sport

Assessment using SALTAPS

In the event of a sporting accident, a sport-specific assessment such as **SALTAPS** should take place to decide whether a player should continue.

Stop	Stop the game and observe the injury.
Ask	Ask questions of the player/participant: how did the injury happen? Where does it hurt?
Look	At the injury site, check for swelling, bruising, deformity or discolouration.
Touch	At the injury site, check for swelling, deformity, lumps and bumps or heat.
Active movement	Ask for active movements from the participant.
Passive movement	Assessor moves the injured limb/body part.
Strength testing	Ask the player to stand, lift and put pressure on the injured area. Ask them if they can continue.

SALTAPS: protocol for the assessment of a sporting injury: stop; ask, look, touch, active movement, passive movement and strength testing.

Acute injury management using PRICE

Soft tissue injuries can be treated by using **PRICE**.

Most minor soft tissue injuries can be managed at home. For the first two to three days after your injury, you should follow the **PRICE** procedure.

PRICE: protocol for the treatment of acute injuries: protect, rest, ice, compress and elevate.

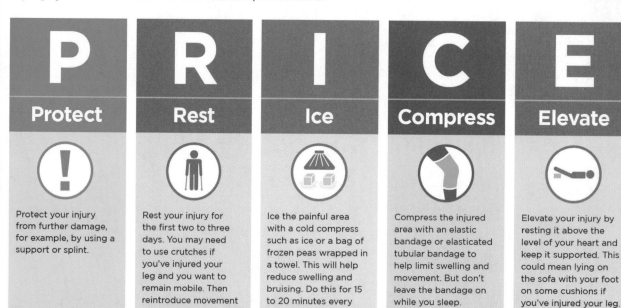

Figure 1.2.18 Bupa's guide to PRICE

Recognising concussion using the six Rs

Concussion is a brain injury and is very serious. World Rugby has launched the 'recognise and remove' campaign, outlined in the table below which involves **six Rs**:

Six Rs: protocol for recognition of concussion: recognise, remove, refer, rest, recover and return.

Recognise	Learn the signs and symptoms of concussion to help identify when an athlete might have a suspected concussion.
Remove	Any athlete who has a concussion or a suspected concussion must be removed from play immediately.
Refer	Once removed, the athlete should be referred immediately to a qualified healthcare professional who is trained in evaluating and treating concussion.
Rest	Athletes must rest from exercise until symptom-free and not be left alone in the first 24 hours following injury.
Recover	Athletes must be fully recovered and symptom-free from the concussion before returning to play. Adults must take a minimum of 1 week and under-18s a minimum of 2 weeks before seeking an authorised return from a healthcare professional.
Return	In order for safe return to play, the athlete must be symptom-free and cleared in writing by a qualified healthcare professional who is trained in evaluating and treating concussion. The athlete completes the GRTP (graduated return to play) protocol.

Now test yourself

TESTED ☐

10 When would you use SALTAPS?
11 With what type of injury would you use PRICE?

Answers on page 169

Rehabilitation of injury

Rehabilitation depends on an accurate diagnosis and specialist treatment. There are three recognised stages of rehabilitation:

1 Early stage: gentle exercise encouraging damaged tissue to heal
2 Mid stage: progressive loading of connective tissues and bones to develop strength
3 Late stage: functional exercises and drills to ensure the body is ready to return to training.

> **Rehabilitation**: the process of restoring full function after an injury has occurred.

Treatment of common sporting injuries

Simple fracture (depending on site and severity)

- Medical attention ASAP
- PRICE
- Immobilisation (plaster cast, sling, crutches)
- Anti-inflammatory and pain medication (**NSAIDs**)
- Severe fractures may require surgery to realign bones or fix pins and wires
- **Physiotherapy** may be needed

> **Non-steroid anti-inflammatory drugs (NSAIDs)**: medication taken to reduce inflammation, temperature and pain following injury.
>
> **Physiotherapy**: physical treatment of injuries and disease using methods such as mobilisation, massage, exercise therapy and postural training.

Stress fracture

- Medical attention required for diagnosis and advice
- PRICE
- Rest for 2 weeks, avoid activity for 8 weeks
- Immobilisation may be needed
- Gentle return to exercise
- Strengthening exercises for surrounding connective tissue

Dislocation (depending on site and severity)

- Medical attention ASAP
- Immobilisation; no attempt to reposition bones unless a medical professional
- PRICE
- Anti-inflammatory and pain medication
- Severe dislocations may require surgery to realign bones and pin them into their original position
- Physiotherapy will strengthen surrounding connective tissue and improve mobility

Sprain (depending on site and severity)

- Medical attention may be required in severe cases
- PRICE
- Immobilisation or support using strapping, a brace, crutches
- Anti-inflammatory and pain medication
- Exercise to strengthen surrounding connective tissue and improve mobility and balance
- Severe sprains may need reconstructive surgery
- **Heat therapy** and **contrast therapy** can be used for pain relief.

> **Heat therapy**: applying heat to an area before training for a therapeutic effect, such as increasing blood flow.
>
> **Contrast therapy**: the use of alternate cold and heat for a therapeutic effect, such as increasing blood flow.

Torn cartilage (depending on site and severity)

- Medical attention
- PRICE
- Support using strapping, a brace (e.g. knee brace)
- Anti-inflammatory and pain medication
- Physiotherapy to strengthen surrounding connective tissue and restore range of motion
- Hydrotherapy to main fitness without weight bearing
- **Arthroscopy** surgery can be used to reshape and resurface torn cartilage

Exercise-induced muscle damage

- In most cases, medical attention is NOT required and symptoms should improve in 5 days
- **Cold therapy** such as ice pack, ice baths post-exercise
- **Massage** and stretching techniques
- Anti-inflammatory and pain medication
- Medical attention may be needed if heavy swelling or dark urine
- Heat therapy and contrast therapy can be used for pain relief.

Arthroscopy: a minimally invasive procedure to examine and repair damage within a joint.

Massage: a physical therapy used for injury prevention and soft tissue injury treatment.

Cold therapy or cryotherapy: applying ice or cold to an injury or after exercise for therapeutic effect, such as reducing swelling.

Summary

You should now have an understanding of:
- acute injuries resulting from a sudden stress to the body: hard tissue injuries, soft tissue injuries, concussion
- chronic injuries resulting from continuous stress to the body: soft tissue injuries, hard tissue injuries
- injury prevention:
  - intrinsic risk factors, individual variables, training effects
  - extrinsic risk factors: poor technique/training, incorrect equipment/clothing, inappropriate intensity, duration or frequency of activity
- the debate surrounding effective warm-up and cool-down

- assessing sporting injuries using 'SALTAPS': stop, ask, look, touch, active movement, passive movement, strength testing
- acute management of soft tissue injuries using 'PRICE': protect, rest, ice, compress, elevate
- recognising concussion – Word Rugby 'recognise and remove' six Rs: recognise, remove, refer, rest, recover, return
- the treatment of common sporting injuries: fractures (simple, stress); joint injuries; dislocation; sprain; strain; torn cartilage; exercise-induced muscle damage
- treatments: stretching; massage; heat, cold and contrast therapies; anti-inflammatory drugs; physiotherapy; surgery.

Exam practice

1 Why do athletes complete a cool-down? [6]
2 Describe the aims of a warm-up. [4]
3 Define rehabilitation and describe the three stages of rehabilitation after injury. [4]

Answers on page 177

Biomechanical principles

REVISED

Biomechanics is the study of human movement and the effect of force and motion on sport performance.

Newton's laws of motion

Using the laws and principles of physics, we can understand why bodies move or do not move.

Law of motion	Definition	Application
First law: law of inertia	A body continues in a state of rest or uniform velocity unless acted upon by an external or unbalanced force.	A golf ball will remain still unless the force applied by a golf club makes it move. Or that same golf ball will continue to move at a constant velocity (speed in a straight line) unless a force acts on it to slow it down (e.g. wind resistance) or change its direction (e.g. gravity).
Second law: law of acceleration	A body's rate of change of momentum is proportional to the size of the force applied and acts in the same direction as the force applied.	When a golf ball is struck by a golf club, the rate of change of momentum (or velocity) of the ball is proportional to the size of the force acted on it by the club. The bigger the force, the greater the acceleration. A popular way of describing Newton's second law of motion, particularly when doing calculations, is F = ma or force = mass × acceleration.
Third law: law of reaction	For every action there is an equal and opposite reaction.	If a tennis player hits a ball, the racquet exerts a force on the ball and the ball exerts an equal and opposite force on the racquet. The racquet exerts what is known as the action force and the ball exerts the reaction force. If the tennis ball then hits the floor, it exerts a force on the floor and the floor exerts an equal and opposite force on the ball.

Key formulae for calculations

The table below summarises the definitions and equations needed for calculations.

Term	Definition	Equation
Velocity (m/s)	Rate of change of displacement (the shortest straight-line route between start and finish points)	Velocity = displacement/time taken
Momentum (kg m/s)	Quantity of motion possessed by a moving body	Momentum = mass × velocity
Acceleration (m/s/s)	Rate of change of velocity	Acceleration = (final velocity – initial velocity)/time taken
Force (N)	A push or a pull that alters the state of motion of a body	Force = mass × acceleration

Force

There are two types of force: external force (comes from outside the body) and internal force (generated by skeletal muscle). Force can have the following effects:

- create motion
- accelerate a body
- decelerate a body
- change the direction of a body
- change the shape of a body.

Net force

If **net force** = 0, there is no change in motion as the forces are balanced.

If a net force is present, there is a change in motion as the forces are unbalanced. This occurs when two forces are unequal in size and opposite in direction.

External forces

The external forces acting on a performer in contact with the ground can be divided into:

- vertical forces: weight and reaction
- horizontal forces: friction and air resistance.

Vertical forces

Weight is the gravitational pull that the earth exerts on a body. Weight is measured in newtons (N), and is calculated by multiplying mass (kg) and acceleration due to gravity (m/s/s).

Reaction is the equal and opposite force exerted by a body in response to the action force placed upon it and is measured in newtons (N). It is a result of Newton's third law of motion and is always present when two bodies are in contact.

Horizontal forces

Friction is the force that opposes the motion of two surfaces in contact. It is measured in newtons (N). Friction is affected by several factors outlined in the following table.

Factors affecting friction	Examples
Roughness of the ground surface	Athletes run on rough, rubberised tracks.
Roughness of the contact surface	Athletes wear spiked shoes.
Temperature	F1 drivers have a warm-up lap, as friction is increased with higher tyre temperatures.
Size of normal reaction	Shot putters have a high mass; due to Newton's third law, this creates an equal and opposite high reaction force, allowing greater friction in the throwing circle and preventing over-rotation.

Air resistance is the force that opposes motion through the air. It is a form of fluid friction, measured in newtons (N). It is affected by several factors outlined in the following table (page 86).

Exam tip

Learn all definitions, equations and correct units.

Revision activity

Add a sporting example to each of the effects of force.

Net force: the sum of all forces acting on a body; also termed resultant force. It is the overall force acting on a body when all individual forces have been considered.

Weight: the gravitational pull that the earth exerts on a body. Weight (N) = mass × acceleration due to gravity.

Reaction: the equal and opposite force exerted by a body in response to the action force placed upon it.

Friction: the force that opposes the motion of two surfaces in contact.

Air resistance: the force that opposes motion through the air.

Factors affecting air resistance	Examples
Velocity	The greater the velocity of a cyclist, the greater the force of air resistance opposing their motion.
Shape	Most cyclists wear a tear-drop or aerofoil shape helmet to minimise air resistance – known as **streamlining**.
Frontal cross-sectional area	The low crouched position of a downhill skier reduces air resistance.
Smoothness of surface	Increased smoothness, e.g. lycra suits, reduces air resistance.

Typical mistake

Biomechanics questions always require a practical example to explain each point. No example = no marks.

> **Streamlining**: the creation of smooth air flow around an aerodynamic shape to minimise air resistance.
>
> **Free body diagram**: a clearly labelled sketch showing all of the forces acting on a body at a particular instant in time.

Now test yourself

TESTED ☐

1 Define Newton's laws of motion.
2 What is net force?
3 Name the two vertical and two horizontal forces.
4 Name four factors that affect friction.
5 Name four factors that affect air resistance.

Answers on page 169

Exam tip

Keep free body diagrams simple. Draw a stick man to represent the athlete and identify all the forces acting upon them at that moment.

Free body diagrams

A **free body diagram** is a clearly labelled sketch showing all of the forces acting on a body at a particular instant in time.

	Vertical forces	
Force (label)	Weight (W)	Reaction (R)
Origin and direction of arrow	From the centre of mass extending vertically downwards	From the point of contact extending vertically upwards
Size of arrow and relationship between forces	If weight is equal in size to reaction (W = R), net force is zero. Forces are balanced (equal in size but opposite in direction). Therefore, the body will remain at rest, for example a basketball player preparing to take a free throw or travelling in constant vertical velocity. If reaction force is greater than weight (R → W), net force is positive. Forces are unbalanced and acceleration in an upward direction will occur, for example a basketball player leaving the ground in the take-off phase of a lay-up shot.	

	Horizontal forces	
Force (label)	Friction (F)	Air resistance (AR)
Origin and direction of arrow	From the point of contact and usually extending horizontally in the same direction as motion (parallel to the surfaces)	From the centre of mass and extending horizontally against the direction of motion
Size of arrow and relationship between forces	If friction is equal in size to air resistance (F = AR), net force is zero. Forces are balanced (equal in size but opposite in direction). Therefore, the body will continue to travel in constant velocity, for example a sprint cyclist who has reached maximum velocity on the track. If friction is greater than air resistance (F → AR), net force is positive. Forces are unbalanced and acceleration in a forward direction will occur, for example a sprint cyclist accelerating away from the starting line. If air resistance is greater than friction (AR → F), net force is negative. Forces are unbalanced and horizontal deceleration will occur, for example a sprint cyclist crossing the finish line sitting up and decelerating.	

Figure 1.3.1 Vertical forces

Figure 1.3.2 Horizontal forces

Examples of free body diagrams

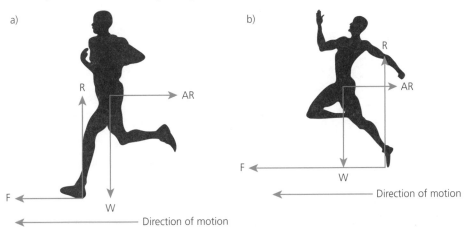

Figure 1.3.3 Free body diagrams: a) marathon runner travelling at a constant velocity: W=R, F=AR, balanced forces, net force = 0; b) long-jumper accelerating forwards and upwards at take-off: R>W, F>AR, unbalanced forces, positive net force, long-jumper experiences forward and vertical acceleration

Centre of mass

- **Centre of mass** is the point at which an object or a body is balanced in all directions.
- It is the point where the weight of the body tends to be concentrated.
- For a round object, this is generally in the middle.
- It can be more complex for the human body, especially when moving.

If an athlete raises their arms, their centre of mass will move up. The centre of mass can also be outside the body and act as a point of rotation.

> **Centre of mass**: the point at which an object or a body is balanced in all directions; the point at which weight appears to act.

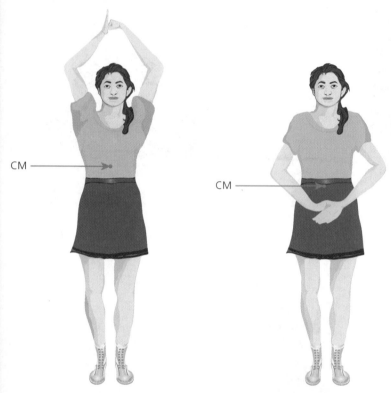

Figure 1.3.4 The location of the centre of mass on a body

Stability

Stability is the ability of a body to resist motion and remain at rest. It is also the ability to withstand a force applied and return to its original position without damage (remain in a balanced position).

Factors that affect stability are outlined in the table below.

Factors	Effect on stability
Mass of the body	The greater the mass, the greater the inertia, e.g. a sumo wrestler
Height of the centre of mass	The lower the centre of mass, the greater the stability
Size of the base of support	The greater the size of the base of support, the greater the stability; this can be increased by more points of contact
Line of gravity	The more central the line of gravity to the base of support, the greater the stability

Quick quizzes at **www.hoddereducation.co.uk/myrevisionnotes**

Maximising and minimising stability: application

- In a sprint start, a sprinter preparing in the blocks has maximum stability.
- When 'set' is called, the sprinter lifts their hips raising their centre of mass, lifts one knee reducing the points of contact and leans forward, thus minimising stability ready for movement.
- When the gun is fired, instability is maximised to aid performance. The chest lifts raising the centre of mass, hands come off the track and the line of gravity falls in front of the base of support, causing the body to fall forwards.
- This must be prevented by driving one leg forward with great speed. This minimises movement time and gives the perfect start from which to drive forwards.

Now test yourself   TESTED

6 What is centre of mass?
7 Name the factors that affect stability.

Answers on page 170

Levers

REVISED

Lever systems are the co-ordination of our bones and muscles, primarily to create human movement. Their two main functions are to:
- generate muscular effort to overcome a given load
- increase the speed of a given movement.

Components of a lever system

The following table outlines the lever system components applied to a biceps curl.

Component	Location in the body	Diagram notation	Example: upward phase of a biceps curl
Lever	Bone	Line	Radius and ulna
Fulcrum	Joint	Triangle	Elbow joint
Effort	Muscular force	Arrow (E)	Force created by biceps brachii
Load	Weight or resistance	Arrow (L)	Weight of the forearm and free weight held

Classification of levers

Most levers in the human body are third class, where the muscle crosses but attaches close to the joint and the load acts at the other end of the lever, such as flexion of the elbow and extension at the knee.

Class	Order of components	Example in the body
First	Fulcrum is in the middle E – F – L or L – F – E 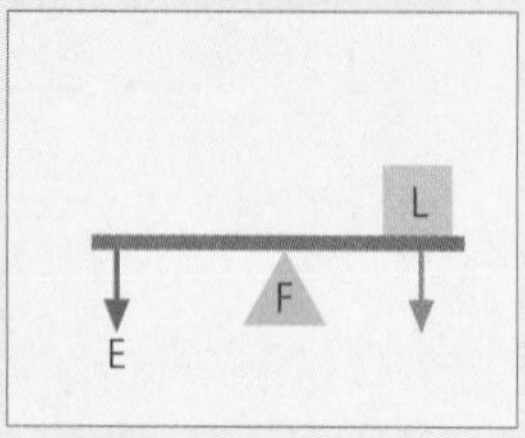	Extension of the neck when preparing to head a football 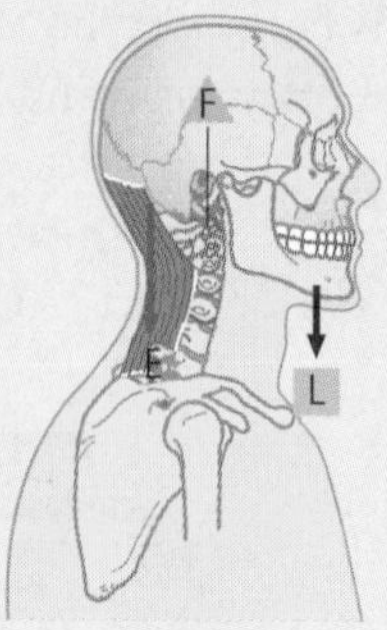
Second	Load is in the middle E – L – F or F – L – E 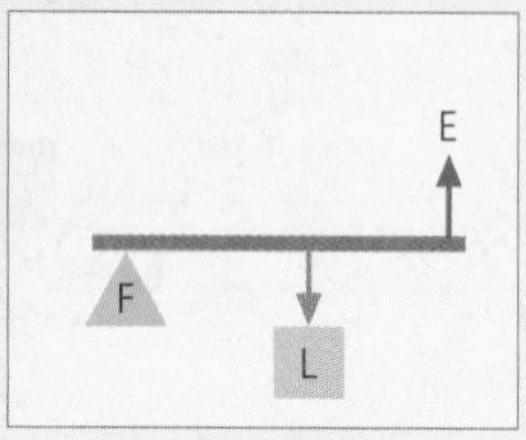	Ball of the foot in the take-off phase of a high-jump 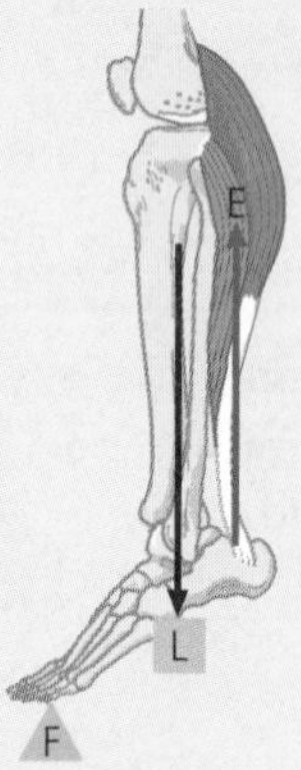
Third	Effort is in the middle L – E – F or F – E – L 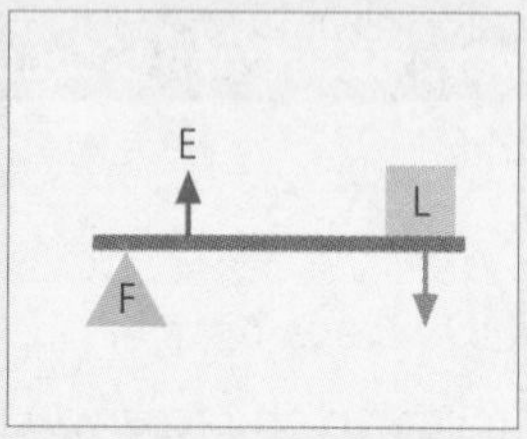	Flexion of the elbow during a biceps curl 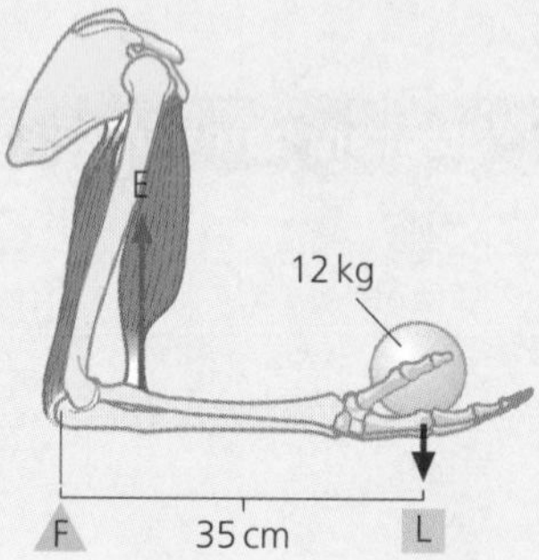

Figure 1.3.5 Classification of lever systems with examples

Efficiency of the lever system

The order and distance of the lever system components from the fulcrum is important to their function:

1 The distance from the fulcrum to the effort is known as the 'effort arm'.
2 The distance from the load to the fulcrum is known as the 'load arm'.

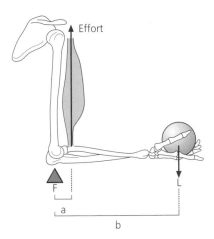

Figure 1.3.6 Third-class lever system at the elbow: a = effort arm, b = load arm

- The greater the distance of the effort or load from the fulcrum, the more significant the effort or load becomes.
- Longer levers generate greater forces, as the load arm becomes longer and therefore can give greater acceleration to projectiles.
- The length of the effort arm and the load arm gives a lever system either the **mechanical advantage** or the **mechanical disadvantage**.
- A second-class lever has the mechanical advantage to move a large load with a small effort, such as at the ball of the foot to vertically accelerate an athlete's whole weight easily.
- A third-class lever has the mechanical disadvantage, requiring a large effort to move a relatively small load.

Mechanical advantage: second-class lever systems where the effort arm is greater than the load arm. A large load can be moved with a relatively small effort.

Mechanical disadvantage: third-class lever systems where the load arm is greater than the effort arm. A large effort is required to move a relatively small load.

Now test yourself

TESTED

8 Name the components of a lever system.
9 What is the mechanical advantage and mechanical disadvantage?

Answers on page 170

Analysis of movement through the use of technology

The following table details different technologies which can be used to analyse movement.

Technology	Definition	Use	Optimising performance
Limb kinematics	Study of movement in relation to time and space	3D or optical motion analysis records an athlete performing a sporting action, allowing the evaluation of the efficiency of movement.	Data produced can be used by coaches to improve performance/specific techniques of athletes.
Force plates	Ground reaction forces are measured in laboratory conditions using force plates	Athletes balance, run and jump on a force plate, which assesses the size and direction of forces acting on the athlete, acceleration rates, work and power output.	Used for sports biomechanics assessment, gait analysis, balance rehabilitation and physical therapy.
Wind tunnels	Steel frame building containing wide fans, where artificial wind is produced	Technology is used to develop the drag reduction system. Objects such as cycle helmets and F1 cars can be tested for aerodynamic efficiency.	Engineers study the flow of air around the object. The aim is to improve the flow of air around an object, streamlining its path through the oncoming air and potentially increasing lift or decreasing drag.

Exam practice

1 Define Newton's laws of motion. Explain how Newton's laws of motion and the application of force can be applied to a tennis serve. [10]

2 Using an example from PE or sport, explain how changes in the position of a performer's centre of mass can affect performance. [5]

Answers on page 177

Summary

You should now have an understanding of:
- Newton's laws of motion
- net force
- balanced and unbalanced force
- weight
- reaction
- friction
- air resistance
- factors affecting friction and air resistance and their manipulation in sporting performance
- free body diagrams showing vertical and horizontal forces acting on a body at an instant in time and the resulting motion
- calculations of force, momentum, acceleration and weight

- the definition of centre of mass
- factors affecting the position of the centre of mass
- the relationship between centre of mass and stability
- components of a lever system:
  - first-class lever, second-class lever, third-class lever; mechanical advantage of a second-class lever
- limb kinematics, force plates, wind tunnels; how each type of technology may be used to optimise performance in sport.

1.3b Linear motion, angular motion, fluid mechanics and projectile motion

Linear motion

REVISED

Linear motion results from a **direct force** being applied to a body, i.e. where force is applied directly to the centre of a body's mass (centre force), for example a skeleton bob at top speed.

Linear motion: movement of a body in a straight or curved line, where all parts move the same distance in the same direction over the same time.

Direct force: a force applied through the centre of mass resulting in linear motion.

Descriptions of linear motion

There are five key descriptors which can be calculated to build data and create a picture of performance.

Descriptor	Definition	Calculation	Unit of measurement
Distance	Total length of the path covered from start to finish	Measured	Metres (m)
Displacement	The shortest straight-line route from start to finish	Measured	Metres (m)
Speed	The rate of change in distance	Speed = distance/time taken	Metres per second (m/s)
Velocity	The rate of change of displacement	Velocity = displacement/time taken	Metres per second (m/s)
Acceleration/ deceleration	The rate of change in velocity	Acceleration/deceleration = (final velocity – initial velocity)/ time taken	Metres per second per second (m/s/s)

Graphs of linear motion

Distance/time graphs

A **distance/time graph** shows the distance a body travels over a period of time. The **gradient** of the curve indicates the speed of a body at a particular instant.

Distance/time graph: a visual representation of the distance travelled plotted against the time taken.

Gradient: the slope of a graph at a particular moment in time. Gradient = change in y axis/change in x axis.

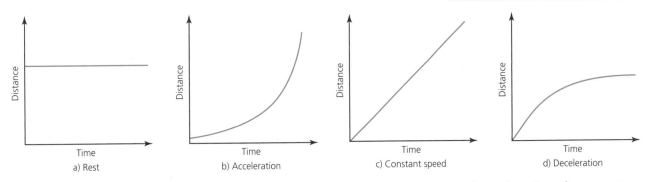

Figure 1.3.7 Stages of motion represented with distance/time graphs: a) rest, b) acceleration, c) constant speed and d) deceleration

Speed/time graphs

A **speed/time graph** shows the speed of a body over a particular time. The gradient of the curve indicates the **acceleration/deceleration** of the body at a particular instant.

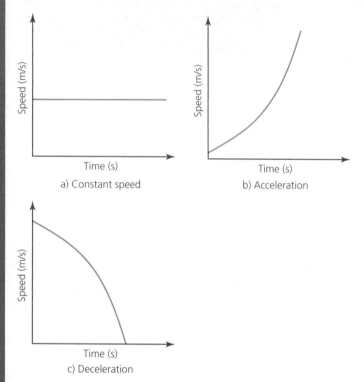

a) Constant speed

b) Acceleration

c) Deceleration

Figure 1.3.8 Stages of motion represented with speed/time graphs: a) constant speed, b) acceleration and c) deceleration

> **Speed/time graph**: a visual representation of the speed of motion plotted against the time taken.
>
> **Acceleration/deceleration**: the rate of change in velocity (m/s/s) calculated using: (final velocity − initial velocity)/time taken.

Velocity/time graphs

A **velocity/time graph** shows the velocity of a body over a period of time. The gradient of the curve indicates the acceleration or deceleration of the body at a particular instant.

> **Velocity/time graph**: a visual representation of the velocity of motion plotted against the time taken.

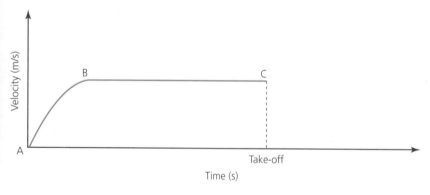

Figure 1.3.9 A velocity/time graph showing the descent of a ski jumper down the ramp prior to take-off

A velocity/time graph can also show any change in direction the body makes. A negative curve below the horizontal axis represents a change in the body's direction.

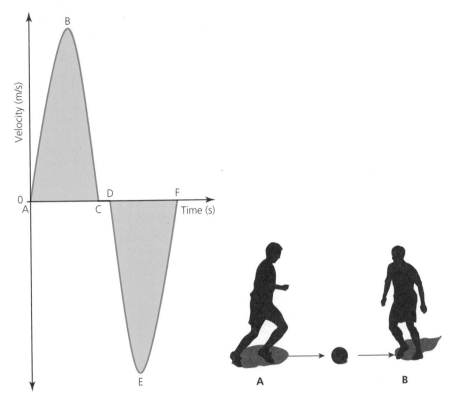

Figure 1.3.10 A velocity/time graph showing the motion of a ball being passed between two players

Now test yourself

TESTED ☐

1 Define linear motion.
2 How is linear motion created?
3 What is the difference between distance and displacement?

Answers on page 170

Angular motion

Angular motion results from an **eccentric force** being applied to a body, i.e. where the force is applied outside the centre of a body's mass. An eccentric force is also known as **torque** – a turning or rotational force, for example a gymnastic somersault.

Principal axes of rotation

If an eccentric force is applied to a body, it will rotate around one (or more) of the three principal axes of rotation.

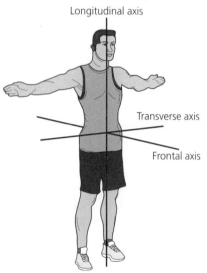

Longitudinal axis

Transverse axis

Frontal axis

Figure 1.3.11 The principal axes of rotation

The following table details the principal axes of rotation with practical sporting examples.

Axis	Location	Example
Longitudinal	Runs from the top to the bottom of the body	A trampolinist performs a full twist turn
Transverse	Runs from side to side of the body	A front somersault
Frontal	Runs from the front to the back of the body	A gymnast performs a cartwheel

Descriptions of angular motion

The table below details the definitions and equations of angular motion.

Descriptor	Definition	Calculation	Unit of measurement
Moment of inertia (MI)	The resistance of a body to change its state of angular motion or rotation	Moment of inertia = sum (mass × distribution of the mass from the axis of rotation²) $MI = \sum m \times r^2$	Kilogram metres² (kgm²)
Angular velocity	The rate of change in angular displacement or rate of rotation	Angular velocity = angular displacement/time taken	Radians per second (rad/s)
Angular momentum	The quantity of angular motion possessed by a body	Angular momentum = moment of inertia × angular velocity	Kilogram metres² per second (kgm²/s)

> **Angular motion:** movement of a body or part of a body in a circular path about an axis of rotation.
>
> **Eccentric force:** a force applied outside the centre of mass, resulting in angular motion.
>
> **Torque:** a measure of the turning (rotational or eccentric) force applied to a body.

Quick quizzes at **www.hoddereducation.co.uk/myrevisionnotes**

Factors affecting the size of the moment of inertia of a rotating body

The two factors that affect moment of inertia are mass and the distribution of mass from the axis of rotation:

1 Mass:
   - The greater the mass, the greater the MI; the lower the mass, the easier it is to change the rate of rotation.
   - Sports with a high degree of rotation (for example high board diving) are typically performed by athletes with a low mass.
2 Distribution of the mass from the axis of rotation:
   - The further the mass moves from the axis of rotation, the greater the MI.
   - Movements where mass is tucked in around the axis of rotation, the lower the MI, for example a tucked somersault.
   - When performing a tucked front somersault, the body will face less resistance to rotation and therefore will rotate more quickly compared with a straight front somersault.

Moment of inertia has a direct effect on angular velocity:
- If MI is high, resistance to rotation is also high, therefore angular velocity is low; the rate of spin is slow.
- If MI is low, resistance to rotation is also low, therefore angular velocity is high; the rate of spin is fast.

a)   b)

Figure 1.3.12 An ice skater manipulating his body position to alter moment of inertia and angular velocity: a) low MI = fast rate of spin and b) high MI = slow rate of spin

Conservation of angular momentum

Angular momentum once generated does not change throughout a movement; it remains constant and therefore is termed a 'conserved' quantity. The **conservation of angular momentum** is a concept associated with the **angular analogue of Newton's first law of motion**.

As angular momentum cannot be changed once in flight, it is important to generate as much angular momentum as possible at take-off. Performers can then manipulate MI and angular velocity to maximise performance.

The following should be considered:
- axis of rotation
- phases of motion.

Practical example

> **Conservation of angular momentum:** angular momentum is a conserved quantity which remains constant unless an external eccentric force or torque is applied.
>
> **Angular analogue of Newton's first law of motion:** the angular equivalent of Newton's first law of motion which states: a rotating body will continue to turn about an axis of rotation with constant angular momentum unless acted upon by an eccentric force or external torque.

Figure 1.3.13 Angular momentum remains constant about the longitudinal axis throughout flight when performing a triple axel jump in ice skating

- At take-off (a), angular momentum is generated by the ice skater applying an eccentric force from the ice to the body.
- Rotation starts about the longitudinal axis.
- Distribution of mass is away from the longitudinal axis. MI is high, angular velocity is low. The ice skater goes into the jump rotating slowly with control.
- During flight (b), mass is distributed close to the longitudinal axis. MI is decreased, angular velocity increases. The ice skater spins quickly, allowing several rotations in the air.
- In preparation for landing (c), mass is distributed away from the longitudinal axis. MI is raised, angular velocity is reduced. The ice skater decreases their rate of spin, increasing control, for landing.
- As they are landing, the ice applies an external torque to remove the conserved quantity of angular momentum.

Graph of angular velocity, moment of inertia and angular momentum

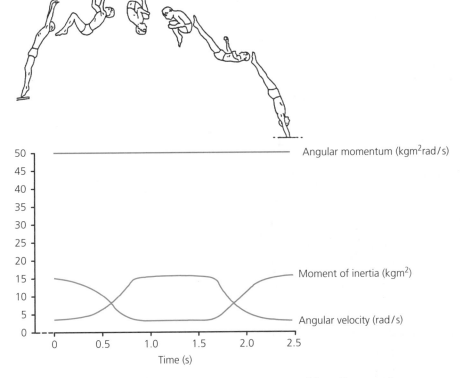

Figure 1.3.14 The relationship between moment of inertia, angular velocity and angular momentum of a diver performing a one-and-a-half backward rotation into the water

- At take-off, angular momentum is generated by an eccentric force from the springboard acting on the body.
- Rotation starts about the transverse axis.
- Straight body position distributes mass away from the transverse axis. MI is high, angular velocity is low. Diver rotates slowly with control.
- During flight, the tucked body position distributes mass close to the transverse axis. MI is decreased, angular velocity is increased. Diver rotates quickly.
- Preparing to enter the water, the straightened body distributes mass away from the transverse axis. MI is increased, angular velocity is decreased. The rate of spin decreases, gaining control on entry.
- Angular momentum is conserved throughout the movement.

> **Exam tip**
>
> Use subject-specific vocabulary to fully explain your answers. For example, 'In the flight phase, the gymnast has a tucked position to distribute the mass close to the transverse axis of rotation. This will decrease the moment of inertia and increase the rate of spin, allowing more rotations'... rather than 'the gymnast tucks to spin faster in the air'.

Now test yourself

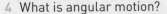

TESTED

4 What is angular motion?
5 How is angular motion created?
6 What are the three principal axes of rotation?
7 Define moment of inertia, angular velocity and angular momentum, stating the units in which they are measured.

Answers on page 170

Fluid mechanics

Fluid mechanics is the study of the forces acting on a body travelling through the air or water.

There are four main factors that affect air resistance and **drag** on the body, outlined in the following table.

> **Drag**: the force that opposes the direction of motion of a body through water.

Velocity	The greater the velocity of a cyclist, the greater the force of air resistance or drag opposing their motion. Freestyle swimming is affected by high levels of drag, due to high velocity.
Frontal cross-sectional area	The low crouched position of a downhill skier reduces air resistance and drag.
Streamlining and shape	The more aerodynamic the shape of a body or equipment, the lower the air resistance or drag. Streamlined body shape out of a tumble turn in swimming reduces drag.
Surface characteristics	E.g. increased smoothness – lycra suits reduce air resistance. Swimmers wear specially designed suits to minimise drag.

Revision activity

Apply the principles above to downhill skiing, track cycling and freestyle swimming.

Projectile motion

Factors affecting the horizontal distance travelled by a projectile

Projectile motion is the movement of a body through the air following a curved flight path under the force of gravity. The table below identifies the factors affecting the horizontal distance travelled by a **projectile**.

> **Projectile**: a body that is launched into the air losing contact with the ground surface, such as a discus or a long-jumper.

Speed of release	Due to Newton's second law, the greater the outgoing speed of the projectile, the further it will travel.
Angle of release	45 degrees is the optimal angle to maximise horizontal distance.
Height of release	45 degrees is the optimal angle if the release height and landing height are equal. Where release height is higher than landing height, optimal angle is less than 45 degrees (e.g. javelin). Where release height is lower than landing height, optimal angle is greater than 45 degrees (e.g. bunker shot in golf).
Aerodynamic factors	Bernoulli and Magnus (see pages 103 and 105).

Projectiles in flight

Once released, projectiles follow a flight path determined by the relative size of the forces acting upon it. Depending on the dominant force, the flight path will be more or less **parabolic** in nature.

If weight is the dominant force and air resistance is very small, a **parabolic flight path** occurs:

- For example, a shot put has a high mass and travels through the air with a low velocity, with a small front cross-sectional area and smooth surface, making air resistance minimal.
- The flight path is parabolic in shape, symmetrical about its highest point.

If air resistance is the dominant force and weight is very small, a **non-parabolic flight path** occurs:

- For example, a badminton shuttle has a very low mass and travels at high velocities with a relatively uneven surface, which all increase air resistance.
- The flight path has a non-parabolic shape, asymmetrical (unequal) about its highest point.

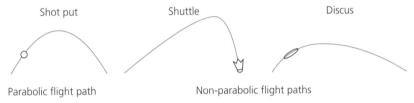

Figure 1.3.15 **The parabolic flight path of a shot compared with the non-parabolic flight paths of a shuttle and a discus**

Free body diagrams

The forces acting on a projectile can be represented with a free body diagram. There are three phases of motion within a flight path to the highest point, after which gravity will accelerate the projectile's mass to the ground. These can be described as start of flight, mid-flight and end of flight. Weight does not change over the three phases. Air resistance will be greater at the start.

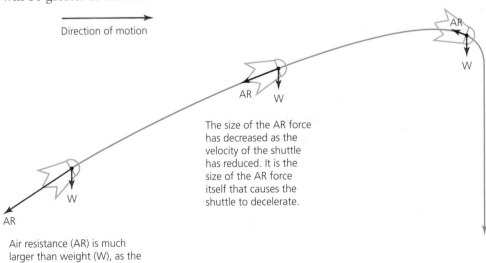

Figure 1.3.16 **Free body diagram of a shuttle in the start, mid- and end of flight phases**

	Free body diagram	Dominant force	Resulting flight path
Shot	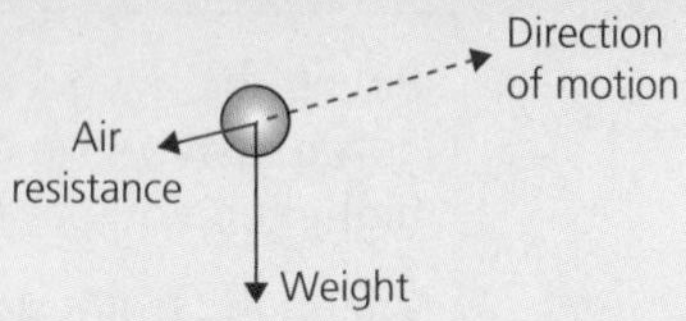 Direction of motion / Air resistance / Weight	Weight → air resistance	Parabolic 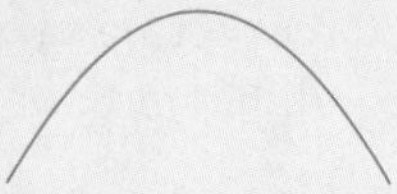
Shuttle	 Direction of motion / Air resistance / Weight	Air resistance ← weight	Non-parabolic 

Figure 1.3.17 Free body diagrams and mid-flight and flight paths of a shot in athletics compared with a hard hit badminton shuttle

Parallelogram of forces

A **parallelogram of forces** can be drawn to consider the result of all the forces acting on a projectile in flight.

How to draw a parallelogram of forces

1 Draw a free body diagram showing weight and air resistance.
2 Add broken parallel lines to weight and air resistance arrows to create a parallelogram.
3 Draw a diagonal line from the origin of the weight and air resistance (centre of mass of projectile) to the opposite corner of the parallelogram with a double arrow labelled 'resultant force'.

Resultant force shows the acceleration of a projectile and the direction in which the acceleration occurs. It will also indicate flight path.
● If resultant force is closer to the weight arrow, weight is more dominant, so the flight path will be more parabolic.
● If resultant force is closer to the air resistance arrow, air resistance is more dominant, so the flight path will be non-parabolic.

> **Parallelogram of forces**: a parallelogram illustrating the theory that a diagonal drawn from the point where forces are represented in size and direction shows the resultant force acting.
>
> **Resultant force**: the sum of all forces acting on a body or the net force acting on a projectile.

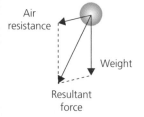

The resultant force shows deceleration to be occurring and weight to be dominant, leading to a parabolic flight path

Figure 1.3.18 Parallelogram of forces for a shot mid-flight showing the resultant force

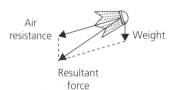

The resultant force shows deceleration to be occurring and air resistance to be dominant, leading to a non-parabolic flight path

Figure 1.3.19 Parallelogram of forces for a badminton shuttle mid-flight showing the resultant force

Exam tip

Do not create the parallelogram on the same free body diagram. Draw a second diagram, to ensure you can gain maximum marks.

Lift and the Bernoulli principle

The Bernoulli principle is the creation of an additional lift force on a projectile in flight resulting from Bernoulli's conclusion that the higher the velocity of air flow, the lower the surrounding pressure.

An **aerofoil** shape has:
- a curved upper surface, forcing air flow to travel further distance and therefore move at a higher velocity
- a flat underneath surface that allows air to travel a shorter distance at a lower velocity.

Therefore:
- As velocity increases, pressure decreases.
- As all fluids move from an area of high to low pressure, a pressure gradient forms, creating an additional **lift force**.
- Additional lift force can increase the time a projectile hangs in the air, extending the flight path and horizontal distance covered, and leading to better results. Examples include discus, ski jumping and javelin.
- **Angle of attack** must be considered for each projectile to maximise lift force.

Aerofoil: a streamlined shape with a curved upper surface and flat lower surface designed to give an additional lift force to a body.

Lift force: an additional force created by a pressure gradient forming on opposing surfaces of an aerofoil moving through a fluid.

Angle of attack: the most favourable angle of release for a projectile to optimise lift force due to the Bernoulli principle.

High velocity
Low pressure
Lift force

Low velocity
High pressure

Direction of motion

Figure 1.3.20 Air flow diagram of a discus in flight

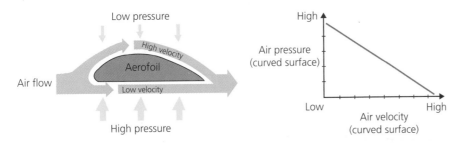

Figure 1.3.21 Air flow, velocity and pressure around an aerofoil in flight

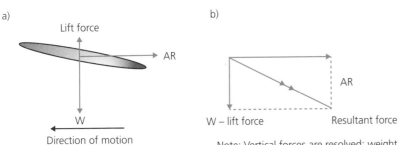

a) Lift force

AR

W

Direction of motion

b) AR

W – lift force   Resultant force

Note: Vertical forces are resolved: weight minus lift force. Resultant force shows the discus is decelerating in flight and closer to AR, therefore the flight path will be non-parabolic.

c) Direction of motion

Note: Non-parabolic flight path. Extended horizontal distance travelled.

Figure 1.3.22 The effects of Bernoulli's lift force on a discus in flight: a) free body diagram, b) resultant force diagram and c) flight path diagram

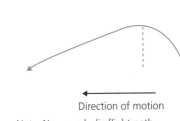

Revision activity

Complete diagrams, as in Figure 1.3.20, applied to the javelin throw and a ski jumper.

Downward lift force

Bernoulli's lift force also works in the downward direction if the aerofoil shape is inverted. This is important in sports such as Formula 1 and track cycling to increase the downward force that holds the car or bike to the track at high speeds around corners.

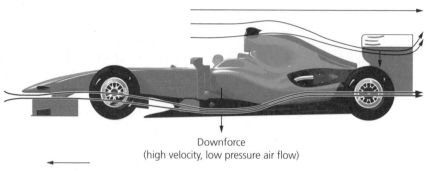

Downforce
(high velocity, low pressure air flow)

Direction of motion

Figure 1.3.23 The downward lift force created by a Formula 1 car design: air flow diagram with high velocity air flow and low pressure underneath the car and spoiler

- The front wing funnels air down through the narrow space underneath the car's chassis.
- The spoiler acts as an inverted aerofoil, forcing air underneath to travel a further distance.
- Air velocity underneath the car is increased, creating areas of low pressure.
- A pressure gradient is formed; additional downward lift force is created.
- The result is increased grip and friction around corners at high speeds.

> **Revision activity**
>
> Apply the downward lift force principles to a track cyclist. Consider the high seat position and helmet design (creating a flat upper body surface).

Now test yourself

TESTED

8 What is air resistance?
9 What is drag?
10 What are four main factors that affect air resistance and drag on a body?
11 What are the factors that affect the horizontal distance travelled by a projectile?
12 Which force is most dominant in a parabolic flight path of a projectile?
13 Which force is most dominant in a non-parabolic flight path of a projectile?
14 What is Bernoulli's principle?

Answers on page 170

Spin and the Magnus force

Spin is created by applying an external force outside the centre of mass. There are four types of spin, outlined in the following table.

Topspin	Eccentric force applied above the centre of mass	Projectile spins downwards around the transverse axis
Backspin	Eccentric force applied below the centre of mass	Projectile spins upwards around the transverse axis
Sidespin hook	Eccentric force applied right of the centre of mass	Projectile spins left around the longitudinal axis
Sidespin slice	Eccentric force applied left of the centre of mass	Projectile spins right around the longitudinal axis

The way a projectile spins determines the direction, velocity and pressure of the air flow around it. A pressure gradient is formed either side of the spinning projectile and an additional **Magnus force** is created which deviates the flight path.

- A topspin rotation creates a downwards Magnus force, shortening the flight path.
- A backspin rotation creates an upwards Magnus force, lengthening the flight path.
- A sidespin rotation creates a Magnus force to the right and left, swerving the projectile right (**slice**) and left (**hook**).

Topspin: tennis example

For a ball with topspin, the additional Magnus force is created by:

1. the upper surface of the ball rotating towards the oncoming air flow, opposing motion, decreasing velocity of air flow and creating a high pressure zone
2. the lower surface of the ball rotating in the same direction as the air flow, increasing velocity of air flow and creating a zone of low pressure
3. a pressure gradient forming and an additional Magnus force being created downwards.

The downward Magnus force adds to the weight of the projectile, the effect of gravity is increased and the projectile 'dips' in flight, giving less time in the air as the flight path shortens.

> **Magnus force**: a force created from a pressure gradient on opposing surfaces of a spinning body moving through the air.
>
> **Slice**: a type of sidespin used to deviate a projectile's flight path to the right.
>
> **Hook**: a type of sidespin used to deviate a projectile's flight path to the left.

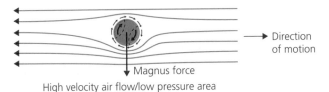

Low velocity air flow/high pressure area

Direction of motion

Magnus force

High velocity air flow/low pressure area

Figure 1.3.24 Air flow diagram illustrating the downward Magnus force created by topspin

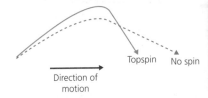

Topspin   No spin

Direction of motion

Figure 1.3.25 Flight path diagram showing the effect of topspin

Spin is useful in tennis and table tennis because:

- it gives the ball stability in flight
- the use of topspin shortens flight path, allowing the ball to be hit harder but still land in court/on the table
- it can confuse opposition.

Use of spin in golf and football

In golf and football, sidespin will allow the ball to swerve in flight, moving around obstacles (For example trees or defensive walls in a free kick).

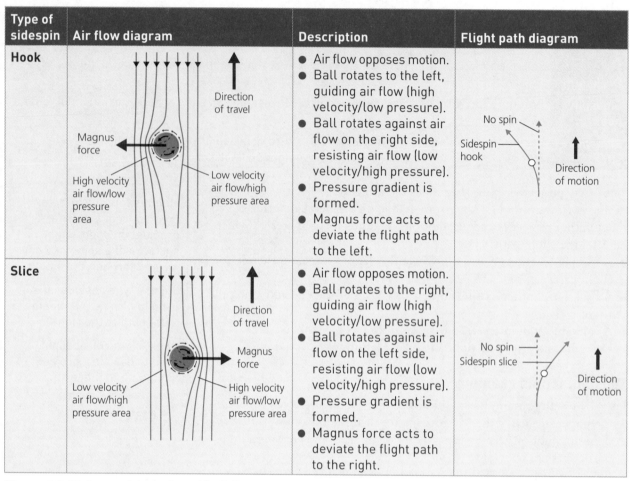

Type of sidespin	Air flow diagram	Description	Flight path diagram
Hook		• Air flow opposes motion. • Ball rotates to the left, guiding air flow (high velocity/low pressure). • Ball rotates against air flow on the right side, resisting air flow (low velocity/high pressure). • Pressure gradient is formed. • Magnus force acts to deviate the flight path to the left.	
Slice		• Air flow opposes motion. • Ball rotates to the right, guiding air flow (high velocity/low pressure). • Ball rotates against air flow on the left side, resisting air flow (low velocity/high pressure). • Pressure gradient is formed. • Magnus force acts to deviate the flight path to the right.	

Figure 1.3.26 An overview of a golfball/football struck with sidespin, hook and slice

Exam tip

When drawing an air flow diagram for a ball with topspin/backspin, it is viewed from the side, whereas sidespin is viewed from above. Air flow diagrams must show a) direction of air flow opposing direction of motion, b) direction of rotation of the ball, c) velocity and pressure labels, d) tighter air flow lines with the direction of rotation side of the ball, e) Magnus force in the direction of the flight path deviation from the centre of mass.

Typical mistake

Always include the direction of travel or direction of motion in an air flow or flight path diagram.

Now test yourself

TESTED ☐

15 What are the four types of spin?
16 What is a Magnus force?
17 Sketch the flight path of a tennis ball with topspin compared to a tennis ball with no spin.

Answers on page 170

Exam practice

1 An athlete performs with rotation prior to the release of a discus. Identify the axis of rotation through which the discus thrower rotates and explain how the thrower uses the law of conservation of angular momentum to enhance performance. [10]

2 A player is kicking a rugby ball. Sketch and label a free body diagram showing the forces acting on the ball at the moment of contact. [2]

3 An association football player is kicking a stationary ball. Using Newton's laws of motion, explain the effect of the resultant force acting on the ball. [4]

4 Identify the three main axes of rotation and give a sporting example for each. [3]

5 What is meant by centre of mass and how does this help to explain why the Fosbury Flop is the preferred technique for the high jump? [4]

6 Explain how a lift force affects a discus during flight. [4]

7 Explain the methods used to reduce the forces acting on a cyclist while racing. [5]

8 Describe a cyclist's use of the Bernoulli principle to increase speed. [6]

9 Use a diagram to work out the resultant force acting on a hard hit badminton shuttle during the early stages of the flight path of a long serve. Explain the effect of the resultant force acting on the flight path of the shuttle. [5]

10 Explain how a performer generates spin on a ball and describe the effects of spin on the bounce of a ball. [5]

Answers on page 178

Summary

You should now have an understanding of:
- the definition of linear motion
- the creation of linear motion by the application of a direct force through the centre of mass
- definitions, calculations and units of measurement for each of the following quantities of linear motion: distance, displacement, speed, velocity, acceleration/deceleration
- how to plot and interpret graphs of linear motion: distance/time graphs, speed/time graphs, velocity/time graphs
- the definition of angular motion
- the creation of angular motion through the application of an eccentric force about one (or more) of the three axes of rotation: longitudinal, frontal, transverse
- definitions, calculations and units of measurement for each quantity of angular motion: moment of inertia, angular velocity, angular momentum
- factors affecting the size of the moment of inertia of a rotating body: mass of the body (or body part), distribution of the mass from the axis of rotation
- the relationship between moment of inertia and angular velocity
- the conservation of angular momentum during flight in relation to the angular analogue of Newton's first law of motion
- how to interpret graphs of angular velocity, moment of inertia and angular momentum
- factors that impact the magnitude of air resistance (on land) or drag (in water) on a body or object
- factors affecting the horizontal distance travelled by a projectile
- free body diagrams showing the forces acting on a projectile once in flight: weight, air resistance
- resolution of forces acting on a projectile in flight using the parallelogram of forces
- patterns of flight paths as a consequence of the relative size of air resistance and weight
- parabolic (symmetrical) flight paths – shot put
- non-parabolic (asymmetric) flight paths – badminton shuttle
- the addition of lift to a projectile through the application of the Bernoulli principle:
  - the angle of attack to create an upwards lift force on a projectile: discus, javelin, ski jumper
  - the design of equipment to create a downwards lift force: F1 racing cars, track cycling
- the use of spin in sport to create a Magnus force, causing deviations to expected flight paths
- imparting spin to a projectile through the application of an eccentric force; types of spin: topspin, sidespin and backspin in tennis and table tennis, sidespin in football, hook and slice in golf.

2.1 Skill acquisition

Classification of skills

Skills are classified using continua, as sometimes skills have more or less of each element depending on the situation.

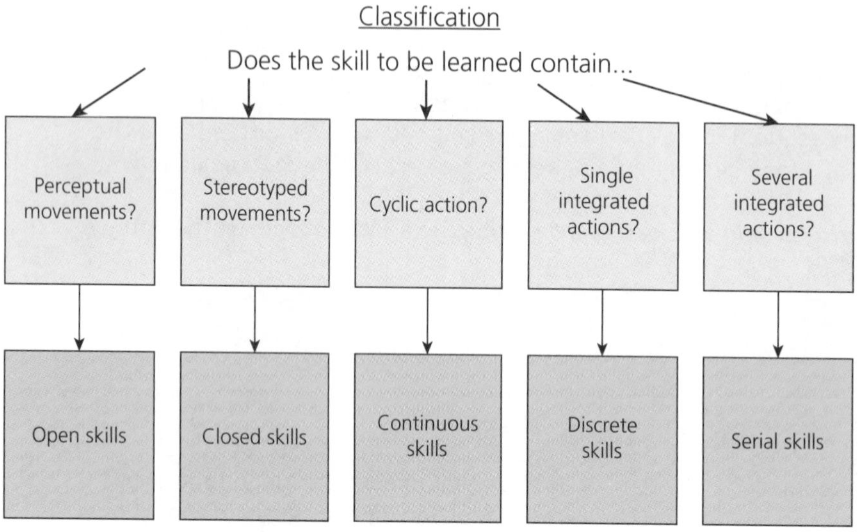

Classification

Does the skill to be learned contain...

Perceptual movements?	Stereotyped movements?	Cyclic action?	Single integrated actions?	Several integrated actions?
↓	↓	↓	↓	↓
Open skills	Closed skills	Continuous skills	Discrete skills	Serial skills

Figure 2.1.1 Identifying the type of skill

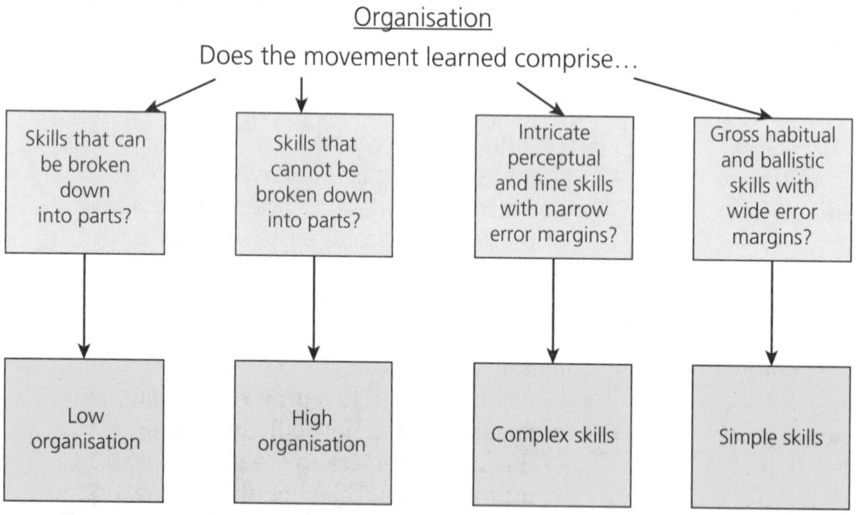

Organisation

Does the movement learned comprise...

Skills that can be broken down into parts?	Skills that cannot be broken down into parts?	Intricate perceptual and fine skills with narrow error margins?	Gross habitual and ballistic skills with wide error margins?
↓	↓	↓	↓
Low organisation	High organisation	Complex skills	Simple skills

Figure 2.1.2 Identifying the organisation level of a skill

Typical mistake

Always refer to a sporting example when classifying skills on a continuum.

Exam tip

It is often helpful to use the same skill, e.g. a tennis serve, throughout your response.

Revision activity

Read the table opposite. Classify the following skills on all six continua and then draw the continua:
- netball pass
- forward roll
- triple jump.

Sub-routines: the elements or separate movements that make up a particular skill. For example, striking a ball in hockey involves grip, stance, back lift, forward swing, strike and follow through.

The table below identifies, describes and gives sporting examples of the skill classification continuum.

Continuum	Description	Sporting example
Muscular movement Gross/fine	Gross skills are large muscle movements using large muscle groups which are not very precise. Movement patterns include walking, running and jumping.	The shot put
	Fine skills are intricate movements using small muscle groups which tend to be precise and generally involve high levels of hand–eye coordination.	A snooker shot
Environmental influence Open/closed	Open skills are affected by the environment (e.g. team games). The environment is constantly changing and so movements have to be continually adapted. Therefore, skills are predominantly perceptual.	Skills in netball, football, hockey, etc., e.g. pass in the game
	Closed skills are not affected by the environment. The environment is predictable and the performer knows exactly what to do and when. Movements follow set patterns and have a clear beginning and end. The skills tend to be self-paced.	A free throw in basketball, serving in squash or tennis
Continuity Discrete, serial and continuous	Discrete skills are brief, well-defined actions that have a clear beginning and end. They are single, specific skills.	A penalty flick in hockey
	Serial skills are a group of discrete skills strung together to make a new and complex movement.	The sequence of skills for the triple jump
	Continuous skills have no obvious beginning or end. The end of one cycle of movements is the beginning of the next, and the skill is repeated.	Swimming, running, cycling
Pacing Externally and internally paced	Internally paced or self-paced skills: the performer controls the rate at which the skill is executed. These skills are usually closed skills.	Javelin throw, discus
	Externally paced skills: the environment controls the rate of performing the skill. The performer must pay attention to external events in order to control rate of movement. These skills involve reaction and are usually open skills.	In ball games, the performer must time their actions with the actions of other players and the ball
Difficulty Simple and complex	Simple skills are straightforward with very few judgements and decisions. They also requires little concentration and cognitive ability of the performer.	Swimming, sprinting
	Complex skills involve many decisions and judgements. They are complicated and are practised in training repeatedly to make it easier to perform in competition.	Somersault, tennis serve
Organisation Low and high	A low organisation skill is very easy and uncomplicated. Moves such as riding a bike and the phases that make the skill are usually discrete and might be practised separately to make technique better. **Sub-routines** are easy to separate.	Swimming strokes, trampolining sequence
	A high organisation skill: many sub-routines are closely linked together to make this skill. They cannot be broken down and practised.	Cartwheel, golf swing

Types and methods of practice

Practice conditions are the type and style of practice administered by the coach. The appropriate type of practice will ensure the opportunity for the performer to make improvements. The conditions in which a skill is learned or practised, as far as possible, replicate the circumstances of real performance.

> **Chaining**: this has the same meaning as the progressive-part method of practice. A serial skill is often broken down into its sub-routines, which can be seen as links of a chain.

Part practice

What is it?	When is it used?	Why is it used?	Practical example
Working on an isolated sub-routine with the aim of perfecting it	• With skills that are low in organisation – easily broken down into separate sub-routines • If the task is complex and dangerous	• Allows performers to make sense of a skill, gaining confidence as they learn each element • Reduces the possibility of overload	Practising the backswing only in the tennis serve

Whole practice

What is it?	When is it used?	Why is it used?	Practical examples
Skills being taught without breaking down into sub-routines or parts	With skills that are high in organisation and need to be taught as a whole	Allows the perfomer to experience the feel of the skill – kinaesthesis	• Sprinting and dribbling, because of their cyclic or continuous nature, will not break down into sub-routines • Golf swing

Whole–part–whole practice

What is it?	When is it used?	Why is it used?	Practical example
Practising the whole skill, then practising a sub-routine in isolation, then practising the whole skill again	With serial skills or skills with low organisation when sub-routines have distinct features	• To recognise strengths and weaknesses, then correct specific skill errors • Allows some feel of the skill	1 Practise whole swimming stroke 2 Practise leg kick in isolation (using a float) 3 Practise whole stroke again

Progressive-part practice

What is it?	When is it used?	Why is it used?	Practical examples
Skills are broken down into sub-routines; performer learns one link, then a second link and practises these, then further links are then added on (known as **chaining**)	• With complex skills as it reduces information load • With low organisation skills • Good for serial skills	Helpful to allow performer to learn links between sub-routines and transfer these into the whole skill	Gymnastic floor routine, triple jump, lay-up shot in basketball, trampoline routine

Massed practice

What is it?	When is it used?	Why is it used?	Practical example
Practice session involves very short or no rest intervals	• Good for discrete skills of short duration • With highly motivated performers with good fitness levels	• To groove skills • Long sessions used when coach wants to simulate elements of fatigue	Basketball players practise their shooting skills by doing drills which involve many shots from different positions around the 'key'

Distributed practice

What is it?	When is it used?	Why is it used?	Practical example
Practice sessions with rest intervals included	• With continuous skills • With beginners or those with low levels of fitness and motivation	• Rest intervals allow performer to receive feedback • Helps maintain motivation and good for dangerous or complex skills	Swimmer swims a width and then has a rest while the teacher gives feedback

Fixed practice

What is it?	When is it used?	Why is it used?	Practical example
A specific movement pattern is practised repeatedly in a stable environment; sometimes called a drill	• With closed skills that require specific movement patterns to become overlearned	• Allow skills to become habitual and automatic • In events where conditions never change, e.g. in discus implement weighs the same, circle is always the same area	Discus thrower practises in the discus circle, using the same weight implement

Varied practice

What is it?	When is it used?	Why is it used?	Practical example
When a skill is practised in many environments	• With open skills • Practice conditions must be as realistic as possible	• Allows the development of experiences in long-term memory, which performer can draw on • Develops performer's perceptual and decision-making skills	Small sided game in football, where performer can work on passing, positional play and strategy

> **Exam tip**
>
> Always give a relevant practical example to support your answer. **No sporting example = no marks.** Learn the practical examples stated above.

Transfer of skills

Learning or regularly performing a skill can affect the learning of a second skill. The types of transfer are outlined in the following table and then discussed in detail below.

Type of transfer	Description
Proactive transfer	When a skill learned previously affects a skill yet to be learned
Retroactive transfer	When learning a new skill affects a skill learned previously
Positive transfer	When the learning and performance of one skill help the learning and performance of another skill
Negative transfer	When the learning and performance of one skill hinder the learning and performance of another skill
Bilateral transfer	The transfer of learning from one limb to another

Positive transfer

- This occurs when the two skills in question are similar in some way.
- Having already mastered one of the skills, it makes learning the second skill easier.
- Coaches can aid this positive transfer by:
  - making sure the individual understands the similarities between the two skills
  - making sure that the basics of the first skill are well learned so that they transfer more easily into the second skill.

For example, the skill of throwing can be transferred to the arm action of the tennis serve.

Negative transfer

- This occurs when having learned one skill, it makes learning the second skill more difficult.
- It happens when a stimulus common to both skills requires a different response.
- Negative transfer can be avoided by:
  - making sure the athlete is aware of the differences
  - making practice sessions similar to match situations, to ensure a larger, generalised motor programme.

For example, a squash player who takes up tennis may find it difficult to learn to not use their wrist during shots.

Figure 2.1.3 A player of both squash and tennis may experience negative transfer

Bilateral transfer

- This involves the transfer of learning from one limb to another.
- It refers to the capacity of a performer who may be dominantly right-sided to perform a skill with the left side of the body.

Bilateral transfer takes place in two ways:
1 cognitive aspects, understanding what is required: 'I swing my left foot in the same way as I swing my right foot'
2 tranfer of the motor programme – the pattern of one movement learned by one limb is used subconsciously by the other limb.

For example, a footballer who can shoot with the right and left foot with matching power and accuracy is a considerable asset to the team.

Optimising positive transfer and limiting negative transfer

- Allow positive transfer by offering variable practices which imitate game situations.
- Make performers aware of transferable elements, e.g. the teacher highlights that throwing a javelin is like throwing a rounders ball – the arm position is the same.
- Give clear and concise demonstrations.
- Diverse childhood experiences enhance probability of transfer; the performer must learn a wide range of fundamental **motor skills**.

> **Motor skill**: an action or task that has a goal and requires voluntary body and/ or limb movement to achieve that goal; it is learned rather than being innate. Also known as movement skill.

Now test yourself

TESTED

1 For each of the following types of practice method, identify the classes of the skill for which they are most suitable and give a practical example for each:
   - part
   - whole
   - progressive-part
   - whole–part–whole.
2 What are the five types of transfer?
3 As a coach, how would you optimise positive transfer?

Answers on page 170

Learning theories

A good understanding of how learning occurs will ensure effective teaching and coaching can take place. The following learning theories are important:

- operant conditioning
- Thorndike's laws
- cognitive theory of learning
- Bandura's observational learning/social learning theory (SLT).

> **Associationist**: a group of theories related to connecting stimulus and response. These theories are often referred to as S–R theories. An individual is conditioned by stimuli which are 'connected' or 'bonded' to appropriate responses.

Learning theory	Description	Sporting example
Operant conditioning	**Associationist view** • Trial and error learning • A correct response is rewarded • This reinforces the correct response • This behaviour is shaped (changed)	During football shooting practice, the coach may direct the players to strike the ball into the right of the goal. If this is done they are rewarded. The area is then reduced to the top half of the right side, and then maybe the top right-hand corner only. Rewarding this behaviour strengthens the link.
Thorndike's laws	**Based on strengthening S–R bonds** • Law of exercise: rehearsing or repeating actions strengthens reinforcement • Law of effect: if followed by a pleasant reaction, then the S–R bond is strengthened; if the following reaction is negative, then the S–R bond is weakened • Law of readiness: the athlete must be both mentally and physically capable of performing the skill efficiently	During hockey: • exercise: repeated dribbling practice strengthens the S–R bond • effect: positive comments about dribbling technique strengthen the S–R bond, negative comments weaken the S–R bond • readiness: if a performer is injured they may not be able to dribble effectively.
Cognitive theory of learning	**Intervening variables and insight learning** • Learning is best achieved by premising the whole skill • Learner must understand and think about the problem as a whole • Thought processes are dependent upon perception • Learner will use intelligence, current knowledge and previous experience to plan or predict a solution	A cricketer learns to swing the ball when bowling by understanding the basic mechanics of movement.
Observational learning/SLT	**Copying behaviour of others** • Behaviour will be copied if the role model is a significant other and of high status • Role models are copied if they are the same gender as the learner • It is a form of visual guidance • A demonstration is presented for the learner to copy • Process involves of attention, retention, motor reproduction and motivation	A young rugby player may copy the behaviour of a professional player they have seen on TV. This could be positive sportsmanship or negative aggressive behaviour.

Quick quizzes at **www.hoddereducation.co.uk/myrevisionnotes**

Stages of learning

Fitts and Posner identified three stages of learning:

- stage 1: cognitive stage (initial)
- stage 2: associative stage (intermediate)
- stage 3: autonomous stage (final).

The following table indicates the key features and sporting examples for the three stages of learning.

Stage of learning	Description	Sporting example
Cognitive	• The learner is trying to create a mental picture of the skill. • Demonstrations are vital. • Teachers should not give too much information. • Give guidance to focus on important cues (selective attention). • Practise the skill with trial and error. • Reinforce success with positive feedback. • Performances will be inconsistent, lack co-ordination and flow and be full of errors. • Specific feedback is needed to correct errors.	A teacher demonstrates a serve to a beginner badminton player. The performer has a mental picture, plus key cues, and practises.
Associative	• This is the practice stage. • The learner attends to relevant cues. • Errors are fewer and smaller. • Big improvements are made in performance • Motor programmes are developed. Sub-routines become more co-ordinated, resulting in the skill becoming smoother. • The learner develops the ability to use internal/kinaesthetic feedback to detect own errors. • Detailed verbal feedback is given.	The badminton player is becoming more consistent with their serve, and is now concentrating on height over the net. The performer can detect errors and make adjustment without the teacher's help.
Autonomous	• The learner can execute the skill with little conscious thought (automatically). • Thus they can concentrate on other factors. • Motor programmes are established and stored in long-term memory and put into action in response to appropriate stimuli. • There is less need for external feedback. • If practice is not maintained, the learner may drop back into the associative stage.	• A tennis player can focus on where to place the ball in relation to their opponent rather than grip, stance, ball toss, etc. • Team players are able to focus on tactics and strategies rather than executing skills.

Guidance

There are four types of guidance that can be used by the teacher or coach to help the learning process:

- verbal
- visual
- manual
- mechanical.

Verbal guidance

- Verbal feedback can be provided by a coach or significant other.
- It is used to describe and explain how to perform an activity.
- It is often used alongside visual guidance.

There are advantages and disadvantages of verbal feedback:

Advantages	Disadvantages
• Can reinforce good movements and identify errors to be corrected • Can hold the attention of the performer and be used to motivate	• Can lead to 'information overload' • If guidance is inaccurate, skills will be hindered

Visual guidance

- Images or demonstrations can be used to help a learner, such as still images (pictures/posters) or moving images (videos or animations – particularly the use of slow motion).
- A coach should highlight key points of the movements. Reinforcing these key points is known as 'cueing'.
- The image or demonstration shown should be accurate.

There are advantages and disadvantages of visual guidance:

Advantages	Disadvantages
• Easy to create a mental picture • Skill can be seen at different stages • Encourages observational learning	• If demonstration incorrect, bad habits could form • Coach may not be able to show accurate demonstration • Visual representation may be unclear or too quick

Manual and mechanical guidance

- This involves physical support by another person or mechanical device, for example a twisting belt in trampolining.
- It may involve a performer being physically directed by another person, for example holding the arms of a performer and forcing their arms through a pattern of movement in a golf swing.
- This type of guidance can reduce fear in dangerous situations.
- It can also give kinaesthetic feel, or remove kinaesthetic feel, depending on performer.
- It could negatively affect motivation and cause negative transfer.

The advantages and disadvantages of manual and mechanical guidance are summaried below:

Advantages	Disadvantages
• Helps with confidence and a sense of safety • Can be used to isolate a skill action, e.g. holding a float to only practise leg kick in swimming – can then concentrate on this aspect	• Can be over-restrictive, performer may feel like they lack control • Can lead to a false kinaesthesis

Now test yourself

4 What are the four learning theories?
5 What are the three stages of learning?
6 What are the four types of guidance?

Answers on page 170

TESTED

Feedback

Types of feedback

There are a number of types of feedback, summarised below.

Intrinsic feedback

- **Intrinsic feedback** is from internal proprioceptors about the feel of the movement. Kinaesthesis is also involved.
- An example would be the feel of whether or not you have hit the ball in the middle of the bat in a cricket shot.

Extrinsic feedback

- **Extrinsic feedback** is from external sources such as the teacher/coach or team mates. It is received by the visual and auditory systems and is used to augment intrinsic feedback.
- An example would be the coach saying 'you need to point your toes in the pike jump'.

Positive feedback

- **Positive feedback** is received when the movement is successful and this reinforces learning.
- For example, in badminton a coach praises the learner when they perform the short serve correctly. Positive feedback can be intrinsic or extrinsic.

Negative feedback

- **Negative feedback** is received when the movement is incorrect. It is then used to correct the movement to make it successful the next time.

Knowledge of results (KR)

- **Knowledge of results** is feedback about the outcome of our movements. It is extrinsic.
- An example would be observing whether the shot went in the basket or watching the movement on a video recording.
- It can be positive or negative.
- It is important in improving the next performance of the movement.

Knowledge of performance (KP)

- **Knowledge of performance** concerns the movement itself and the quality of it.
- Normally it comes from external sources but it can be internal arising from kinaesthetic awareness.
- It can come from a teacher/coach, explaining what went well and not so well.
- It can also come from a video recording or the feeling of the movement.

Intrinsic feedback: a type of continuous feedback that comes from the proprioceptors – nerve receptors found in muscles, ligaments and joints that pick up movement information.

Extrinsic feedback: feedback that comes from external sources, for example a teacher/coach.

Positive feedback: reinforces skill learning and gives information about a successful outcome.

Negative feedback: information about an unsuccessful outcome, which can be used to build more successful strategies.

Knowledge of results: a type of terminal feedback that gives the performer information about the end result of the response.

Knowledge of performance: information about how well the movement is being executed, rather than the end result.

The table below looks at the advantages and disadvantages of the different types of feedback.

Type of feedback	Advantages	Disadvantages
Intrinsic	• Occurs as movement happens – so movements can be corrected immediately • Performer does not have to rely on anyone	• If in the cognitive stage, performer may not be able to interpret information correctly and performance will deteriorate
Extrinsic	• Coaching points can lead to improvements, as long as information is accurate	• Inaccurate feedback can negatively affect performance • If the source is unreliable, motivation can drop • Does not encourage kinaesthetic awareness
Positive	• Can lead to positive reinforcement, correct S–R bond is formed • Extremely motivating • Helps build self-esteem and confidence	• If undeserved can lead to inappropriate S–R bonds and performance will deteriorate • Some performers do not respond to praise and may ignore it
Negative	• Some are motivated by negative feedback – resulting in a more determined performer • Allows performer to be clear which aspect needs improvement • Best suited to autonomous learners who require skill refinement	• Can be demotivating • Can be detrimental to learning
Knowledge of results	• Allows performer to see the outcome of their action • Can motivate performer	• May demotivate if performers are unsuccessful
Knowledge of performance	• Allows performer to know what good performance feels like • Can motivate performer	• May demotivate if performers are unsuccessful

Effective feedback

The type, amount and timing of feedback are crucial. The following should be considered to ensure feedback is effective:
- Feedback should correspond to the skill level of the performer (cognitive/associative/autonomous).
- Limit the amount of information given.
- Feedback should be give immediately or as soon as possile.
- Feedback should relate to the individual.
- Try to facilitate internal feedback/kinaesthesis.

Revision activity

Draw a table to include all the different types of feedback. Give a practical example from your own sport of each type of feedback.

Now test yourself

TESTED

7 What are the six types of feedback?
8 What is the difference between knowledge of results and knowledge of performance?

Answers on page 171

Memory models

Atkinson and Shiffren's multi-store memory model

Memory is so important for sports performers. It is used when learning
new skills, developing skills already acquired and remembering tactics
and strategies. There are three stages of remembering information:

- short-term sensory store
- short-term memory
- long-term memory.

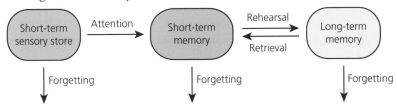

Figure 2.1.4 Adapted from Atkinson and Shiffren's multi-store memory model

Short-term sensory store (STSS)

- The STSS is a limitless memory store for holding information for about
  1 second.
- It is viewed as a subdivided part of short-term memory (STM).
- Streams of sensory stimuli/information are passed into and stored
  very briefly in the STSS and processed simultaneously before the next
  streams enter and are processed.
- **Selective attention** selects the relevant stimuli in the STSS and directs
  them into STM for further processing. Irrelevant stimuli are lost.

Short-term memory (STM)

- STM represents 'a working memory space' where information from the
  STSS and LTM are received and brought together.
- STM has a limited capacity to store information for around seven
  items. The information is held for as long as attention is held.
- STM is limited to the amount of time that information can be
  stored < 1 minute.
- Information can also be held in STM through a process called
  chunking. For example, instead of trying to remember each separate
  move made by each player in a lineout in rugby or penalty corner in
  hockey, a player might remember the whole drill as a single number.

Long-term memory (LTM)

- LTM contains well-learned, retained and permanent coded
  information collected over past experiences.
- LTM is limitless in capacity and length or retention, for example
  learning to ride a bike.
- Well-learned and rehearsed **movement skills** from STM will
  eventually be stored in LTM as motor programmes for future use.
- Relevant information from LTM can be retrieved into STM workspace
  to be used for comparison, to identify stimuli (perception), for decision
  making or to select an appropriate motor programme.

Selective attention: relevant
information is filtered
through into short-term
memory and irrelevant
information is lost or
forgotten.

Chunking: different pieces of
information can be grouped
(or chunked) together and
then remembered as one
piece of information.

Movement skills: an action
or task that has a goal and
requires voluntary body and/
or limb movement to achieve
that goal; it is learned rather
than being innate. Also
known as motor skill.

Advantages and disadvantages of the multi-store memory model approach

Advantages	Disadvantages
<ul><li>Simplifies the memory process</li><li>Explains how those with brain damage may have a dysfunctional memory or amnesia</li></ul>	<ul><li>Too simplified – does not explain why we remember different sorts of information</li><li>Does not prove the distinction between STM and LTM and does not explain the interaction between STM and LTM</li></ul>

Craik and Lockhart's levels of processing model

This approach is used to explain how memory works; it opposes the view that there are set memory stores. It seeks to explain what we do with information rather than how it is stored. According to this approach, meaning of the information is more relevant than repetition.

Information received by the brain will be transferred to the long-term memory (and remembered) if it is:

- considered
- understood
- has meaning (is related to past memories).

How much this information is considered is called the depth of processing. The deeper the information is processed, the longer the **memory trace** will last. There are three levels related to the processing of verbal information:

1 Structural level: paying attention to what words look like (shallow processing level)
2 Phonetic level: processing words and sounds
3 Semantic level: considering the actual meaning of words (deepest level of processing).

Memory trace: when the brain cells retain or store information.

Practical example: a gymnastics coach explains why it is important to tuck in a somersault to ensure there is greater rotation. The performer is more likely to understand why the tuck is important and therefore more likely to remember it.

Advantages and disadvantages of the levels of processing model approach

Advantages	Disadvantages
<ul><li>Explains that if we understand information, we are likely to remember it</li><li>Explains that the longer we consider and analyse information, the more we remember it</li></ul>	<ul><li>The longer it takes to process information does not always lead to better recall</li><li>It is difficult to know what 'deep' processing involves</li><li>It does not take into account individual differences</li></ul>

Relating both memory models to learning and performance of physical activity skills

To make our memory processes more effective to learn and perform skills, there are a number of ways in which our memory can be improved:

- rehearsal – a tennis player will rehearse a serve physically and mentally
- meaningfulness – a tennis coach will show that coaching information being given will raise the player's performance levels
- association – a tennis coach will show the player that new information regarding the serve technique is simply an adaptation of the old serve, so learning a whole new skill is not required
- avoiding overload – a tennis coach will only give the player a few points to remember before the match
- organising information – a trampolinist will remember a complex sequence by mentally putting together the small moves to make bigger ones
- mental imagery – the trampoline coach demonstrates the move or shows a video of the sequence so that the performer can remember it more effectively.

Now test yourself

TESTED

9 What are the three key features of the multi-store memory model?
10 What is a memory trace?
11 How can you make memory processes more effective when learning and performing skills?

Answers on page 171

Exam practice

1 The classification of skills can help us to understand and learn new movement skills. Using a practical example for each, describe what is meant by a simple skill and a complex skill. [4]
2 Part, whole, progressive part and whole–part–whole are all methods of practice. Describe each of these four methods of practising movement skills, giving a practical example for each. [4]
3 For the three phases of learning, describe the use of different types of guidance to improve the performance of movement skills. [6]
4 Describe each part of the multi-store memory model and give a practical example to show how each part contributes to the performance of physical activities. [6]

Answers on page 179

Summary

You should now have an understanding of:
- classification of skills
- types and methods of practice
- transfer of skills
- how to optimise positive transfer
- how to limit negative transfer
- theories of learning
- stages of learning
- types and uses of guidance
- types and uses of feedback
- advantages and disadvantages of using each type of feedback
- Atkinson and Shiffren's multi-store memory model
- uses of selective attention
- Craik and Lockhart's levels of processing model
- how to relate both memory models to learning and performing physical activity skills.

2.2 Sports psychology

Individual differences

REVISED

Personality

Trait theories of personality

Personality traits are innate characteristics and are thought to be relatively stable. They are highly consistent attributes that exert a widely generalised causal effect on behaviour, for example outgoing, aggressive, tense, shy, relaxed, sensitive, etc.

- Trait theories do not believe that the situation or environment has any bearing on a person's behaviour.
- Behaviour is said to be consistent.
- Trait theory attempts to predict behaviour.

> **Personality**: the patterns of thoughts and feelings and the ways in which we interact with our environment and other people that make us a unique person.
>
> **Anxiety**: a negative emotional state that is closely associated with arousal. It is experiencing apprehension and being aware of high arousal linked to our fears and worries.

Type A and B personalities (narrow band approach)

This approach recognises two distinct personality types, each of which highlights its own characteristics. A coach may be able to be more aware of a performer's **anxiety** levels and therefore be able to suggest intervention strategies.

Type A characteristics	Type B characteristics
<ul><li>Highly competitive</li><li>Strong desire to succeed</li><li>Works fast</li><li>Likes to be in control</li><li>Prone to suffer stress</li></ul>	<ul><li>Non-competitive</li><li>Unambitious</li><li>Works more slowly</li><li>Does not enjoy being in control</li><li>Less prone to stress</li></ul>

Stable and unstable personality traits, extroversion and introversion

Stable personality trait	Someone who does not swing from one emotion to another but is usually constant in emotional behaviour
Unstable (neurotic) personality trait	Someone who is highly anxious and has unpredictable emotions
Extroversion	A person who seeks social situations and likes excitement but lacks concentration
Introversion	A person who does not seek social situations but likes peace and quiet and is good at concentrating

Social learning and personality

Social learning theory suggests that rather than being born with characteristics, we learn them from other people, especially from those we hold in high esteem, such as parents, coaches, role models, friends and other people of significance to us.

- Behaviour changes depending on the situation and is therefore a product of our interaction with the environment.
- Personality is learned by observing, modelling and imitating behaviour, and through experience. Psychological functioning occurs as a result of environmental determinants affecting behaviour.

Interactionist approach

- This approach recognises that trait theory and social learning theory both have a role in determining behaviour and personality.
- It offers a more realistic explanation of personality, explaining how different behaviours are produced for different situations.
- It suggests that we base behaviour on inherent traits that we then adapt to the situation we are in.

Attitudes

Attitudes are used to explain a pattern of behaviour or a response in a given situation.

Attitude is an enduring emotional and behavioural response, and although it can be established firmly, an attitude is unstable and can be changed and controlled. Attitudes are directed towards attitude objects, which can be places, situations and the behaviour of other people.

> **Attitude:** a predisposition to act in a particular way towards something or someone in a person's environment.

Factors affecting attitude formation

Positive attitudes are formed by:	Negative attitudes are formed by:
• belief in the benefits of exercise • enjoyable experiences in sport • being good at a particular sport • being excited by the challenge of sport • using sport as a stress release • the influence of others where participation is the norm	• not believing in the benefits of exercise • a bad past experience, e.g. injury • a lack of ability • fear of taking part in sport • suffering stress when taking part • the influence of others when non-participation is the norm

> **Revision activity**
>
> Use practical examples to explain how positive and negative attitudes are formed.

Components of attitudes

According to the triadic model, attitudes have three elements (components):
- cognitive component – what we know and believe about the attitude object (beliefs)
- affective component – how we feel about the attitude object (emotions)
- behavioural component – how we behave towards, respond to or intend to respond to the attitude object (behaviour).

> **Revision activity**
>
> Give each component of the triadic model a sporting example.

Methods of changing attitudes

There are two ways of changing attitudes used particularly in sport:
1 persuasive communication
2 cognitive dissonance.

Persuasive communication

This is an active, non-coercive attempt to reinforce, modify or change the attitude of others. The effectiveness of the persuasion depends on:

● the persuader: the person attempting the change (coach, team manager, teacher, captain)
● the message: the quality of the message the persuader is giving
● the receiver: the person whose attitude the persuader is trying to change.

Cognitive dissonance

According to this theory, individuals like to be consistent in what they do, feel and believe (triadic model). This theory results in individuals having contradictory thoughts about something or someone, which creates an attitude. For example, a rugby player might believe that aerobics is too 'girlie', so the coach tells him that some of the fittest people do it to improve stamina. This attack on the player's beliefs causes a change in attitude and the player now does aerobics to keep fit.

Now test yourself

TESTED ☐

1 Define personality.
2 Name the three personality theories.
3 Define attitude.
4 Name three factors that affect attitude formation.
5 What are the three components of attitude?

Answers on page 171

Motivation

Motivation is the psychological **drive** to succeed. Without it, there is no reason for anyone to want to acquire and develop motor skills in sport. Motivation has three key considerations:

1 our inner drive towards achieving a goal
2 external pressures and rewards we perceive
3 the intensity (arousal level) and the direction of our behaviour.

There are two types of motivation:

1 Intrinsic motivation is the drive from within, for example wanting to achieve mastery for its own sake. This includes feelings of fun, enjoyment and satisfaction.
2 Extrinsic motivation comes from an outside source, for example a trophy or rewards. It is a valuable motivator for the beginner, but will eventually undermine intrinsic motivation.

> **Motivation**: 'the internal mechanisms and external stimuli which arouse and direct our behaviour' (Sage 1974).
>
> **Drive**: directed, motivated or 'energised' behaviour that an individual has towards achieving a certain goal.

Arousal

Motivation is related to the intensity and direction of behaviour. **Arousal** represents the intensity aspect of motivation. Arousal can be somatic or cognitive and can be a positive or negative influence on performance.

> **Arousal**: the 'energised state' or the 'readiness for action' that motivates us to behave in a particular way.

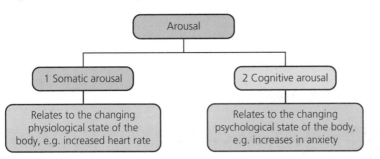

Figure 2.2.1 Diagram of arousal

As a performer's arousal increases, the state of readiness and expectation increases, but if the arousal gets too high, a performer can lose concentration and feel over-aroused. It is essential to understand the three theories of arousal:
1 drive theory
2 inverted U theory
3 catastrophe theory.

Drive theory

This demonstrates a linear relationship between performance and arousal. This means at low levels of arousal, performance is low; performance increases in line with an increase in arousal.

Key points of drive theory

- Quality of performance depends on how well the skill has been learned.
- Motor programmes that have already been learned are said to be the dominant response.
- A dominant response or behaviour is most likely to emerge when a performer experiences an increase in arousal.
- Hull predicted that as arousal increases in a competitive situation or when a learner feels the pressure of assessment, there is a greater likelihood of the dominant response occurring.
- Behaviour = habit × drive (arousal).

Practical application

- High arousal is beneficial to expert performers (autonomous learning stage) because their dominant behaviour would tend to produce a response which is fluent and technically correct.
- The opposite would be true for a novice learner.
- High arousal also helps the performance of gross and simple skills.

Inverted U theory

This theory states that arousal improves performance up to an optimal point. Past this point, performance begins to decrease. The conditions of both under- and over-arousal severely limit the capacity to learn skills and perform them up to potential.

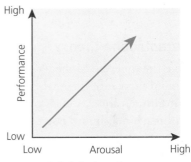

Figure 2.2.2 Drive theory

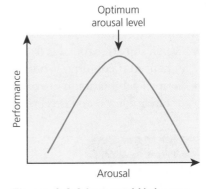

Figure 2.2.3 Inverted U theory

Key points of inverted U theory

It is important to consider:

- personality: extroverts learn best under conditions of high arousal, introverts under conditions of low arousal
- type of task: gross/simple/ballistic/closed – high arousal; fine/complex/open – low arousal
- stage of learning: cognitive/associative – low arousal; autonomous – high arousal
- level of experience: experienced – high arousal; novice – low arousal.

Arousal levels can impact performance, and this is outlined in the following table.

Under-arousal	Optimum arousal	Over-arousal
- Difficult to direct and focus attention and concentration onto relevant environmental cues - Concentration is lost because attentional field is too wide - Many unwanted cues in the environment – learner may be daydreaming - Selective attention, cannot operate - Information overload prevents decision making	- Perfect state - Attentional field is ideal width - Performer is able to learn or concentrate fully - Increased capacity to concentrate means the most important cues can be absorbed from the environment – accurate decision making - Cue utilisation theory predicts that the detection of the most important information occurs at the optimum point of arousal	- Causes attentional field to narrow - Relevant environmental cues are lost - Performer is often in a state of panic - Also known as hypervigilance - Selective attention, cannot operate - Concentration is seriously impeded

Catastrophe theory

Like the inverted U theory, catastrophe theory claims that as somatic arousal increases, the quality of performance improves. However, a third dimension is added to this prediction by stating that performance will reach maximum potential at the optimum level only if cognitive arousal anxiety is kept low. If high **cognitive anxiety** coincides with high **somatic anxiety,** the athlete will go beyond the optimum level of arousal and is thought to have 'gone over the edge'. Under these conditions performance drops.

Key points of catastrophe theory

- The drop is not on a smooth curve as predicted in inverted U theory but plummets vertically.
- The vertical descent depicts a performance disaster or catastrophe.
- After a catastrophe, the performer can re-join the upward curve of arousal and once again attain the optimum threshold.
- This return requires the athlete to reduce cognitive anxiety.
- When somatic arousal is low, skill learning and performance can be enhanced if cognitive arousal is increased.
- Serious debilitation in learning performance will arise when low levels of physiological and psychological arousal converge.

Cognitive anxiety: anxiety experienced by the mind, for example worry about failing.

Somatic anxiety: anxiety experienced physiologically, for example sweating.

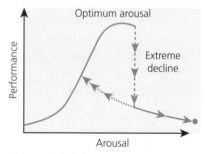

Figure 2.2.4 Catastrophe theory

Revision activity

Create three revision cards highlighting the key points of drive, inverted U and catastrophe theories. Include practical examples and diagrams on your cards.

Now test yourself

TESTED ☐

6 What are intrinsic and extrinsic motivation? Give an example of each.
7 What are somatic and cognitive arousal?
8 What are the three theories of arousal?

Answers on page 171

Exam tip

Drawing a diagram is an excellent way to help you explain. Diagrams such as the inverted U theory can help you gain marks. Ensure they are accurate and fully labelled.

Anxiety

Anxiety is the negative aspect of experiencing stress and can be caused by worry, apprehension or fear of failure. **Trait anxiety** relates to personality. A performer with high trait anxiety is likely to feel anxious in any stressful situation, such as exams or interviews. **Competitive trait anxiety** is the worry or apprehension experienced during or about competition. The sport competitive anxiety test (SCAT) is used to help predict how anxious a performer will be in future competitions – their **state anxiety**.

Trait anxiety: a trait that is enduring in an individual. A performer with high trait anxiety has the predisposition or the potential to react to situations with apprehension.

Competitive trait anxiety: a tendency to perceive competitive situations as threatening and to respond to these situations with feelings of apprehension or tension.

State anxiety: the athlete's emotional state at any given time; variable from situation to situation.

Somatic and cognitive anxiety

Two types of anxiety have been identified: somatic and cognitive. Both can be experienced at different levels before, during and after sports performance. The control of both types of anxiety is very important to ensure optimal performance.

Anxiety type	Possible symptoms
Somatic	Increased BP, sweating, adrenaline boost, need to urinate, muscle tension, pacing, yawning, nausea, vomiting, diarrhoea, loss of appetite
Cognitive	Indecision, confusion, negative thoughts, poor concentration, irritability, loss of confidence, images of failure

Zone of optimal functioning

The zone of optimal functioning is thought of as an important state of well-being. This zone is an emotional response that facilitates top performance and is often referred to as the peak flow experience.

Top performer 'in the zone' are:
- relaxed
- confident
- completely focused – concentrating on cues that are relevant (cue utilisation)
- find activity is effortless
- find movements are automatic
- have fun
- are in control.

Aggression in sport

Aggression is the intent to harm or injure outside the rules of the game. Assertion is forceful behaviour within the laws of an event.

Theories of aggression

Instinct theory of aggression	Frustration–aggression hypothesis	Social learning theory	Aggressive cue hypothesis
• Views aggression as being a natural response, innate and instinctive • Animalistic • Humans developed aggression as survival instinct	• Frustration will always lead to aggression • Any blocking of goals that an individual is trying to reach increases an individual's drive, thus increasing aggression and frustration • If success follows then aggression leads to catharsis	• Aggression is learned by observation of others' behaviour • Imitation of this aggressive behaviour is then reinforced by social acceptance • For example, if we see a team mate fouling an opponent and this stops them from playing well, it is reinforced and copied	• For aggression to occur certain stimuli must be present • These stimuli are cues for the performer which are subconsciously linked to aggression, for example baseball bats, ice hockey sticks • Frustration causes anger and arousal and this creates a readiness for aggression • For example, a player sees a colleague fouled then decides to join in

Social facilitation and social inhibition

The effect of having others present during performances can be either positive or negative:

- positive = **social facilitation**
- negative = **social inhibition.**

Other performers are known as co-actors; the spectators are known as the audience.

Zajonc identified the following factors as affecting performance:
1 The presence of an audience increases arousal.
2 Increases in arousal will trigger the dominant response.
3 If a skill is well-learned, response will be correct.
4 If the skill is new or poorly learned, the response will be incorrect.

> **Social facilitation**: the positive influence on sports performance of others who may be watching or competing.
>
> **Social inhibition**: the negative influence on sports performance of others who may be watching or competing.

Evaluation apprehension

Performers can suffer with evaluation apprehension. This increases arousal levels, which in turn increases heart rate and causes other detrimental effects. For example, a person who is trying out for cheerleading may feel a heightened sense of arousal leading to incompetence not just because others are around, but because of the fear that others are observing and ridiculing them.

Effects of social facilitation and social inhibition on performance

The presence of an audience will spur some athletes on to great performances, while others may 'choke', adversely affecting their performance. Some of the effects of social facilitation and social inhibition are outlined in the following table.

Effect	Explanation
Home v away	● Teams more often win at home, maybe due to the nature of the audience. ● Some research suggests it is harder to win at home due to increased pressure.
Personality factors (introverts v extroverts)	● Type A (high anxiety) personalities perform worse in front of an audience than Type B (low anxiety) personalities. ● Extroverts tend to perform better than introverts in front of a crowd.
Levels of experience (beginners v experts)	● Previous experiences in front of an audience can help alleviate nerves and improve performance. However, if a performer has failed in front of an audience previously, they may expect to fail again. ● Elite/higher skilled perform better than beginners/novices, due to the dominant response being correct. ● Performing in front of peers can aid experts but increase anxiety of novices.
Types of skills/ activities	● Gross skills are helped by high arousal, therefore an audience can facilitate performance. ● Fine or complex skills are more desirable at lower levels of arousal, so an audience could inhibit performance.
Other influences	● The nature of the crowd – if hostile or noisy, a performer may feel more anxious. ● The proximity of the audience, e.g. a close audience could make a performer feel threatened and increase arousal.

Strategies to minimise social inhibition

The following strategies may be used by athletes to copy with the negative effects of an audience:

- imagery techniques to 'shut out' the audience
- relaxation techniques
- training with an audience present
- preparing to deal with negative reactions of co-actors
- decreasing the importance of an event
- remaining calm and focused.

Now test yourself

TESTED

9 What is cognitive anxiety? State two symptoms.
10 What is somatic anxiety? State two symptoms.
11 What performance characteristics would a performer who was 'in the zone' display?
12 What is the difference between social facilitation and social inhibition?
13 Name the four theories of aggression.

Answers on page 171

Groups and teams

Group or sports team formation

Tuckman (1965) identified **group** development in the model 'Forming-Storming-Norming-Performing' as shown in the following table.

> **Group**: a collection of people who both share similar goals and interact with one another.

Forming	• High dependence on leader for guidance • Group members are getting to know each other • Very little agreement on the aims of the team • Individual roles are unclear • Team leader needs to give strong direction
Storming	• Group decisions are difficult • Team members are establishing themselves in the group • Focus is clearer • Cliques form, there may be power struggles • Need for environmental compromise • Leader has a more advisory role
Norming	• Much more agreement and consensus of opinion • Roles and responsibilities are accepted • Decisions are made through group agreement • Strong sense of commitment and unity • Team members are social and friendly with each other • Respect for the leader and leadership is shared
Performing	• More strategies, a clear vision and aim • No interference of participation from the leader • Focus is on achieving goals • Team is trusted to get on with the job in hand • Disagreements occur but are resolved within the team • Team is able to work and be personable • Team does not need to be instructed or assisted • Team members may ask for assistance from the leader with personal and interpersonal issues

Team cohesion

Cohesion is used when describing group dynamics. Festinger (1963) states that cohesiveness is 'the total field of forces which act on members to remain in the group'.

According to Carron (1980), cohesion has two dimensions:
- group integration – how the individual members of the group feel about the group as a whole
- individual attraction to the group – how attracted the individuals are to the group.

Group or sports team performance

Steiner (1972) proposed the following model, which is helpful when looking at the relationship between individuals and group performance:

Actual productivity = potential productivity − losses due to faulty process

Potential productivity refers to the best possible performance of the group, taking into account resources available and the ability of the players. For example, a non-league team losing 4–0 to Chelsea might well be reaching their full potential but are not winning due to their limited resources.

Losses due to faulty processes are caused by two factors:

1 Co-ordination problems: if co-ordination and timing of team members do not match, team strategies that depend on them will suffer. An example would be positional error or an ill-timed move.
2 Motivational problems: if individual members of a team are not motivated to the same extent, they will be 'pulling in different directions' and players will withdraw effort.

The Ringelmann effect

This occurs when individual performances decrease as group sizes increase.

Research on co-ordination and motivational losses was based on studies into tug of war, where it was found that a team of eight did not pull eight times as hard as solo performers.

Latane (1979) found that group performance suffered as a group got larger; he termed the motivational losses **social loafing**. For example, a water polo team may not play very well because one particular player is not trying very hard.

Social loafing is undesirable in teams and should be eliminated as far as possible. Strategies to eliminate social loafing include:
- highlight individual performances
- support from others in the team – social support
- feedback
- peer pressure to reinforce individual effort.

Social loafing: some individuals in a group seem to lose motivation. It is apparently caused by the individual losing identity when placed in a group. Individual efforts may not be recognised by those who are spectating or by those who are taking part.

Goal setting

Goal setting can develop positive self-perception and reduce the anxiety that may arise prior to and during performance. The correct use of goal setting can help improve confidence and motivation levels of the athlete.

Goal setting influences performance in a number of ways:

1 It directs the attention of the performer onto the required task or strategy.
2 It increases the effort applied by the performer.
3 It improves persistence when a task becomes difficult or when failure is experienced.
4 The performer becomes increasingly motivated to learn and to apply different approaches to learning in order to complete a task successfully.
5 Successful completion of a goal will help raise confidence and self-efficacy.
6 Goals can help break down performance into manageable tasks, helping to control arousal and anxiety.

SMART goal setting

● **S**pecific – goals must be clear and specific.
● **M**easurable – goals must be assessed and therefore need to be measurable.
● **A**chievable – goals that are shared by performers and coaches are more likely to be achievable, as all interested parties have a common purpose and the goals set are realistic to the ability of the performers.
● **R**ecorded – goals should be recorded so that progress can be monitored.
● **T**ime-phased – goals should be split into short-term goals leading to long-term goals.

Different types of goal

● Performance goals – for example to achieve a certain time, such as 100 m in under 10 seconds
● Process-oriented goals – for example to ensure front crawl arm technique is correct
● Outcome goals – for example to win the race

Now test yourself

14 What is a group?
15 Explain the Ringelmann effect.
16 What is social loafing?
17 What does SMART stand for?
18 Give three reasons why a coach might use goal setting with an athlete.

Answers on page 171

Attribution in sport

Attribution is the perceived cause of a particular outcome. It comprises the reasons, justifications and excuses we give for winning, losing and drawing in sport. Attribution theory is linked to motivation, as our attributions will directly affect future efforts and performances.

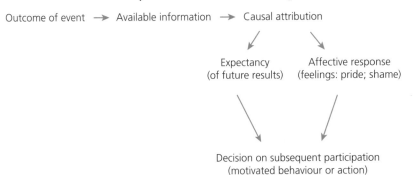

Outcome of event → Available information → Causal attribution

Expectancy (of future results)

Affective response (feelings: pride; shame)

Decision on subsequent participation (motivated behaviour or action)

Figure 2.2.5 **The process of attribution**

The model in Figure 2.2.5 is a well-known representation of the process of attribution. Often attributions are inappropriate or unreal; it is important to change these, in order to have a positive effect on future performance. This is known as attribution retraining (see page 134).

Weiner's model of attribution

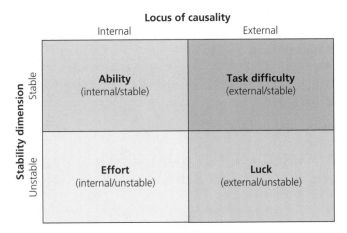

Figure 2.2.6 **Weiner's model of attribution**

Weiner's model is not sport-specific. The locus of causality refers to whether attributions come from within the person (internal) or the environment (external). Stability refers to whether the attribution is changeable or unchangeable.

If reasons for winning are stable, the individual is motivated to achieve again. If failure is attributed to an unstable factor, the individual is more likely to try again because there is a good chance the outcome will change.

Sports performers who lose tend to attribute their failure to external causes, while those who succeed attribute their success to internal causes. This is known as the **self-serving bias**.

Self-serving bias: a person's tendency to attribute their failure to external causes ('I lost the badminton match because the floor was too slippery') and their success to internal causes.

Controllability

Weiner added a third dimension to his attribution model – **controllability**. This dimension takes into consideration whether a cause for sports outcome is controllable or uncontrollable.

Controllability: whether attributions are under the control of the performer or under the control of others, or whether they are uncontrollable, i.e. nothing can be done by anyone (e.g. luck, weather).

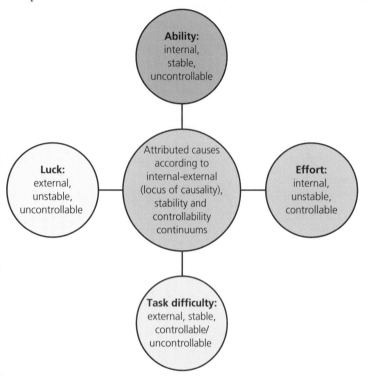

Figure 2.2.7 Attribution theory: how each attributed cause links to controllability

Learned helplessness and mastery orientation

- Learned helplessness is the belief that failure is inevitable and that the individual has no control over the factors that cause failure.
- Low achievers often attribute their failures to uncontrollable factors, which can lead to learned helplessness.
- Mastery orientation is the view that an individual will be motivated by becoming an expert (master) in skill development.
- An athlete who is mastery oriented will often attribute failure to internal, controllable and unstable factors.

Attribution retraining

Attributions should be encouraged to be controllable, unstable factors. For example, a hockey team that has just lost narrowly should be encouraged to 'try harder next week'. This is more likely to result in mastery orientation.

Revision activity

Sketch Weiner's model diagram (Figure 2.2.6). Add a sporting example from your own experience to each box.

Now test yourself   TESTED ☐

19 What is an attribution?
20 What are the three dimensions of Weiner's model?
21 What is learned helplessness and mastery orientation?

Answers on page 171

Confidence and self-efficacy in sports performance

REVISED

Levels of **sport confidence** have an effect on:
- performance – you will be more motivated to achieve and will take firm decisions that are more likely to have positive outcomes
- participation – low levels of sport confidence may mean you shy away from activities; high levels enable people to participate and not feel inhibited
- **self-esteem** – high levels of sport confidence will mean high self-esteem; those with low levels may experience low self-esteem and feel they are not good enough.

> **Sport confidence:** the belief or degree of certainty individuals possess about their ability to be successful in sport.
>
> **Self-esteem:** the feeling of self-worth that determines how valuable and competent we feel.

Vealey's sport confidence model

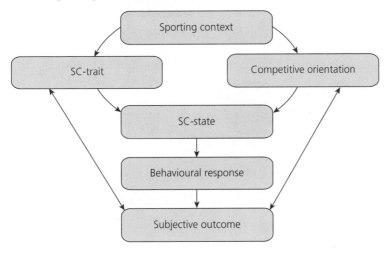

Figure 2.2.8 Vealey's sport confidence (SC) model

The following table explains the key points of Vealey's model.

Component	Explanation	Sporting example
Sporting context	The sporting situation you are in	Penalty kick in football
SC-trait	Everyone has an existing level of sport confidence	High levels of confidence in football (high levels of SC-trait)
Competitive orientation	Everyone has an existing level of competitiveness	Enjoying highly competitive situations
SC-state	• The confidence that can be shown in a specific situation in sport • SC–state = (SC – trait) + (competitive orientation)	• Experienced penalty taker has been successful in same situation many times = high levels of SC-state so likely to be successful • If SC-state was low, an inexperienced, nervous penalty taker would be unlikely to be successful
Behavioural response	Response to the situation	Penalty is scored or not scored
Subjective outcome	• The emotion felt towards the behavioural response • These perceived feelings affect future SC-trait and competitive orientation: positive perceived feelings may increase confidence and negative perceived feelings may decrease confidence	• Satisfaction if penalty is scored • Disappointment if penalty is not scored • Increased future confidence if outcome is successful, possible decreased confidence if outcome is poor

Bandura's theory of self-efficacy

According to Bandura (1977), our expectations of **self-efficacy** depend on four types of information:

- performance accomplishments: a reminder of previous successes in the related skill or situation
- vicarious experiences: watching others perform the skill in question
- verbal persuasion: convincing the athlete of their ability to perform the skill
- emotional arousal: the evaluation the performer makes of a physiological state.

Self-efficacy: the confidence we have in specific situations.

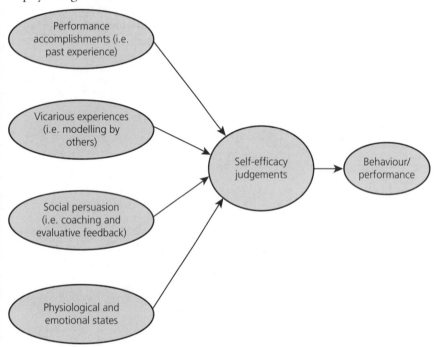

Figure 2.2.9 Bandura's model of self-efficacy

> **Exam tip**
>
> When explaining a model or theory, use the same practical example throughout, showing the examiner you are able to apply theory to practice consistently.

Now test yourself

TESTED ☐

22 On what three things can sports confidence have an effect?
23 What are the six components of Vealey's model of sport confidence?
24 According to Bandura, what four things can affect self-efficacy?

Answers on page 171

Leadership in sport

There are many leadership positions in sport, for example captain, manager, director, coach, physiotherapist and team sport psychologist.

Characteristics of effective leaders

Qualities of effective leaders include:
- good communication skills
- high motivation
- enthusiasm
- a clear goal or vision of what needs to be achieved
- empathy
- comprehensive knowledge of the sport/being good at the sport
- charisma.

Emergent and prescribed leaders

An emergent leader becomes a leader through their hard work and determination. People who look up to and respect them help them to become a leader. They may be skilful in their sport and they become a leader to show others how well they can do and inspire team mates.

A prescribed leader is someone appointed by people of a higher authority. For example, Gareth Southgate was appointed manager of the England men's football team by the Football Association in 2016.

Leadership styles

Leadership style	Description	Explanation of when used
Authoritarian	• Task-oriented and dictator style • Leader makes all the decisions and is very direct in their approach	• When discipline or control is needed • With hostile groups or if there is a lack of time • If the situation is dangerous or task is clear • Novice performers and males tend to like this style
Democratic	Person-oriented and takes into account team members' ideas and feelings, leader shows interest in others	• When group members want to be involved in decision making • If the situation is not dangerous and the task requires greater interpersonal communication • With small teams or individuals • Advanced performers and females tend to like this style
Laissez-faire	Leader provides little support or input and lets team members do as they wish	• With high-level performers or elite athletes • With developing creativity for team members • When leader can fully trust member capabilities • When group is being assessed • If leader is incompetent

Theories of leadership

Leadership theory	Explanation	Evaluation
Trait theory	<ul><li>Leaders are born with their leadership qualities.</li><li>These traits are stable and enduring and can be generalised across different situations.</li></ul>	<ul><li>Popular belief that 'great leaders are born not made'. Leaders have characteristics which make them effective.</li><li>People in sport tend to be quite specific in their leadership skills, which works against the generalised trait approach.</li></ul>
Social learning theory	<ul><li>Leadership characteristics can be learned from others.</li><li>Behaviour of others is watched and copied – **vicarious learning**.</li></ul>	High-status models are more likely to be copied. This theory shows the importance of the social environment for adopting leadership qualities, rather than the trait approach which does not take the environment into account.
Interactionist theory	An individual may have certain in-born traits, such as assertiveness, but they are not evident unless a situation (state) demands the leadership behaviour.	This theory accounts for the fact that people may not be leaders in everyday life but show leadership qualities in sports situations.

Chelladurai's multi-dimensional model of leadership

The most prevailing view of leadership is that people learn to be leaders through social learning and interactions with the environment. Chelladurai's multi-dimensional model of leadership (1984) shown in Figure 2.2.10 is a popular approach to the study of leadership in sport.

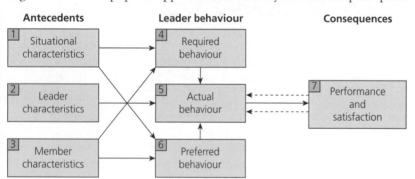

Figure 2.2.10 Chelladurai's multi-dimensional model of leadership

The more the elements of this model match each other, the more effective the leadership is likely to be. If the leadership qualities are what the group members want and expect, then they are more likely to follow the leader. If the leadership style matches the situation, again leadership is likely to be more effective.

Vicarious learning: the person observes that a reward is given to another person for certain behaviour and learns to emulate that same behaviour.

Typical mistake

Do not mix up the leadership theories with the personality theories.

The following table explains Chelladurai's model further.

Number	Part of model	Explanation
1	Situational characteristics	Environmental conditions e.g. activity (football, rock climbing), number of people in the group, time constraints, strength of opposition, etc.
2	Leader characteristics	The personality/skill level/experience of the leader. The leader may have a preferred style of leadership.
3	Member characteristics	What is the group like? Skill level/attitudes/experience/age/personalities.
4	Required behaviour	What style of leadership is needed for this task? The situation (and the member characteristics) dictates the appropriate style of leadership.
5	Actual behaviour	What does the leader actually choose to do? The behaviour the leader displays as a result of the situation and the member characteristics and the leader characteristics.
6	Preferred behaviour	What leadership style do the group prefer? Member characteristics (and the situation) dictate the appropriate style of leadership.
7	Performance and satisfaction	The overall performance of the members and the leader and the level of satisfaction.

Now test yourself

TESTED

25 What is the difference between a prescribed leader and an emergent leader?
26 What are the three main leadership styles?
27 Sketch Chelladurai's multi-dimensional model of leadership.

Answers on page 171

Stress management to optimise performance

REVISED

Stress causes a release of hormones in the body. In the short term, adrenaline is released which increases heart rate, raises blood pressure and gives extra energy that is beneficial. Stress that is long term, or too intense, can increase the risk of health problems and have a negative effect on a performer's readiness to perform.

Causes of stress

A number of things may cause stress; these are termed stressors. Stressors are environmental changes that induce a stress response. They generally arise when there is an imbalance between the person's perception of the demand being made on them by the situation and their ability to meet that demand. In sport, there are many stressors:
- competition (a powerful stressor)
- conflict (with other players or the opposition)
- frustration (with your own or team members' performances)
- climate (excessively hot or cold).

> **Stress**: in sport, stress is more often linked to negative feelings and can be seen as a psychological state produced and perceived by physiological and psychological forces acting on our sense of well-being.

Stress/anxiety management techniques

Two types of state anxiety have been recognised:
- cognitive anxiety (stress response of the mind)
- somatic anxiety (stress response of the body).

The ways in which performers control the amount of stress can be cognitive or somatic, or in many cases a mixture of both.

Cognitive stress management techniques

Technique	Description	Evaluation
Mental rehearsal	Recalling movement experiences from memory or creating a mental picture of new experiences. Forming a mental image of the skill you are about to perform, for example seeing yourself score the goal.	• For a novice, it may help improve confidence and control arousal levels. • Research has shown that it can create optimism in performance.
Positive thinking/ positive self-talk	Used to motivate and 'psyche up'. Being positive about your past performance, by talking to yourself can help confidence and performance, for example saying to yourself 'I am going to score today'.	It is only of value if performers are experienced and of a high standard.
Goal setting	Setting SMART goals can break tasks down and reduce levels of anxiety. Setting short-term goals, which lead to long-term goals, will make a performer feel in control and reduce stress.	• Goals need to be clearly defined and decisions shared. • Performers should be aware of outcome, performance and process goals.
Negative thought stopping	Instructions aimed at halting negativity, for example stopping feelings of 'I can't score'.	Individuals prone to learned helplessness may find stopping negative thoughts difficult.
Rational thinking	Challenging any negative thoughts by looking at logical and real aspects of a situation, for example thinking about an extensive training programme and how this will have prepared them.	Perception is the key because it is the interpretation of the situation that dictates the level of stress the performer experiences.
Mindfulness	A therapeutic technique, often involving meditation, with the individual taking into account the present. It concerns our environmental awareness and our relationships with others at a particular point in time. For example, if a golfer is worrying about her next hole, she should concentrate on her peaceful surroundings and the 'flow' of her golf swing.	Can lead to the 'peak flow experience' of the zone of optimum functioning.
Imagery • External (seeing yourself from outside your body) • Internal (seeing yourself from within)	Can help improve concentration and develop confidence. Imagery involves the formation of mental pictures that are often unrelated to the actual activity. Imagery can be visual, auditory, kinaesthetic or emotional. For example, pictures of escape, such as lying on a beach, sounds of the sea, etc., may help control stress.	Internal imagery is more effective than external imagery. To be effective you must: practise in a relaxed environment, keep exercises short but frequent, set goals for each session and evaluate your programme at regular intervals.

Somatic stress management techniques

Technique	Description	Evaluation
Centering	Combines somatic and cognitive responses. Similar to mindfulness in that you focus on the here and now. Concentration is shifted to the centre of the body. The mind recognises that the body is responding to a stressful event. Through centering, the athlete will redirect energy to the centre of the body and then achieve a calm steady state.	Skill needs to be mastered, focusing on breathing. It requires regular practice so it can be used automatically.
Progressive muscular relaxation	Developed by Jacobsen (1932), sometimes called Jacobsen technique. Athletes have to learn to be 'aware' of tension in muscles and then 'let it go'. Gradually, muscle groups should be combined until the whole body can be relaxed on one command.	Takes longer to learn than self-directed relaxation but is thought to be more effective.
Biofeedback	Performers are taught to control muscular tension by relaxing (by any chosen method) the specific muscles showing tension on a machine. The degree of tension is noted by the sound the machine makes. By linking the feeling with the noise, the performer eventually can identify the tension without assistance.	The machine provides objective biological feedback about muscle activity, skin temperature, heart rate and electromyography which informs about the performer's success at relieving the tension.
Breathing control	Slow deep breaths ensure you get enough oxygen and feel more relaxed and in control. Focusing on breathing can help take your mind off things.	It can be helpful as part of a routine, for example between serves in tennis.

Revision activity

Create a spider diagram of the stress management techniques. Include pictures to help you revise and remember.

Now test yourself

TESTED ☐

28 What is stress? Name possible causes of stress in sport.
29 Name the seven cognitive techniques used to reduce stress.
30 Name the four somatic techniques used to reduce stress.

Answers on page 172

Exam practice

1 Identify two characteristics of an extroverted performer and two characteristics of an introverted performer and explain why a coach may take personality type into account during training.   [6]
2 Identify what is meant by an attitude and describe the components of attitudes that young people might have towards sport and PE.   [4]
3 Use practical examples from sport to describe type A and type B trait personalities.   [2]
4 Briefly describe the difference between aggression and assertion. Use an example from sport in your answer.   [4]
5 Anxiety is a negative aspect of stress. What is meant by the terms 'trait anxiety' and 'state anxiety'? Use examples from a practical activity to illustrate your answer.   [4]
6 The audience or crowd at a sports event may help or hinder performance. Using psychological theories and practical examples from sport, explain how an audience can affect performance.   [10]
7 Why is goal setting relevant to managing anxiety in sport?   [4]
8 With reference to Chelladurai's multi-dimensional model of leadership, explain how effective leadership can encourage participation in sport.   [6]
9 Using one example from sport, explain Vealey's model of sport confidence.   [6]
10 Describe the methods that might be used to raise self-efficacy in sports performance.   [4]

Answers on page 180

Summary

You should now have an understanding of:
- the definition of personality
- theories of personality
- the definition of attitude
- factors affecting attitude formation/ components of attitude: cognitive, affective, behavioural
- methods of attitude change: persuasive communication, cognitive dissonance
- the definitions of intrinsic motivation and extrinsic motivation
- uses and effects of intrinsic motivation and extrinsic motivation
- the definition of arousal
- the effects of arousal: drive theory, inverted U theory, catastrophe theory
- the definition of anxiety
- types of anxiety: state and trait
- the response to anxiety: somatic and cognitive
- the zone of optimal functioning
- the definition of aggression
- theories of aggression
- the definition of social facilitation and social inhibition
- the effect of an audience on: introverts/ extroverts, beginners/experts, simple/complex skills, gross/fine skills
- evaluative apprehension
- strategies to minimise social inhibition

- the definition of a group
- the formation of groups and sports teams using stages of group development: forming, storming, norming and performing
- Steiner's model of group effectiveness
- the Ringelmann effect and social loafing
- the importance and effectiveness of goal setting: the SMART principle (specific, measurable, achievable, recorded, timed)
- Weiner's model of attribution
- learned helplessness as a barrier to sports performance; mastery orientation to optimise sports performance
- the definitions of sport confidence and self-efficacy and the impact of sport confidence on: performance, participation, self-esteem
- Vealey's model of sport confidence
- characteristics of effective leaders
- emergent or prescribed leaders
- leadership styles
- theories of leadership
- Chelladurai's multi-dimensional model of leadership
- the definition and causes of stress
- the use of cognitive stress management techniques
- the use of somatic stress management techniques.

3.1 Sport and society

Emergence and evolution of modern sport

REVISED

How social and cultural factors shaped sports and pastimes in pre-industrial Britain

The following factors had a major influence on sports and pastimes in pre-industrial Britain.

Revision activity

Outline the main characteristics of a) mob football, b) real tennis, and c) prize fighting.

Social class

Class	Description	Examples of sports and pastimes
Upper class	Aristocracy or gentry who were hereditary landowners	• Real tennis and fox hunting: sophisticated activities with complex rules which required money to participate • Pedestrianism: as patrons (sponsors) of lower-class competitors; derived from putting wagers on footmen • Cricket: played as 'gentleman' amateurs
Lower/peasant class	Peasants who worked manually, mainly on the land	• Mob football, dog fighting, prize fighting: simple activities, often violent, with few rules • Pedestrianism: as competitors, racing (walking or running); derived from footmen racing and beating others • Cricket: played as 'player' lower-class professionals

Gender

Class	Influence
Upper and lower	Women participated in very different activities to men
	Women were seen as the 'weaker' sex
	Activities women participated in were not 'too strenuous' or 'dangerous'
Upper	Women could take part in archery
Lower	During country fairs, women were allowed to take part in 'smock races'

Law and order

Class	Influence
Upper and lower	There was little law and order, reflected in the activities undertaken
Lower	Involved in bare-knuckle fighting or animal baiting, reflecting lack of order and animal cruelty
	Games like mob football had few rules, showing lack of law and order in society at this time

Education and literacy

Class	Influence
Upper	Educated and literate
	Could read and write and understand written rules of sophisticated activities like real tennis
Lower	Uneducated and illiterate
	Could understand simple activities with few rules, like mob football

Availability of time

Class	Influence
Upper	Had more time and could be involved in longer-lasting activities, e.g. fox hunting
Lower	Worked long exhausting hours, so had little time or energy for physical activities
	The few activities they participated in were confined to festivals or holy day fairs, based around pubs, e.g. drinking contest, bare-knuckle fighting

Availability of money

Class	Influence
Upper	More money therefore more opportunities to be involved in physical activity of their choice
	Could afford horses, clothing and equipment, e.g. hunting, real tennis
	Had access to specialist facilities, e.g. real tennis courts
Lower	Had no spare money to spend on physical activities

Type and transport available

Class	Influence
Upper and lower	Activities were local; transport was generally horse and cart or walking
Upper	Had more opportunity to travel further by horse and carriage, but this was often limited by the state of the roads
	Could get to facilities such as real tennis courts; some gentry would even build the facility within the grounds of their stately homes
Lower	Roads were in a poor state, preventing people from leaving their villages; this influenced the simple, local and unwritten rules, varying from village to village

How social and cultural factors shaped sports and pastimes in post-1850 industrial Britain

The industrialisation of Britain changed the way people lived and worked, as there was much more distinction between work and leisure. The following factors enable us to analyse how sports and pastimes were shaped.

Social class

- The upper and lower (working) classes were now accompanied by a middle class.
- The middle class included professionals, factory owners and managers, who did not own big estates and were not born into aristocracy.
- Many members of the middle class went to **public schools**, which were influential in the development of sports such as rugby and football.

Amateurism and professionalism

- **Amateurs** were not paid; this status suited the upper and middle classes.
- Cricket: amateurs and **professionals** played in the same team but social distinction was preserved through different changing rooms; also the lower-class professionals bowled and cleaned the kit.
- Soccer and rugby: professionalism was the most controversial. The growth of social mixed northern teams led to broken-time payments, where lower classes were paid in order to miss a day's work to play. These payments were against the amateur principles of the upper classes. Tensions led to the splitting of rugby into two codes, league and union, in 1895.
- Golf: before 1861 there were separate Open Championships for amateurs and professionals. The professionals did not fit in with the image of the gentlemanly game.

> **Public school**: a place of education of old standing which the sons of gentlemen traditionally attended in large numbers from 8 to 18 years old.
>
> **Amateurs**: people who compete in sporting activities but do not receive monetary reward for participating
>
> **Professionals**: people who compete in sporting activities and earn an income by participating

Gender and the changing status of women

- In the early nineteenth century, women were expected to marry, have children and be financially dependent on their husbands. Many people regarded education for women as pointless.
- Schooling for girls was initially limited, compared to boys. Women were allowed to become teachers, but this was a low-status, poorly paid job.
- During the late nineteenth century, the status of women began to change; a shortage of men, due to high mortality rates and a large number serving in the armed forces, suppressed the assumption that women had to marry.
- Limitations on schooling for women were identified by the Taunton Royal Commission Report in 1868. Efforts formed part of a wider movement of campaigners who fought for equal rights to study, work, own property and, eventually, vote.
- This had an encouraging effect on women to be more involved in sport and physical education in schools.

Law and order

- The development of laws affected the type of activities undertaken, especially for the lower (working) class.
- Laws led to a decline in blood sports, for example animal baiting and cock fighting.
- Upper classes held onto their sports, such as fox hunting.
- Law makers were from the upper and middle classes, so it was in their interest to support the sports they enjoyed.

Education and literacy

- The vast majority of the working classes had very little interest in education because it was perceived to be of little relevance.
- Child labour was still common practice; working-class families were reluctant to give up the earnings of their children for the benefits of education.
- The employment of children continued to increase even after 1850.
- The 1870 Forster Act modernised education in England. Elementary education became free with the passing of the 1891 Education Act. Education became more accessible to the working classes, allowing them to understand more sophisticated rules in sport. Sport became widespread.

Availability of time and money

- An increase in leisure time after the mid-nineteenth century allowed sport to develop quickly.
- However, the working class still found participation difficult due to lack of disposable income.
- The growth of factories meant that for many working hours were long and pay was poor.
- 72-hour working weeks were common, leaving little energy and time for sport.
- Introduction of the Saturday half-day, for skilled workers initially then for labourers, allowed more time for sport and leisure.
- Living conditions remained poor, deprivation and poverty were high, but some sports clubs developed.
- Factory owners recognised a happy, healthy work force as being more productive, so some organised annual excursions to the seaside.
- By 1965, the working week was 40–45 hours, reducing by the end of the twentieth century to 37–40 hours, increasing the amount of time available for sport.
- Law today states workers must have four weeks' holiday a year, allowing time for playing and watching sport.

Type and availability of transport

- The railways were important in the development of seaside resorts and, in sport, allowed fixtures to be played and spectators to visit venues around the country.
- Cars were mass produced in the twentieth century, and the majority of households have a car nowadays; compared to 50 years ago, it is much easier both to follow and participate in sport.

Quick quizzes at **www.hoddereducation.co.uk/myrevisionnotes**

Influence of public schools

The promotion and organisation of sport and games

- Public schools were influential in the development of modern sports, both at home and abroad.
- At the beginning of the nineteenth century, sport was unorganised, reflecting society. Bullying and exploitation of younger boys was common in public schools. Headmasters were not in favour of sport.
- In the middle of the nineteenth century, with the changing ethos of public schools, sport became an important element of the education of upper- and middle-class boys in these schools.

The promotion of ethics through games and sports

- Thomas Arnold, headmaster at Rugby School, wanted pupils to grow up as Christian gentlemen. He revised the fagging system (whereby younger boys were required to act as personal servants to older boys) and promoted more regulated sports, which provided exercise and encouraged healthy competition.
- Arnold developed the house system, influencing the formation of competitive teams.
- Arnold also established prefects, who organised sports.

The 'cult' of athleticism

- The ideas of muscular Christianity linked sport with being a Christian gentleman, establishing a connection between sports and games and a moral and ethical character.
- The development of character through sport is referred to as the cult of **athleticism**.

> **Athleticism**: a combination of physical endeavour (trying hard) and moral integrity, (being honourable, truthful and showing good sportsmanship).

The spread and export of games and the games ethic

- By 1845, pupils at Rugby wrote down the rules of football at their school to ensure fair play.
- Pupils took the games with them to university, but played many different versions.
- In 1863, a common set of rules was decided for football. At the end of that year, players from around the country came together to form the Football Association (FA).
- Other sports followed suit: the Amateur Athletic Club (AAC) formed in 1866, the Rugby Football Union (RFU) formed in 1871 and the Lawn Tennis Association (LTA) formed in 1888.

How social factors shaped sport in the twentieth century

There was a massive development of scientific and technological innovation throughout the twentieth century. Sport in Britain had taken the shape it would keep, more or less, until the television boom of the 1960s and 1970s. The following social factors enable us to analyse how sport was shaped in the twentieth century.

Class, gender, law and order

Class	• The pub was the centre of sporting activity for working-class men. • In horse racing and boxing, the middle class and upper class put up the money and the lower class took part. • In team sports such as cricket, the working class and middle class would compete side by side. • Working-class men and women had less free time for sport than the upper and middle classes. • Sport played an important part in troop morale during the First World War. In the aftermath of the war, spectator sport reached new heights of popularity. • Crowds were mostly well behaved, leading to the view that sport was a symbol of orderliness and good nature of the British working class. • Unemployed and unskilled workers could not afford to spectate.
Gender	• Participation of women in physical recreation had dropped dramatically in 1900. • Crowds at professional football and rugby league games became male dominated, showing a shared sense of community and class. • Professional sport was mainly watched by male skilled workers, with only a few women and middle-class spectators. • Working-class women were excluded from professional sport by the constraints of time and money.
Law and order	• Fields of play were enclosed, formal games were timetabled, there were written codes of conduct, e.g. in rugby and football, and most cruel sports had disappeared. • Spectators had to pay to watch; in boxing, gloves were worn, and numbered kit to assist spectators appeared in football. There was a fixed number of players per side in most sports. • Teams and spectators were able to travel widely. Sports events were held on Saturdays rather than on festival days. • Professional teams formed in football, rugby and cricket. • Growing crowds demanded purpose-built grounds and stadia. Spectatorism emerged, with more watching than participating. • Gambling was still an essential part of sport. • A sports press developed.

Education

The Education Act of 1944 (Butler Act) stated: 'It shall be the duty of the local education authority for every area, so far as their powers extend, to continue the spiritual, mental and physical developments of the community.'

Before the introduction of comprehensive schools, the state education system was made up of grammar schools, secondary modern schools and secondary technical schools.

- All schools' curricula included physical education and some elements of sport.
- Grammar schools often emulated the public school provision of sport and ran competitive sports teams in major sports.
- Secondary modern schools ran a range of sports teams.
- Sport was also promoted through extra-curricular provision in schools.

Availability of time, money and space for sport

- With the gradual increase in leisure time and money, men played as well as watched sport.
- Towns offered many different sports, from water polo in public baths to pigeon races on allotments and quoits in fields behind pubs.
- The availability of money enabled darts, dominoes and billiards to flourish inside pubs.
- Space was a key requirement but it was at a premium and the land that was available was heavily used.

Transport

- Public and private transport became much more available to everyone; increased numbers could now participate in and spectate sport.
- In the late 1940s, radio coverage increased the spectacle of football, rugby and cricket, attracting large crowds.
- Large crowds were at the 1948 London Olympics, rejuvenating tourism and the economy.
- International competitions, accessible by international travel, served as a 'shop window' for the host city.

> **Typical mistake**
>
> Learn specific facts and give practical examples; candidates can often be very vague.

Now test yourself

TESTED

1. Outline the differences between the upper and lower classes in pre-industrial Britain. How did the activities they participate in differ?
2. When and why did the middle class emerge?
3. How did education and literacy and law and order impact the development of sport in Britain post-1850?
4. What are the key factors that shaped the development of sport in the twentieth century?

Answers on page 172

How contemporary factors are shaping sport in the twenty-first century

Class

- Sport is still associated with those who are perceived to be of a certain social class.
- Traditionally, football was played and watched by the working classes, but it is now much more mixed. Middle classes are now likely to state they are football fans.
- Tennis, golf and polo are still associated with the upper/middle classes because of the expense and social elitism associated with joining such clubs.
- Elite Olympic sport has a disproportionate number of privately educated and, therefore, more middle-class athletes.
- Sport participation of over 16-year-olds is greater among higher socio-economic groups.
- Social mobility can be achieved through sports.

Amateurism and professionalism

- Social class is a factor in whether someone is likely to be an amateur or a professional in sport.
- Amateurs in cricket and rugby have traditionally been middle class.
- Professionals in football have traditionally been working class.
- Rugby now consists of a broad range of professionals from all backgrounds.

Gender

- More men than women still participate in or watch sport.
- Sport is still regarded by some as 'unfeminine', reinforcing male dominance in sport and sports coverage.
- Certain activities are traditionally linked to males (team sports) and females (dance).
- However, more women than ever are now involved in physical exercise and there is more interest in health and fitness activities.
- Participation rates of women in football and rugby are continuing to grow.
- There is an increased number of female sports presenters, encouraging interest and female role models.

Law and order

- Legislation that affects sport is sophisticated and specific to sport.
- The rights of athletes and spectators and their safety are now protected by law.
- The law has also been used increasingly to protect or to litigate against officials and referees.
- Banning orders have been used in football to stop disruptive fans from travelling abroad.
- The law has been involved in the misuse of drugs, misconduct on and off the field and 'match fixing'.
- Laws to prevent discrimination based on race, gender, disability, age, sexual orientation and religion exist in the UK, and these have had an impact on sport.

Education

- Children between the ages of 5 and 16 must receive an education.
- Examinations and qualifications in physical education and sport, including sports science, have increased in availability in the twenty-first century.
- GCE A Level, GCSE, Cambridge National, BTECs and Cambridge Technical qualifications are available in PE/sport.
- Universities offer a wide range of PE/sport-related degrees.

Availability of time, money and transport

- Society has become much more technological, increasing time available.
- Flexible working conditions increase time available.
- Most people are better off, although a substantial number of people struggle to make ends meet.
- The global recession has affected disposable income; less money is being spent on sport and exercise, and participation rates are down since 2012.
- The availability of transport has increased; access to cars, buses, trains and cheap air fares have increased sport participation and spectatorship.

Globalisation of sport

International sport is a big business, with massive investment involved as well as the reputations of countries and international companies. It has been affected by the following key factors:

- freedom of movement for performers
- greater exposure of people to sport
- media coverage.

> **Globalisation**: a process that involves sport as a worldwide business and features corporate brands, media coverage and freedom of movement of sport participants, officials and spectators.

Freedom of movement for performers and greater exposure of people to sport	Media coverage (TV, press, radio, internet, cinema)
• Sport is a global marketplace for participants to demand high wages for their skills, e.g. football. • National and international laws allow freedom of movement (particularly in the EU). • Some performers change nationality (athletics). • Many spectators now travel to support teams or watch international competitions (Olympics); cheap air travel is available.	• Increased TV coverage due to the commercial boost of the late 1990s (satellite TV) led to the **globalisation** of sport. • Media increased the number of people who watched televised sport – rugby league changed seasons to fit in with this. • Very little media attention has been devoted to sporting inequalities based on class, gender and ethnicity. • Rules have been influenced and timings of games are fixed to suit TV. • Olympic Games events are often scheduled at unsuitable times, due to TV. • In cricket, the third umpire has come into play due to the influence of TV.

Now test yourself

TESTED ☐

5 How has education affected sport in the twenty-first century?
6 What is the globalisation of sport?

Answers on page 172

Global sporting events

The modern Olympic Games

In 1896, Baron Pierre de Coubertin established the first modern Olympic Games, held in Athens.

The aims of the games are to:
- promote development of the physical and moral qualities of sport
- spread Olympic principles, creating international goodwill
- bring together athletes of the world every four years
- educate young people through sports in a spirit of better understanding between each other and of friendship, thereby helping to build a peaceful world.

The Olympic values

1 Encourage effort – striving for **excellence** (determination)
2 Preserve human dignity – demonstrating **respect** (courage, inspiration)
3 Develop harmony – celebrating **friendship** (equality)

The British Olympic Association (BOA) and International Olympic Committee (IOC)

BOA	IOC
<ul><li>Formed in 1905</li><li>Responsible for planning and execution of GB's Olympic Team participation in the winter and summer games</li><li>Responsible for developing the Olympic movement in the UK</li><li>Not funded by government, no political interest, dependent on commercial sponsorship and fundraising income</li></ul>	<ul><li>Created by Paris Congress in 1894</li><li>Owns all rights to the Olympic symbol and the Olympic Games themselves</li><li>Administers the Olympic movement and has headquarters in Lausanne, Switzerland</li><li>Members are appointed to the IOC and are responsible for selecting host cities</li></ul>

Political exploitation of the modern Olympic Games

The Olympic Games have been used as a tool to make political points, due to their extensive global publicity.

> **Propaganda**: a type of communication that seeks to influence people towards a certain cause and, in this case, a political philosophy. The information given as part of this communication is biased towards a certain belief or set of values.
>
> **Apartheid**: a range of policies of racial segregation under a system of legislation. Apartheid existed in South Africa from 1948 to 1994. Under apartheid, non-white South Africans (the vast majority of the population) were forced to live in separate areas from white South Africans and use separate public facilities, and contact between the two groups was limited by law.

The table below provides an overview of political exploitation of the Olympic Games.

Games	Politics
Berlin 1936 – Third Reich ideology	The Games were used by Hitler and the Nazi Party as a stage for political **propaganda** for the Third Reich – an ideology that viewed Germany as a superior 'empire'. German athletes trained full time, undermining the amateur ideal of the games. Hitler refused to place gold medals around Jesse Owens (African-American) after he beat the German athlete Luz Long in the long jump.
Mexico City 1968 – 'Black Power' demonstration	South Africa's invitation to the Games was withdrawn because of other countries threaening to boycott the games due to its **apartheid** regime. African-Americans were able to protest to the world when two black athletes used a medal ceremony to protest about the lack of civil rights in the USA. They raised black-gloved fists – a gesture called the black power salute.
Munich 1972 – Palestinian terrorism	A day before the Games, Palestinian terrorists entered the Olympic village and seized 11 Israeli athletes. The terrorists made a political request to release 234 Palestinians imprisoned in Israel. The German authorities attempted a rescue, but all hostages and five terrorists were killed.
Moscow 1980 – boycott led by the USA	In December 1979, the Soviet Union invaded Afghanistan, which created a conflict that would last ten years and extended the Cold War. The USA boycotted the Games, alongside some British athletes. In all, an estimated 4,000 athletes boycotted the Games.
Los Angeles 1984 – boycott led by the Soviet Union	In response to the events of the 1980 Games, the Soviet Union, East Germany, Poland, Bulgaria, Hungary and Cuba announced they would boycott the 1984 Games. A total of 14 nations refused to take part. The Soviet Union blamed the commercialisation of the Games and the lack of security measures.

Hosting global sporting events

Many cities bid to host global sporting events (for example the Olympics and the FIFA World Cup). Hosting an event can bring many advantages and disadvantages.

	Advantages	Disadvantages
Sporting impact	• It raises the profile of the sport; this may lead to increased participation, e.g. cycling from London 2012. • New or upgraded venues are built, e.g. Sir Chris Hoy Velodrome, Glasgow 2014. • The event can focus on minority sports, which may inspire participation, e.g. Boccia and wheelchair rugby. • There is an increase in funding for sports involved, e.g. 2015 Rugby World Cup. • The event can bring increased sponsorship and commercial income for individuals and the governing body.	• 1.4 million more people are playing sport than in 2005, but this increase came in two short bursts, after the London 2012 winning bid (2005) and around the 2012 Games themselves. The current trend is a gradual decline in participation. • New facilities can end up not being used after the event, e.g. Barcelona 1992. • Lesser-known non-global sports can suffer, e.g. squash is not an Olympic sport and attracts little funding, with participation figures dropping. • Sports deviance is likely to be highlighted by media at global events, e.g. hooliganism at the Brazil World Cup in 2014.

→

	Advantages	Disadvantages
Social impact	<ul><li>More money is brought into a city or country, which can be used to benefit the local population.</li><li>Events can give pride to the host nation or city and help with 'nation-building'.</li><li>There will be improved use of sport facilities by local communities.</li><li>It can improve transport systems.</li><li>Accommodation built for the event can be used by the community, e.g. the Olympic Village built for London 2012 has been used for housing.</li></ul>	<ul><li>Some areas of the country may not get the same benefits as the host city.</li><li>Some areas of the host country do not benefit from improved infrastructure and transport.</li><li>Local inhabitants may have to vacate land being used for sport venues, e.g. be re-housed.</li></ul>
Economic impact	<ul><li>Increased income leads to positive economic impact. More money is brought to the host city by those who participate or spectate.</li><li>More jobs are created through building of facilities, transport infrastructure and support for the event.</li><li>There is an increase in tourism and related economic benefits during and after the event.</li><li>There are commercial benefits related to goods sold in the area of the event and also in the sale of event-related goods.</li></ul>	<ul><li>Bidding to host an event can be expensive, e.g. the failed 2018 FIFA World Cup bid, estimated cost £21 million.</li><li>Events can cause an overall economic loss, e.g. the 1976 Montreal Olympics took 30 years to pay off.</li><li>Benefits to employment and long-term jobs are often exaggerated.</li><li>If events or participants are linked with failure, e.g. the Rugby World Cup 2015, it can lead to loss of revenue in merchandising sales.</li></ul>
Political impact	<ul><li>Individual political parties and their leaders can gain credit and therefore more votes and reflect well if a bid is successful.</li><li>Staging an event can bring unity and a sense of purpose to a country.</li><li>The country or city can be used as a 'shop window' for its culture and commerce, and therefore raise its status in the eyes of the world.</li></ul>	<ul><li>If the cost is too high or over budget, it can be a political disadvantage, losing votes and decreasing economic resources.</li><li>If something goes wrong, e.g. a terrorist attack, politicians have to shoulder responsibility.</li><li>If the host nation does poorly, it can reflect badly on the political party.</li><li>Negative environmental impacts can decrease political popularity.</li><li>If the legacy of the event is negative, this can be politically damaging.</li><li>Protests by athletes or spectators can be embarrassing, e.g. Black Power, Mexico 1968.</li></ul>

Exam tip

If a question asks for an evaluation of global sporting events, ensure you mention advantages and disadvantages alongside relevant examples from sport.

Now test yourself

TESTED

7 What are the aims of the Olympic Games?
8 What are the values of the Olympic Games?
9 Give three examples where the Olympic Games have been the subject of political exploitation.

Answers on page 172

Exam practice

1 How did social class influence the physical activities of people in pre-industrial Britain? [4]
2 With reference to practical examples, outline the difference between amateurism and professionalism in post-1850 industrial Britain. [4]
3 Public schools experienced a 'cult of athleticism'. What is athleticism? [2]
4 Explain the impact of gender on sport in the twentieth century. [3]
5 Evaluate the various impacts of hosting a global sporting event. Refer to specific sporting examples in your answer. [10]

Answers on page 182

Summary

You should now have an understanding of:
- how social and cultural factors shaped the characteristics of, and participation in, sports and pastimes in pre-industrial Britain:
  - social class, gender, law and order, education/literacy, availability of time/money/transport
- how social and cultural factors shaped the characteristics of, and participation in, sport in post-1850 industrial Britain:
  - social class, amateurism and professionalism, gender/changing status of women, law and order, education/literacy, availability of time/changing work conditions, availability of money, transport (notably the railways)
  - influence of public schools on: the promotion and organisation of sports and games, the promotion of ethics through sports and games, the 'cult' of athleticism, the spread and export of games and the games ethic
- how social factors shaped the characteristics of, and participation in, sport in twentieth-century Britain:
  - class, amateurism and professionalism, gender/changing role and status of women, law and order, education, availability of time/money/transport

- how contemporary factors are shaping the characteristics of, and participation in, sport in the twenty-first century:
  - class, amateurism and professionalism, gender/changing role and status of women, law and order, education, availability of time/money/transport
- the globalisation of sport, media coverage, freedom of movement for performers, greater exposure of people to sport
- the modern Olympic Games; background and aims (1896)
- political exploitation of the Olympic Games: Berlin 1936 Third Reich ideology; Mexico City 1968 'Black Power' demonstration; Munich 1972 Palestinian terrorism; Moscow 1980 boycott led by the USA; Los Angeles 1984 boycott led by the Soviet Union
- hosting global sporting events; positive and negative impacts on the host country/city of hosting a global sporting event (such as the Olympic Games or FIFA World Cup): sporting, social, economic, political.

Ethics and deviance in sport

REVISED ☐

Doping and drugs in sport

Ethics are rules that dictate an individual's conduct. They form a system of rules upon which groups and societies are judged. An ethic in sport would be that an athlete sticks to the spirit of the rules of the game. Both **blood doping** and the illegal consumption of performance-enhancing drugs have been a feature in many sports and are an example of **deviance**.

Blood doping

- A process that increases a person's red blood cell (RBC) count
- More RBCs = higher volumes of haemoglobin
- Extra O_2 can be transported to working muscles
- Allows higher level of performance
- Involves the removal of approximately 2 pints of blood
- Blood is then frozen, thawed and re-injected prior to competition
- Used by endurance athletes, for example runners and cyclists

Performance-enhancing drugs

- Anabolic steroids: allow athletes to train harder for longer, and often increase strength and aggression
- Beta blockers: control heart rate and keep an athlete calm
- Stimulants: increase alertness, for example amphetamines

Other prohibited substances are: narcotic analgesics, anabolic agents, diuretics, peptide hormones, mimetics and analogues, substances with anti-oestrogen activity and masking agents.

Prohibited methods are: enhancement of oxygen transfer, blood doping and gene doping.

> **Blood doping:** defined by the World Anti-Doping Agency (WADA) as the misuse of techniques and/or substances to increase one's red blood cell count.
>
> **Deviance:** unacceptable behaviour within a culture. Any behaviour that differs from the perceived social or legal norm is seen as deviant.

Advantages and disadvantages of legal supplements

Advantages	Disadvantages
• Dietary supplements claim to help to build muscle, increase stamina, control weight, etc. • Ergogenic aids claim to increase strength, performance and recovery. Creatine supplements can help performance during high-intensity exercise. • Staying hydrated through the drinking of water or energy drinks can improve and aid performance.	• Some supplements may not be what they seem and could contain banned substances or be contaminated. • Health implications over the long-term use of creatine supplements have been suggested, e.g. effects on the digestive system and increasing the risk of cancer. • Energy drinks contain high levels of sugar, contributing to obesity and tooth decay. • Philosophical argument – it is not in the spirit of fair play.

Reasons why elite performers use doping and illegal drugs

- Pressure to succeed can affect a performer's judgement and decision making
- Pressure from coaches
- Political pressures – for example the Russian doping scandal
- High monetary rewards for winning and lucrative sponsorship deals
- Some performers think 'everyone else is doing it'

Consequences of drug taking in sport

Societal consequences	• Society seen as corrupt and full of unethical citizens who will do anything to 'win at all costs'
Sporting consequences	• Concept of fair play is severely challenged • Cheating • Sports become 'tainted', struggling to gain sponsorship, e.g. cycling – loss of public support
Performer's consequences	• Severe dangers to health and well-being • Possible death

Strategies to stop the use of doping and illegal drugs

- WADA draws up a list of banned substances. It provides assistance to countries' own anti-doping programmes and funds research.
- Drug testing can be carried out in and out of competitions.
- Drug education can be provided for athletes and coaches.
- A culture of keeping sport free from drugs cheats should be created and reinforced.
- Punishments for drug use are to be more rigorous and longer. WADA doubled the ban in 2015.

> **Typical mistake**
>
> Focus on the societal impact of doping and drugs, rather than the physiological impact on a performer, when answering a question from this area. Try to be clear and not confuse elements of other chapters.

Violence in sport

Causes of violence in sport (players and spectators)

- Desire to win so overwhelming it leads to **violence** – importance of result
- Nature of activity – physical sports like ice hockey
- Frustration of events
- Alcohol and social drugs or performance-enhancing drugs
- Rivalries
- Media increasing tensions
- Perception of unfairness or poor officiating
- **Deindividuation**

> **Violence**: intense physical force that is directed towards harming another individual or groups of individuals and can cause injury and death.
>
> **Deindividuation**: when you lose your sense of being an individual; this can cause violent behaviour.

Implications of violence in sport

Societal implications	• If violence is to be tackled in sport, then violent behaviour in society should also be tackled. Sport is often a reflection of society. • Spectators relish violence in sports such as boxing. Should a sporting action on the field of play be treated the same as a violent act on our streets?

→

Sporting implications	• Governing bodies have their own disciplinary processes to ensure standards and maintain non-violent behaviour. • Playing strategies that promote violence should be punished. • Rule changes should be adopted to make violence less likely.
Performer's implications	• Education of performers is important; performers are responsible for their individual actions and fair play at all times. • Performers need to be aware that they are role models and their behaviour is likely to be copied.

Strategies to prevent violence in relation to players and spectators

- Education of performers, encouraging awareness of their emotions and stress levels
- Punishments at the time: fines, bans, docking points
- Encouraging coaches to promote assertion rather than aggression in players
- Law enforcement (in spectator violence) – banning orders have been served in football
- Sophisticated policing methods, CCTV, etc.

Gambling in sport

Gambling is not an example of deviant behaviour, as it is legal in the UK. Sport lends itself to gambling because the outcomes of events are supposed to be unpredictable and there is an element of chance in most competitions. Gambling is a big business.

However, **match fixing**, bribery and illegal sports betting are designed to make individuals and illicit organisations a great deal of money.

> **Match fixing**: when a sports competition is played to a completely or partly pre-determined result. This is against the law. Match fixing requires contacts to be made between corrupt players, coaches and team officials.

Now test yourself

TESTED

1 What is deviance? Give two examples of deviance in sport.
2 Why might a performer use performance-enhancing drugs?
3 Name three causes of violence in sport.
4 What is match fixing?

Answers on page 172

Commercialisation and the media

REVISED

Factors leading to the commercialisation of contemporary physical activity and sport

Growing public interest and spectatorship	More people now play sport at least once a week. There has also been growth in the numbers that spectate. The greater the **spectatorship** the more money is attracted to sports.
More media interest	Events are televised, leading to companies wanting to sponsor events and their participants.
Professionalism	Sporting professionals are now likely to attract **sponsorship** from commercial organisations.

> **Spectatorship**: the act of watching something without taking part; often related to sports spectators.
>
> **Sponsorship** (in sport): to support an event, activity or person related to sport by providing money or goods.

Advertising	Sports present opportunities to sell more goods and can be used as a 'billboard'. In return, the sport concerned is promoted, which can improve participation rates.
Sponsorship	Sponsorship leads to increased publicity and sales for the sponsor and provides free clothing/equipment or financial support for the performer. For example, Andy Murray has a sponsorship deal to wear a particular brand of clothing.

Positive and negative impacts of the commercialisation of physical activity and sport

Positive impacts	Negative impacts
Individual sports	
• Sports can promote themselves, attracting more participants or spectators, which can lead to increased revenue. • More money for sports can mean more facilities can be built and development takes places. • Commercial investment into sports can develop all areas from grassroots to international teams.	• Less popular sports attract less sponsorship and therefore are unable to develop as much as others. • Female and disabled events may lose out on commercial investment, as they are less popular and therefore attract less media exposure for a potential sponsor.
Society	
• In the UK we hold the view that sport is about fair competition and everyone has an equal chance to participate and win. Sponsorship supports this ideal, in that it can help to support training and competition.	• Attracting sponsorship can depend on a number of factors. Some sportspeople are more 'marketable' than others. This is a reflection of our society in that success can be based on factors other than talent and ability.
Performers	
• Performers can receive kit and equipment from companies wishing to promote their products. • Commercial organisations can fund athletes' accommodation and travel. • Athletes can spend more time training and competing, rather than having to go to work.	• There is pressure to perform well to secure and keep sponsorship deals. • Pressure to win could lead to deviant behaviour. • Companies can demand a great deal of a performer's time to promote their products. • Performers may find they have little control over their careers, with sponsors demanding they enter specific tournaments.
Spectators	
• A commercially supported event can provide a more exciting spectacle and additional entertainment. • Giant video screens and play-back technology provide more information. • Due to commercial investment, there are more competitions in some sports, increasing accessibility for a greater range of spectators.	• Actual sporting action can take second place to advertisements for goods. • At live events, advertising can be overwhelming and may spoil enjoyment. • Spectators may not agree with a particular company's ethics, e.g. does alcohol advertising have a place in sport? • Spectators may not want their team to be associated with particular brands. • The cost to watch sport is high; commercialism can be seen as doing little to make spectatorship more affordable.

Coverage of sport by the media today

Coverage of sport today is extensive and different types of media make it accessible to many people. Types of media include:

- television – terrestrial, satellite, pay-per-view
- printed press – newspapers, magazines
- radio – local and national stations, dedicated sports stations
- the internet
- social media
- cinema.

Reasons for changes since the 1980s

- In the 1980s, media coverage was different from how it is today. Sports presenters were generally male and very little attention was paid to female sport.
- Football hooliganism was rife and often the media were dominated by reports of the negative behaviour of sports spectators.
- Changes occurred with the introduction of satellite television in the 1990s. Sky spent money on securing the rights to prominent football events. Other companies have now followed suit to show other sporting events.
- Now, different types of media are available to most people. Media coverage is more global; events are recorded or streamed online.
- Many different sports are now accessible, although minority, female and disabled sports are still underrepresented.

Positive and negative effects of the media on sport

Positive effects	Negative effects
Performers	
- Can raise the profile of a performer - Can help develop a performer's career	- Can highlight and promote sensational news, which can increase pressure to perform
Individual sports	
- Can raise the profile of a sport - Can boost participation numbers, e.g. Wimbledon - Can increase financial revenues, in terms of sponsorship and funding for sports events and facilities - Can attract more funds for international teams - Can give more coverage to minority sports and disability sports, e.g. the Paralympics	- Can highlight negative aspects of sport, e.g. hooliganism in football
Spectators	
- Increases number of people watching - Rules have been influenced to make sports more accessible to a wider audience - Different types of media are available 24/7 and sport is broadcast live all over the world	- Can provide negative coverage – possibly promoting hooliganism and unrest among some countries, e.g. England v Germany (football) - Cost of subscriptions to satellite TV can be prohibitive

Relationship between sport and the media

Sport is viewed as a **commodity** by commercial organisations, and the media help to promote both sport and its commercial partners. The relationship between sport, sponsorship and the media is often referred to as the '**golden triangle**'.

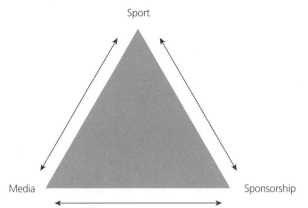

Figure 3.2.1 **The golden triangle: sport, sponsorship and the media**

> **Commodity**: an article that can be traded. In this case, sport is the article that can be sold to different media outlets or companies that wish to associate their brand with a particular sport.
>
> **Golden triangle**: the interdependence and influences of three factors of sport, sponsorship and the media – each aspect influences the others.

Now test yourself

TESTED

5 What are the five factors that have led to the commercialisation of contemporary physical activity and sport?
6 Name the different types of media that cover sport.
7 What is a commodity?
8 What is the golden triangle?

Answers on page 173

Routes to sporting excellence in the UK

REVISED

From talent identification to elite performance

The identification of potential elite athletes has been formalised and organised by **UK Sport**. This organisation develops elite athletes by:
1 Identifying potential talent in sport:
   ○ testing phases 1, 2 3
      ○ phase 1: a range of generic physical and skill-based tests; also includes an in-depth analysis of each athlete's training and competition history
      ○ phases 2–3: tests in functional movement screening, medical screening, performance lifestyle workshops and psychology and behavioural assessments
      ○ confirmation phase: selected athletes embark on a 6–12-month confirmation phase during which they are immersed in the sport's training environment; unsuccessful athletes are provided with opportunities to continue the sport through the club system
   ○ #DiscoverYour Gold: over 20 sports are involved in #DiscoverYour Gold, a partnership between UK Sport, the English Institute of Sport (EIS) and a range of national governing bodies, targeting 15–24-year-olds to be fast-tracked into the world of high-performance sport
2 Supporting an athlete's lifestyle
3 Supporting an athlete's coaching

> **UK Sport**: an organisation whose aim is the development of the UK's sportsmen and sportswomen. It is funded jointly by the government and the National Lottery.

4 Supporting, through research, sports science and sports medicine, via the English Institute of Sport
5 Providing a World Class Programme or pathway to success:
   ○ podium: athletes with realistic medal-winning capabilities at the next Olympic or Paralympic Games (i.e. maximum four years from podium)
   ○ podium potential: athletes whose performance suggests that they have realistic medal-winning capabilities at the subsequent Olympic or Paralympic Games (i.e. maximum eight years from podium).

The role of UK Sport in developing elite sport

The main role of UK Sport is to invest National Lottery funds and income from central government to maximise the performance of UK athletes in the Olympic and Paralympic Games and global sporting events. Success is measured by medals won and the number of medallists developed.

UK Sport invests about 70 per cent of its income in two ways:
1 to national governing bodies (NGBs), enabling them to operate a World Class Programme
2 funding athletes directly through the Athlete Performance Award.

The role of National Institutes of Sport in developing elite sport

Each country that makes up the UK has a National Institute of Sport. Their role is to:
● provide sports science and technological help to elite sportsmen and women
● work with coaches and sports administrators to help improve the performance of their athletes
● give technical support that enables athletes and coaches to optimise their training programmes, maximise competition and improve their health and availability to train.

The EIS (English Institute of Sport) has a dedicated team of sports scientists who support coaches and their athletes.

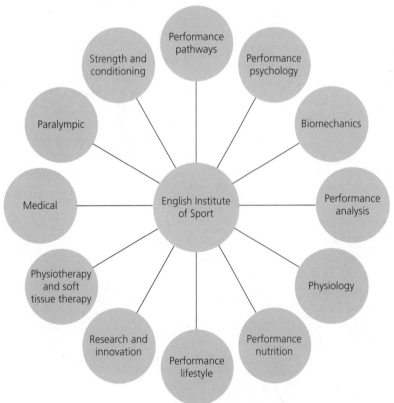

Figure 3.2.2 The main services available from the EIS for elite performers

The role of schools, colleges, clubs and universities in contributing to elite sport success

Schools, colleges and clubs

- These provide PE for all young people and often extra-curricular activities and clubs for those who are keen to participate or who might excel in a particular sport.
- The government supplies schools with funds to support school sport and the development of elite sports performers.
- FA, ECB (England and Wales Cricket Board), RFU, LTA and Premier League send coaches to primary schools to improve sports provision.
- Sport England encourages schools and colleges to link with community sport to increase sports participation and the likelihood of students realising their potential and becoming elite performers.
- Schools and colleges offer qualifications in sports at GCSE and A Level. All these have sports performance as part of the qualification.
- Schools and colleges often run sport teams, playing fixtures. This helps to develop sports talent in the UK.
- Advanced Level Apprenticeships in Sporting Excellence (AASE) offer a structured training and development route across a number of sports for talented young athletes (16–19 years).
- Sports clubs are often in leagues or national competitions, which enable those with talent to gain competitive experience.
- Sports clubs nurture and encourage talent, often giving financial concessions and providing coaching and guidance to develop sports performers.

Universities

- Most higher education (HE) institutions offer university sports scholarships or bursaries. This enables access to special support services.
- Many top sports facilities are located at universities, so HE is increasingly involved in the development of sporting excellence in the UK.
- The Talented Athletes Scholarship Scheme (TASS), and in Scotland the Winning Students Scheme (WSS) are both government-funded sport programmes, delivered through a partnership between universities and NGBs.
- Some universities host centres of sporting excellence, which can be linked to a National Sports Institute.

Strategies to address drop-out or failure rates from elite development programmes and at elite-level sport

Drop-out and failure in elite sport can be a result of poor performances, injury, pressures from outside sport such as family commitments, pressure from the media, or the stress relating to the financial impact of training, travelling, competing and fulfilling commitments outside of sport.

The programmes run by UK Sport include a lifestyle component that attempts to help athletes cope with the pressures and demands of elite sport. 'Lifestyle' is available to all athletes on World Class Programmes. Training advisers at the EIS give athletes the necessary skills to cope with the special demands of being an elite performer and to prepare them for life after sport.

Now test yourself

9 State the five ways UK Sport identifies and supports elite athletes.
10 What is the role of UK Sport in developing elite sport?
11 Give two roles of universities in contributing to elite sport success.

Answers on page 173

TESTED ☐

Modern technology in sport

Elite performance and general participation

Modern technology can be beneficial in the following instances:
- when assessing whether someone has the potential to be an athlete, for example assessing bone density and internal body fat
- health screening devices
- **prosthetic** devices developed for athletes who have lost a lower limb, for example Springlite
- wheelchair devices with slanted back wheels allowing tennis players to move across the court quickly
- improved access to buildings, for example specialist hoists at swimming pools
- rehabilitation and elite training facilities with state of the art equipment
- different simulated competitive environments, for example surf simulators
- improved sports surfaces and artificial lighting
- provision of equipment for elite athletes
- use of composite material in rackets and protective gear, making them lighter
- improvement in the design of trainers/sports footwear
- development of the **hypoxic chamber**
- **precision hydration** techniques
- more effective physiological laboratory testing for athletes
- gait analysis in runners to help avoid injury
- heart rate monitors and GPS watches helping to monitor activity and motivate performance.

> **Prosthetic**: an artificial device that substitutes or supplements a defective part of the body.
>
> **Hypoxic chamber**: a sealed room that simulates high altitude.
>
> **Precision hydration**: the monitoring of sodium loss during sweating leading to more effective replacement in the body of essential salts.

The extent to which modern technology has limited or reduced participation

There are some drawbacks for sport with the increased use of modern technology:
- Cost of equipment and facilities:
  - Equipment is expensive and has led to inequality for both elite and recreational performers.
  - In developing countries, the expense of sophisticated equipment and facilities is prohibitive.
- Range of alternatives to physical activity and sport:
  - Computers, game consoles, etc. can make people sedentary and less likely to take part in sport.

Revision activity

Create a spider diagram about the use of modern technology in sport. Include small diagrams; this may help you remember important information in an exam.

Fair outcomes

Modern technology has had an influence on producing fair results or outcomes in important competitions.

Advantages and examples

- Most professional sports use instant replay to help officials make the right decision.
- Rugby uses video-replay systems to check referees' decisions.
- Basketball referees use video-replay systems to make sure players are shooting within the allotted time.
- In international cricket, the third umpire sits off the ground with access to video replays of, for example, disputed catches; the umpires on the field communicate with the third umpire via wireless technology.
- Hawk-eye is the name of a computer and camera system which records a ball trajectory; it is used in tennis and cricket. Goal-line decisions in football are being trialled.
- There is improved detection of doping.
- There is improved detection of foul play.
- Better timing devices are available.

Disadvantages

- Many sports officials report feeling under pressure to use the technology more, rather than making their own decisions.
- It enables the media to highlight an official's mistake during a sports competition, which can lead to judgements from the public and high levels of anxiety for the official.
- Advances in genetic technology are relevant to doping in sport. **Gene therapy** is being developed, with the potential for this to affect athletic performance.
- Performance-enhancing drug detecting technology cannot keep up with new drug development.
- Access to modern technology can be limited.

> **Gene therapy:** the use of genes and genetic elements to treat human disease.

Entertainment

Modern technology can enhance or hinder the enjoyment of sport.

Advantages

- Modern technology has increased entertainment through the use of action-replays and slow-motion playback.
- During live sports events, giant screens show the action and also replays.
- Multiple camera angles allow spectators to enjoy every aspect of performance, and see whether officiating decisions are correct.

Disadvantages

- Performance is analysed at intervals by pundits, using motion-capture analysis.
- Constant interruptions can interfere with the flow of an event and can irritate viewers.
- It could potentially reduce the number of people attending live sport events.

> **Exam tip**
>
> Always give a relevant sporting example to improve your answer.

Now test yourself

TESTED

12 Give four examples of how modern technology can benefit sport.
13 Give two examples of how modern technology can affect fair outcomes.
14 Give two examples of how modern technology can enhance or hinder the enjoyment of sport.

Answers on page 173

Exam practice

1 Describe two social implications of violence in sport. [2]
2 Discuss the reasons why new technology has divided opinion among many who participate in sport. [6]
3 Outline the reasons for the growth of commercialisation in contemporary sport. [5]
4 Discuss the positive and negative effects of the media on all aspects of sport. [10]

Answers on page 184

Summary

You should now have an understanding of:
- drugs and doping in sport
- legal supplements versus illegal drugs and doping
- reasons why elite performers use illegal drugs/doping; consequences/implications for society, sport and performers
- strategies to stop the use of illegal drugs and doping
- violence in sport – causes in relation to players and spectators; implications for society, sport and performers
- strategies to prevent violence in relation to players and spectators
- gambling in sport, match fixing/bribery, illegal sports betting
- factors leading to the commercialisation of contemporary physical activity and sport
- positive and negative impacts of the commercialisation of physical activity and sport on society, individual sports, performers and spectators
- coverage of sport by the media today and reasons for changes since the 1980s
- positive and negative effects of the media on sport, individual sports, performers and spectators
- the relationship between sport and the media
- sport as a commodity; links with advertising and sponsorship (the 'golden triangle')
- development routes from talent identification through to elite performance: the role of schools, colleges, clubs and universities in contributing to elite sporting success
- the role of UK Sport and National Institutes of Sport in developing sporting excellence/high-performance sport
- strategies to address drop-out/failure rates from elite development programmes/at elite level
- modern technology in sport: its impact on elite-level sport, participation, fair outcomes and entertainment
- the extent to which modern technology has affected elite-level sport
- the extent to which modern technology has increased participation in sport
- the extent to which modern technology has limited or reduced participation in sport
- the extent to which modern technology has increased or decreased fair outcomes
- the extent to which modern technology has increased entertainment.

Now test yourself answers

Chapter 1.1a

1

Joint	Agonist	Antagonist
a) Wrist	Wrist flexors	Wrist extensors
b) Elbow	Biceps brachii	Triceps brachii
c) Shoulder	Anterior deltoid	Posterior deltoid
d) Hip	Iliopsoas	Gluteus maximus
e) Knee	Biceps femoris	Rectus femoris
f) Ankle	Tibialis anterior	Gastrocnemius and soleus

2 Sagittal plane: vertical – divides body into left/right. Frontal plane: vertical – divides body into anterior/posterior. Transverse plane: horizontal – divides body into upper/lower.

3 Agonist: a muscle responsible for creating movement at a joint. Antagonist: a muscle that opposes the agonist, providing a resistance for co-ordinated movement. Fixator: a muscle that stabilises one part of the body while another part moves.

4 Concentric: the muscle shortens to produce tension. Eccentric: the muscle lengthens to produce tension.

5 Motor neuron and its muscle fibres

6 Slow oxidative, fast oxidative glycolytic, fast glycolytic

Chapter 1.1b

1 Heart rate (HR): the number of times the heart beats per minute. Stroke volume (SV): the amount of blood ejected from the left ventricle per beat. Cardiac output (CO): the amount of blood ejected from the left ventricle per minute. HR × SV = CO

2 Diastole (relaxation phase); systole (contraction phase)

3 SA node, AV node, Bundle of His, Bundle branches, Purkinje fibres

4

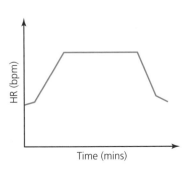

5

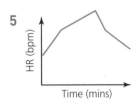

6 Medulla oblongata in the brain

7 Skeletal pump, respiratory pump, pocket valves, gravity, smooth muscle

8 Neural (proprioceptor, baroreceptors, chemoreceptors); intrinsic (temperature, venous return); hormonal (adrenaline and noradrenaline)

9 Breathing rate: the number of inspirations or expirations per minute. Tidal volume: the volume of air inspired or expired per breath. Minute ventilation: the volume of air inspired or expired per minute: TV × f = VE (tidal volume × breathing rate = minute ventilation).

10 At rest: active process. External intercostal muscles between the ribs contract, pulling the chest walls up and out. The diaphragm muscle below the lungs contracts and flattens, increasing the size of the chest.
During exercise: active process. In addition to the external intercostal muscles and diaphragm, the sternocleidomastoid lifts the sternum, the scalenes and pectoralis minor contract and lift the ribs more.
Effect: volume of the thoracic cavity increases, creating a larger concentration gradient between inside the lungs and outside the body, therefore more air enters the lungs quicker.

11 At rest: passive process. External intercostal muscles between the ribs relax so that the chest walls move in and down. The diaphragm muscle below the lungs relaxes and bulges up, reducing the size of the chest.
During exercise: active process. In addition to the external intercostal muscles and diaphragm, the internal intercostal muscles contract and pull the ribs down and in. The rectus abdominus contracts and pushes the diaphragm up.
Effect: a decrease in volume of the thoracic cavity, increases pressure in the lungs, therefore air is forced out quickly because of the larger concentration gradient.

12 Chemoreceptors, thermoreceptors, proprioceptors, baroreceptors

13 Oxygen unloading from haemoglobin

14 Partial pressure (pp) is the pressure a gas exerts within a mixture of gases.

15 The difference between the high and low pressure is called the diffusion gradient.

Chapter 1.1c

1 ATP is adenosine triphosphate. This compound is the only immediately usable form of energy stored in our bodies. ATP is readily available as it is stored in the muscle cell.

2 ATP/PC system, glycolytic system, aerobic system

3 Aerobic glycolysis, Krebs cycle, electron transport chain

4 The relative contribution of each energy system to overall energy production, depending on intensity and duration of the activity

5 Fast component of recovery (alactacid); slow component of recovery (lactacid)

6 Warm-up, active recovery, cooling aids, intensity of training, work:relief ratios, strategies and tactics, nutrition

Chapter 1.1d

1 Altitude is the height or elevation of an area above sea level.

2 As altitude increases, the diffusion gradient decreases.

3 Rate of oxygen diffusion decreases, reducing haemoglobin saturation and resulting in poor transport of O_2. Blood volume decreases – plasma volume decreases by 25 per cent to allow increase in density of RBCs. Stroke volume decreases, which increases heart rate. Maximal cardiac output, stroke volume and heart rate decrease during maximum-intensity exercise.

4 Breathing frequency increases at rest and during exercise; there is a reduced aerobic capacity and VO_2max, impacting on the intensity and duration of an athlete's performance.

5 Acclimatisation is a process of gradual adaption to a change in environment, for example lower pO_2 at altitude.

6 Cardiovascular drift is an upward drift in heart rate associated with a rise in body temperature (1 °C increases heart rate by 10 bpm).

7 Pre-competition: 7–14 days of acclimatisation in the same conditions to increase the body's tolerance to heat; using cooling aids such as ice vests to reduce core temperature and delay effects of dehydration. During competition: pacing strategies to reduce the feelings of exertion at low-exercise intensities; wearing suitable clothing to maximise heat loss; rehydrating as often and as much as possible with a hypotonic or isotonic solution.

Post competition: Using cooling aids such as cold fans; rehydrating using isotonic solutions to replace lost fluids, glucose and electrolytes.

Chapter 1.2a

1 Carbohydrates (CHOs), fat, protein, vitamins, minerals, fibre, water

2 Saturated fatty acids (bad fats): solid at room temperature, typically animal products, associated with heart disease. Unsaturated fatty acids (good fats): liquid at room temperature, sunflower/olive oil, can help lower cholesterol.

3 The ability to perform work, measured in joules or calories.

4 Energy expenditure = BMR + TEF + physical activity energy expenditure. It is important as it will allow athletes to plan their diet to facilitate effective training and performance.

5 EPO: benefits = increased RBCs and haemoglobin count, increased O_2 transport and aerobic capacity, increased intensity and duration of performance. Drawbacks = increased blood viscosity, decreased cardiac output, increased risk of blood clots and heart disease, decreased natural production of EPO.
Glycogen loading: benefits – increased glycogen stores, increased endurance capacity, increased time to exhaustion (up to 30 per cent), delays fatigue. Drawbacks – hypoglycaemia and poor recovery rates in depletion phase, lethargy and irritability, gastrointestinal problems, increased risk of injury, affects mental preparation.
Creatine supplements: benefits – increased PC stores – more fuel for high intensity training (ATP-PC system), increased intensity and duration of training, increased maximum and explosive strength. Drawbacks – increased weight gain, increased water retention, muscle cramps and gastrointestinal problems, long-term effects unclear.

Chapter 1.2b

1 Specificity, progression, overload, variance, moderation and reversibility

2 Macro-, meso-, micro-cycles

3 Aerobic capacity: the ability of the body to inspire, transport and utilise oxygen to perform sustained periods of aerobic activity. VO_2max: maximum volume of oxygen inspired, transported and utilised per minute during exhaustive exercise.

4 Direct gas analysis, Cooper 12-minute run, NCF multi-stage fitness test, Queens College step test

5 Similarities: both used to improve aerobic capacity; both use activities such as swimming, cycling and running. Differences: continuous – work interval is 20–80 mins; intensity is 60–80% max HR; low to moderate intensity; no breaks in activity. HIIT: 20–60 minutes; intensity is 80–95% max HR; high intensity; has recovery periods built in.

6 Cardiac hypertrophy: increased SV at rest and during exercise and increased CO (at rest), increased filling capacity and force of ventricular contraction, decreased resting and sub-maximal HR (<60 bradycardia), decreased HR and recovery after exercise. Health and performance effects: easier to perform exercise, reduced onset of fatigue, delayed OBLA, increased intensity and duration of performance, lower risk of CHD, hypertension and stroke.

7 Maximum strength: one repetition maximum test or grip strength dynamometer. Strength endurance: UK abdominal curl test. Explosive strength: vertical jump test.

8 Cross-sectional area of muscle, age, gender, fibre type

9 Rower: strength to develop – strength endurance, at least 12 weeks; frequency 2+ times a week; intensity – 50–80 per cent of 1RM; duration: 3–6 sets/15+reps; type – weight training; work:relief ratio 1:2.
Shot putter: strength to develop – explosive strength/power, at least 12 weeks; frequency 2+ times a week; intensity – 75–100 per cent of 1RM; duration 2–6 sets/1–10 reps; type – weight training; work:relief ratio; 1:3+.

10 Static flexibility: the range of motion about a joint without reference to speed of movement. Dynamic flexibility: the range of motion about a joint with reference to speed of movement.

11 Type of joint, length and elasticity of surrounding connective tissue, gender, age

12 Goniometry: 360-degree protractor; difference in starting angle and full range of motion calculated. Sit and reach test: test box placed against wall, straight legs at full stretch, best score is recorded.

13 Static stretching: can be active (on own) or passive (with partner); isometric stretching; PNF; ballistic stretching; dynamic stretching.

Chapter 1.2c

1 Acute injury is a sudden injury associated with a traumatic event. Chronic injury is a slowly developed injury associated with overuse.

2 Fracture, dislocation

3 Any two from: contusion/haematoma, sprain, strain, abrasion, blister.

4 A stress fracture is a tiny crack in the surface of a bone caused by overuse. Shin splints are chronic shin pain due to the inflammation of muscles and stress on the tendon attachments to the surface of the tibia.

5 Signs: possible post-traumatic seizure, loss of consciousness, balance problems, disorientation/confusion. Symptoms: lying motionless/slow to get up, headache/dizziness, visual problems/light sensitivity, nausea/vomiting.

6 Any two from: previous injury, posture and alignment issues, age, nutrition, poor preparation, inadequate fitness level, inappropriate flexibility level.

7 Any two from: poor technique and training, incorrect equipment and clothing, inappropriate intensity duration or frequency of activity, warm-up and cool-down ineffectiveness.

8 Any three from: raising body temperature, preparing body physiologically, preparing body psychologically, minimising the risk of injury.

9 Maintaining heart rate, aiding the removal of lactic acid, aiding the healing process

10 In the event of a sporting accident, to consider whether a player should continue.

11 Soft tissue injuries

Chapter 1.3a

1 First law, law of inertia: a body continues in a state of rest or uniform velocity unless acted upon by an external or unbalanced force.
Second law, law of acceleration: a body's rate of change of momentum is proportional to the size of the force applied and acts in the same direction as the force applied.
Third law, law of reaction: For every action there is an equal and opposite reaction.

2 Net force is the sum of all forces acting on a body; it is also termed resultant force. It is the overall force acting on a body when all individual forces have been considered.

3 Vertical forces: weight and reaction. Horizontal forces: friction and air resistance.

4 Roughness of the ground surface, roughness of the contact surface, temperature, size of normal reaction

5 Velocity, shape, frontal cross-sectional area, smoothness of surface

6 Centre of mass is the point at which the object or body is balanced in all directions. It is the point where the weight of the body tends to be concentrated.

7 Mass of the body, height of the centre of mass, size of base of support, line of gravity

8 Lever, fulcrum, effort, load

9 A second-class lever has the mechanical advantage to move a large load with a small effort, such as at the ball of the foot to vertically accelerate an athlete's whole weight easily. A third-class lever has the mechanical disadvantage, requiring a large effort to move a relatively small load.

Chapter 1.3b

1 Linear motion is the movement of a body in a straight or curved line, where all parts move the same distance in the same direction over the same time.

2 Linear motion results from a direct force being applied to a body, i.e where force is applied directly to the centre of a body's mass.

3 Distance is the total length of the path covered from start to finish. Displacement is the shortest straight-line route from start to finish.

4 Angular motion is the movement of a body or part of a body in a circular path about an axis of rotation.

5 Angular motion results from an eccentric force being applied to a body, i.e. where the force is applied outside the centre of a body's mass.

6 Longitudinal, transverse, frontal

7 Moment of inertia: the resistance of a body to change its state of angular motion or rotation. MI = $\sum$ m × r^2, measured in kilogram metres^2 (kgm^2).
Angular velocity: the rate of change in angular displacement or rate of rotation. Angular velocity = angular displacement × time taken, measured in radians per second (rad/s).
Angular momentum: the quantity of angular motion possessed by a body. Angular momentum = moment of inertia × angular velocity, measured in kilogram metres^2 per second (kgm^2/s).

8 Air resistance is the force that opposes the direction of motion of a body through air.

9 Drag is the force that opposes the direction of motion of a body through water.

10 Velocity, front cross-sectional area, streamlining and shape, surface characteristics

11 Speed of release, angle of release, height of release, aerodynamic factors (Bernoulli and Magnus)

12 Weight: if weight is the dominant force and air resistance is very small, a parabolic flight path occurs.

13 Air resistance: if air resistance is the dominant force and weight is very small, a non-parabolic flight path occurs.

14 The Bernoulli principle states that there is the creation of an additional lift force on a projectile in flight resulting from Bernoulli's conclusion that the higher the velocity of air flow, the lower the surrounding pressure.

15 Topspin, backspin, hook (sidespin), slice (sidespin)

16 Magnus force is a force created from a pressure gradient on opposing surfaces of a spinning body moving through the air.

17

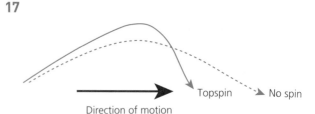

Chapter 2.1

1

Type of practice	Classes of skill most suitable	Practical examples
Part	Low organisation, serial, complex	Backswing of a tennis serve
Whole	High organisation, low in complexity	Golf swing, sprinting
Progressive-part	Complex, low organisation, serial	Triple jump, trampoline routine
Whole–part–whole	Low organisation	Swimming strokes

2 Proactive transfer, retroactive transfer, positive transfer, negative transfer, bilateral transfer

3 Offering variable practice, make aware of transferable elements, give clear and concise demonstrations, ensure diverse childhood experiences

4 Operant conditioning, Thorndike's laws, cognitive theory of learning, observational learning/social learning theory

5 Stage 1: cognitive stage (initial). Stage 2: associative stage (intermediate). Stage 3: autonomous stage (final).

6 Verbal, visual, manual and mechanical

7 Intrinsic, extrinsic, positive, negative, knowledge of results (KR), knowledge of performance (KP)

8 Knowledge of results (KR) is feedback about the outcome of our movements, e.g. did the ball go in the net? Knowledge of performance (KP) concerns the movement itself and the quality of it, i.e. was the shooting technique correct?

9 Short-term sensory store (STSS), short-term memory (STM), long-term memory (LTM)

10 When the brain cells retain or store information

11 Rehearse information physically and mentally, ensure information is meaningful, associate information with already learned skills/tactics, avoid overload – only give a few key points, organise or chunk information, create a clear mental image

Chapter 2.2

1 The patterns of thoughts and feelings and the ways in which we interact with our environment and other people that make us a unique person

2 Trait theories (type A/type B, stable/unstable and extroversion/introversion), social learning theory, interactionist theory

3 A predisposition to act in a particular way towards something or someone in a person's environment

4 Beliefs, experiences, ability, fear, influence of others

5 Cognitive, affective, behavioural

6 Intrinsic motivation is the drive from within, for example wanting to achieve mastery for its own sake. It includes feelings of fun, enjoyment and satisfaction. Extrinsic motivation comes from an outside source, for example a trophy or reward. It is a valuable motivator for the beginner, but will eventually undermine intrinsic motivation.

7 Somatic arousal relates to the changing physiological state of the body, e.g. increased heart rate. Cognitive arousal relates to the changing psychological state of the body, e.g. increases in anxiety.

8 Drive theory, inverted U theory and catastrophe theory

9 Cognitive anxiety: anxiety experienced by the mind; symptoms include worry about failing, indecision, confusion, negative thoughts, poor concentration, irritability, loss of confidence, images of failure.

10 Somatic anxiety: anxiety experienced physiologically; symptoms include increased BP, sweating, adrenaline boost, need to urinate, muscle tension, pacing, yawning, nausea, vomiting, diarrhoea, loss of appetite.

11 They are relaxed, confident and completely focused; activity is effortless; movements are automatic; they have fun and are in control.

12 The effect of having others present during performances can be either positive or negative: positive = social facilitation; negative = social inhibition.

13 Instinct theory of aggression, frustration–aggression hypothesis, social learning theory, aggressive cue hypothesis

14 A collection of people who both share similar goals and interact with one another

15 This occurs when individual performances decrease as group sizes increase.

16 Some individuals in a group seem to lose motivation. It is apparently caused by the individual losing identity when placed in a group. Individual efforts may not be recognised by those who are spectating or by those who are taking part.

17 Specific, Measurable, Achievable, Realistic, Time-phased

18 Any three from: to direct attention, increase effort, increase persistence, help improve confidence/self-efficacy, increase motivation and control arousal/anxiety

19 The perceived cause of a particular outcome

20 Locus of causality, stability, controllability

21 Learned helplessness is the belief that failure is inevitable and that the individual has no control over the factors that cause failure. Mastery orientation is the view that an individual will be motivated by becoming an expert (master) in skill development.

22 Performance, participation, self-esteem

23 Sporting context, SC-trait, competitive orientation, SC-state, behavioural response, subjective outcome

24 Performance accomplishments, vicarious experiences, verbal persuasion, emotional arousal

25 A prescribed leader is someone appointed by people of a higher authority. An emergent leader becomes a leader through their hard work and determination. People who look up to and respect them help them to become a leader. They may be skilful in their sport and they become a leader to show others how well they can do and inspire team mates.

26 Authoritarian, democratic, laissez-faire

27

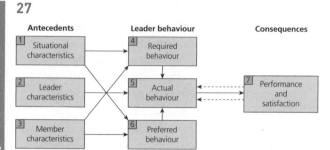

28 Stress in sport is more often linked to negative feelings and can be seen as a psychological state produced and perceived by physiological and psychological forces acting on our sense of well-being. Stressors: competition, conflict, frustration, climate.

29 Mental rehearsal, positive thinking/positive self-talk, goal setting, negative thought stopping, rational thinking, mindfulness, imagery

30 Centering, progressive muscle relaxation, biofeedback, breathing control

Chapter 3.1

1 Upper class: aristocracy or gentry who were hereditary landowners. Activities: real tennis and fox hunting – sophisticated activities with complex rules which required money to participate; pedestrianism – as patrons (sponsors) of lower-class competitors – derived from putting wagers on footmen; cricket – played as 'gentleman' amateurs.
Lower/peasant class: peasants who worked manually, mainly on the land. Activities: mob football, dog fighting, prize fighting – simple activities, often violent with few rules; pedestrianism – as competitors, racing (walking or running) – derived from footmen racing and beating others; cricket – played as 'player' lower-class professionals.

2 Post-industrial Britain – 1850 onwards. The middle class included professionals, factory owners and managers who did not own big estates and were not born into aristocracy. Many members of the middle class went to public schools, which were influential in the development of sports such as rugby and football.

3 Education and literacy: the vast majority of working classes had very little interest in education because it was perceived to be of little relevance. Child labour was still common practice; working-class families were reluctant to give up the earnings of their children for the benefits of education. The employment of children continued to increase even after 1850. The 1870 Forster Act modernised education in England. Elementary education became free with the passing of the 1891 Education Act. Education became more accessible to the working classes, allowing them to understand more sophisticated rules in sport. Sport became widespread.
Law and order: the development of laws affected the type of activities undertaken, especially for the lower (working) class. Laws led to a decline in blood sports, e.g. animal baiting and cock fighting. Upper classes held onto their sports, such as fox hunting. Law makers were from the upper and middle classes, so it was in their interest to support the sports they enjoyed.

4 Class, gender, law and order, education, availability of time, availability of money, availability of space, transport

5 Children between the ages of 5 and 16 must receive an education. Examinations and qualifications are now available in physical education and sport, including sports science. GCE A Level, GCSE, Cambridge National, BTECs and Cambridge Technical qualifications are available in PE/sport. Universities offer a wide range of PE/sport-related degrees.

6 The globalisation of sport is a process that involves sport as a worldwide business and features corporate brands, media coverage and freedom of movement of sport participants, officials and spectators.

7 Promote development of the physical and moral qualities of sport; spread Olympic principles, creating international goodwill; bring together athletes of the world every four years; educate young people through sports in a spirit of better understanding between each other and of friendship, thereby helping to build a peaceful world.

8 Excellence, respect, friendship

9 Any three from: Berlin 1936 – Third Reich ideology; Mexico City 1968 – 'Black Power' demonstration; Munich 1972 – Palestinian terrorism; Moscow 1980 – boycott led by USA; Los Angeles 1984 – boycott led by Soviet Union

Chapter 3.2

1 Deviance describes unacceptable behaviour within a culture. Any behaviour that differs from the perceived social or legal norm is seen as deviant. In sport this may be in the form of illegal performance-enhancing drugs/doping, violence, match fixing, bribery or illegal sports betting.

2 Pressure to succeed can affect a performer's judgement and decision making, pressure from coaches, political pressures, high monetary rewards for winning and lucrative sponsorship deals, some performers think 'everyone else is doing it'

3 Any three from: desire to win so overwhelming it leads to violence, nature of activity – physical sports like ice hockey more prone to violence, frustration of events, alcohol and social drugs or performance-enhancing drugs, rivalries, media increasing tensions, perception of unfairness or poor officiating, deindividuation.

4 Match fixing is when a sports competition is played to a completely or partly pre-determined result. This is against the law. Match fixing requires contacts to be made between corrupt players, coaches and team officials.

5 Growing public interest and spectatorship, more media interest, professionalism, advertising, sponsorship

6 Television: terrestrial, satellite and pay-per-view; radio: local and national stations, dedicated sports stations; printed press: newspapers and magazines; the internet; social media; cinema

7 A commodity is an article that can be traded. In this case, sport is the article that can be sold to different media outlets or companies that wish to associate their brand with a particular sport.

8 The golden triangle is the interdependence and influences of three factors of sport, sponsorship and the media – each aspect influences the others.

9 Identifying potential talent, supporting an athlete's lifestyle, supporting an athlete's coaching, supporting through research sports science and sports medicine, providing a World Class Programme or pathway to success

10 The main role of UK Sport is to invest National Lottery funds and income from central government to maximise the performance of UK athletes in the Olympic and Paralympic Games and global sporting events. Success is measured by medals won and the number of medallists developed.

11 Any two from: 1 Most HE institutions offer university sports scholarships or bursaries. This enables access to special support services. 2 Many top sports facilities are located at universities, so HE is increasingly involved in the development

of sporting excellence in the UK. 3 The Talented Athletes Scholarship Scheme (TASS), and in Scotland the Winning Students Scheme (WSS), are both government-funded sport programmes, delivered through a partnership between universities and NGBs. 4 Some universities host centres of sporting excellence, which can be linked to a National Sports Institute.

12 Any four from: 1 When assessing whether someone has the potential to be an athlete, e.g. assessing bone density and internal body fat. 2 Health screening devices. 3 Prosthetic devices (e.g. Springlite). 4 Wheelchair devices with slanted back wheels allowing tennis players to move across the court quickly. 5 Improved access to buildings, e.g. specialist hoists at swimming pools. 6 Rehabilitation and elite training facilities with state of the art equipment. 7 Different simulated competitive environments, e.g. surf simulators. 8 Improved sports surfaces and artificial lighting. 9 Provision of equipment for elite athletes. 10 Use of composite material in rackets and protective gear, making them lighter. 11. Improvement in the design of trainers and sports footwear. 12 Development of the hypoxic chamber. 13 Precision hydration techniques. 14 More effective physiological laboratory testing for athletes. 15 Gait analysis in runners to help avoid injury. 16 Heart rate monitors and GPS watches helping to monitor activity and motivate performance.

13 Any two from: 1 Sports use instant replay to help officials make the right decision. 2 Improved detection of doping. 3 Improved detection of foul play. 4 Better timing devices.

14 Any two from: 1 It has increased entertainment through the use of action-replays and slow-motion playback. 2 During live sports events, giant screens show the action and also replays. 3 Multiple camera angles allow spectators to enjoy every aspect of performance, and see whether officiating decisions are correct. 4 Performance is analysed at intervals by pundits, using motion-capture analysis. 5 Constant interruptions can interfere with the flow of an event and can irritate viewers. 6 It could reduce the numbers of people attending live sport events.

Exam practice answers

Chapter 1.1a

1 [2 marks] Movement: plantar flexion; agonist: gastrocnemius/soleus.

2 [1 mark for each] A ball and socket; B (medial) deltoid; C latissimus dorsi/pectoralis major; D concentric.

3 Upward [sub max 2]: 1 It is the agonist or prime mover. 2 It causes extension or movement (of the elbow joint). 3 This is a concentric contraction/it shortens under tension.
Downward [sub max 2]: 4 It is (still) the agonist or prime mover. 5 It controls flexion or movement (of the elbow joint). 6 This is an eccentric contraction/it lengthens under tension.

4 (4 marks from) 1 High/higher proportion of slow twitch or type 1 or SO muscle fibres most likely to perform successfully in or choose aerobic or endurance or low intensity, long duration activities. 2 Any suitable example of endurance activity e.g. marathon running. 3 High/higher proportion of type 2a or FOG muscle fibres most likely to perform successfully in or choose speed endurance activities or team games. 4 Any suitable example of speed endurance activities e.g. 400 m, 800 m, 1500 m. 5 High/higher proportion of fast twitch or type 2b or FG muscle fibres most likely to perform successfully in or choose anaerobic or explosive or high intensity, short duration activities. 6 Any suitable example of explosive activity e.g. throwing event, 100 m sprint. 7 (mix) (more even) mix of muscle fibre types may perform successfully in both aerobic and anaerobic activity/they may be good at team games (with varying intensities of activity). 8 Type 1, 2a and 2b (for mix)/any suitable example of aerobic and anaerobic activity e.g. 'can do both sprinting and long distance runs'.

Chapter 1.1b

1 [5 marks from] 1 (Venous return) Increased venous return/more blood enters the atria or heart/increased blood flow back to the heart. 2 (Atrial stretch) The right atrium stretches. 3 (SA node) SA node increases rate of firing/SA node increases heart rate. 4 (Ventricular stretch) More blood enters ventricles causing them to stretch further/increased EDV or end diastolic volume. 5 (Strength of contraction) This increases the strength of contraction or recoil (of heart wall or ventricles)/ESV or end systolic volume. 6 (Stroke volume) This increases stroke volume/forces more blood out per beat. 7 (Temperature) Body temperature increases which increases heart rate. 8 (Nerve impulses) This increases speed of nerve impulses (to SA node). Outcome: 9 (Cardiac output increases) CO = SV × HR/cardiac output = SV × HR.

2 [5 marks from; sub max 4 for contraction phase] (Contraction phase) 1 (SA node) Sinoatrial or SA node or SAN receives or initiates or sends an impulse. 2 (Atria contract/impulse spreads across atria) This causes atrial systole or contraction of atria/atrial depolarisation. 3 (Blood to ventricles) This causes the remaining blood (in the atria) to be pushed (actively) into the ventricles (during ventricular diastole). 4 (AV node) Impulse reaches atrio-ventricular or AV node or 5 (Purkinje) impulse distributed or continues down the bundle(s) of His/impulse distributed throughout or to the Purkinje fibres (and only if point 4 or 5 awarded or BofH or Purkinje fibres identified) 6 (Ventricles contract) This causes ventricular systole or contraction of ventricles/ventricular depolarisation/blood pushed or ejected from ventricles. (Relaxation phase) 7 (No impulse) Repolarisation occurs/there is no impulse. 8 (Atria fill) Atria fill with blood (during atrial diastole). 9 (Atrial pressure) (pressure builds in atria) Blood travels (passively) into the ventricles.

3 [2 marks] 1 (Combines) with or in haemoglobin/as oxyhaemoglobin or HbO_2. 2 (Dissolved) in plasma.

4 [3 marks from] 1 Oxygen diffuses or moves from the alveoli to the blood/oxygen diffuses down the diffusion or pressure or concentration gradient/oxygen travels from high partial pressure or concentration to low partial pressure or concentration. 2 There is a high partial pressure or concentration of oxygen or pO_2 in the alveoli. 3 (During exercise) muscles use more oxygen. 4 (So) there is a low(er) partial pressure or concentration of oxygen or pO_2 in the blood. 5 There is a large(r) or steep(er) or increased diffusion or pressure or concentration gradient of oxygen. 6 More oxygen diffuses or moves (from the alveoli) to the blood/increased or faster rate of diffusion of oxygen (from the alveoli) to the blood.

5 [4 marks from] 1 (Active) Expiration becomes active. 2 (Muscles relax) External intercostals and diaphragm relax. 3 (Additional muscles contract) Internal intercostals or rectus abdominus or transverse abdominus or obliques contract. 4 (Rib cage) (This) pulls the rib cage or ribs down and in 5 (Diaphragm) (and) forces the diaphragm up (further or with more force). 6 (Thoracic cavity volume) Decreasing the volume of the thoracic cavity/decreasing the volume in the lungs. 7 (Thoracic cavity pressure) Increasing the pressure within the thoracic cavity or in the lungs. 8 (Air) Forcing (more) air out of the lungs/increasing tidal volume/increasing volume of air expired/increasing rate of breathing or expiration.

Chapter 1.1c

1 [3 marks from] 1 The only usable form of energy in the human body/energy currency that powers all forms of biological work. 2 High energy phosphate compound/the phosphate bonds are high energy bonds/a store of potential energy. 3 When the phosphate bond is broken, energy is released/ATP is broken down to release energy/$ATP \rightarrow ADP + P + energy$. 4 An exothermic reaction/facilitating enzyme is ATPase. 5 Can be resynthesised (via the energy systems/with or without oxygen). 6 The breakdown and resynthesis of ATP is a reversible reaction.

2 [5 marks in total] 1 The alactacid component occurs first 2 using some of the excess post-exercise oxygen consumption. 3 This process restores the ATP (and) PC stores depleted during exercise. 4 The energy for these (reversible) endothermic reactions 5 is made available by the aerobic breakdown of fats and carbohydrate/uses aerobic system. 6 The alactacid component takes between 2 and 3 minutes for full recovery 7 and uses up to 4 litres of oxygen/O_2 consumption remains high. 8 It takes approximately 30 seconds to resynthesise 50 per cent of PC stores. 9 During this component the myoglobin oxygen stores are replenished.

3 Levels mark scheme
At Level 3 [8–10 marks] the candidate explains fully ATP/PC and glycolytic energy system, explaining advantages and disadvantages. Many relevant practical examples are used.
At Level 2 [5–7 marks] the candidate explains, but is at times descriptive. There are few advantages and disadvantages fully explained. There are few relevant practical examples.
At Level 1 [1–4 marks] the candidate is mostly descriptive with little or no detail. Very few or no practical examples are used.

Indicative content

1 (ATP) – energy currency of body/stores last up to 2 seconds/ATPase/structure of ATP. 2 (ATP resynthesis)/reversible reaction/exothermic/endothermic reactions. 3 Energy continuum (accept graph)/systems do not work in isolation/they interact to resynthesise ATP/energy system thresholds/the point at which one system is taken over by another as the predominant system. 4 Exercise intensity and duration of the activity being undertaken will affect which energy system is predominant: high intensity/short duration – predominant systems are ATP/PC and LA; low to medium intensity/long duration – predominant system will be aerobic. 5 Fitness level of the performer will affect which energy system is used/and when/thresholds will change depending upon training done/oxygen supply will vary/fuel available will vary/enzyme activation levels will vary. 6 ATP/PC system: ATP can be resynthesised via ATP/PC system/alactic system/PC system/sufficient detail about this system, e.g. involves coupled reactions/PC is broken down into P + C + energy. This is an exothermic reaction. Energy released + ADP + P ------ATP. Site = muscle cell sarcoplasm. Enzyme = creatine kinase. 7 Identify use with a high intensity and short duration activity: suitable example/up to 10 seconds. 8 Advantages of this system identified : no fatiguing by-products are produced/allows for the quick resynthesis of ATP/doesn't need oxygen or few reactions/PC can be quickly resynthesised (so recovery is quick)/50 per cent recovery in 30 seconds/100 per cent recovery in 180 seconds/PC is readily available in the muscle. 9 Disadvantages of this system identified: only small amounts of fuel stored in muscle cell (PC)/low energy yield/only 1 ATP resynthesized/can only provide energy for short period of time/210 seconds. 10 Lactic acid system: ATP can be resynthesised via lactic acid system/lactacid system/anaerobic glycolysis/sufficient detail about this system e.g. glucose is (partially) broken down by the enzyme phosphofructokinase (PFK) into pyruvic acid/pyruvate. This is further broken down into lactic acid by the enzyme lactate dehydrogenase (LDH). Site = muscle cell sarcoplasm. Glucose is stored as glycogen. Glycogen is broken down by the enzyme glycogen phosphorylase (GPP) into glucose. 11 Identify use with a high intensity and short duration activity: suitable example 10–180 seconds. 12 Advantages of this system identified: large potential fuel store of glycogen available (stored in muscles and liver)/requires few reactions/can work anaerobically/in the absence of oxygen/can provide energy quickly/faster/quicker (than the aerobic energy system). 13 Disadvantages of this system

identified: produces the by-product lactic acid/ reduces pH/inhibits enzyme action/causes pain/ stimulates pain receptors/causes fatigue/(relatively) low yield of ATP (in comparison to aerobic system)/ long recovery.

Chapter 1.1d

[5 marks total] [sub max 4 marks from] 1 Decrease in (atmospheric) pressure causes increase in breath frequency or breathing or ventilation rate. 2 Partial pressure of oxygen or of pO_2 in the (atmospheric) air or the alveoli is low or reduced or less (than at sea level). 3 This reduces or gives low(er) concentration or diffusion gradient of oxygen at the alveoli or between the alveoli and blood. 4 Less oxygen diffuses into the capillaries or blood. 5 Less oxygen combines with haemoglobin/haemoglobin not fully saturated (at lungs)/less oxygen is transported/ less oxygen in the blood. 6 This reduces or gives a low(er) concentration or diffusion gradient of oxygen at muscle or tissue or between blood and muscle or tissue. 7 Less oxygen diffuses into the muscle (cell) or tissue or myoglobin. 8 Less oxygen available for (aerobic) respiration. 9 Hypoxia or hypoxic conditions at high altitude/impact on overall performance while at altitude.

[sub max 1 mark] 10 Performance (of endurance events) deteriorates or decreases at altitude/ performers fatigue faster/accelerated OBLA/decrease in VO_2max or aerobic capacity/detraining occurs/ increase muscle fatigue. 11 Increased altitude can cause hyperventilation which will decrease performance.

Chapter 1.2a

1 [4 marks from] 1 Method used = glycogen loading/CHO loading. 2 Starts 1 week before competition. 3 Day 1: intense exercise (deplete glycogen stores). 4 Days 2–3: high protein/ high fat diet. 5 Day 4: intense exercise (deplete glycogen stores further). 6 Days 5–7: high CHO diet and tapering training or rest. 7 This super-compensates and muscles store more CHO than usual.

2 [4 marks from] 1 Named aid – HGH, anabolic steroid or EPO. 2 Benefits: increased muscle mass and strength. 3 Increased recovery rate. 4 Increased intensity and duration of training. 5 Risks: HGH – abnormal bone and muscle development. 6 Enlargement of vital organs. 7 Increased risk of cancer and diabetes. 8 Anabolic

steroids – liver damage. 9 Heart failure. 10 Acne, hormonal disturbances. 11 EPO increased blood viscosity. 12 Decreased cardiac output. 13 Increased risk of blood clots and heart disease.

3 [3 marks from] 1 Used post-event to speed up recovery. 2 Blood vessels constrict and blood is drained away from muscles, removing LA. 3 Once out of ice, capillaries dilate and 'new' blood flows back to the muscles, bringing fresh oxygen. 4 Reduced core body temperature, decreased sweating, dehydration and early fatigue. 5 Decreased chance of injury pain and swelling.

Chapter 1.2b

1 [3 marks from] Identification of adaptation and explanation (both needed to gain mark). 1 Muscle hypertrophy/muscles bigger – muscles therefore stronger. 2 Hyperplasia/more fibres/fibres split – muscle fibres therefore generate more force. 3 Increase in mitochondria/increase in myoglobin stores – more oxygen transported within muscle cell/increases endurance capability/delays fatigue/ delays OBLA. 4 Increase in glycogen/fat stores – more food fuel for aerobic respiration/medium/ low intensity work. 10 Increased efficiency of lactic acid system/anaerobic glycolysis. 5 Increase in ATP/PC stores – more fuel for anaerobic respiration/high intensity work. 6 Increased buffering capacity – greater tolerance to lactic acid/delays threshold. 7 Recruitment of more motor units – generates greater strength of contraction. 8 Improved co-ordination of muscle fibre recruitment – FOG/FG motor units can be recruited quicker/allowing for a larger force in a shorter space of time

2 a) Test A – (NCF) multi-stage fitness test/Queens College step test/Cooper 12-minute run test. NB: Any suitable test that gives a 'predicted' VO_2max score, so direct gas analysis would be incorrect. Fitness component B – Muscular/ strength endurance

b) Answers MUST be explained. Both heart and muscles must be addressed. [sub max 2 for either] Reason/explanation Heart: 1 Large/strong heart/hypertrophy able to contract with more force/contractility of myocardium – improved/greater efficiency at pumping blood/O_2 to the muscles. 2 Low resting heart rate/bradycardia – greater efficiency at pumping blood/oxygen to the working muscles 3 Larger stroke volume/ (maximal) cardiac output – more blood/

oxygen pumped per beat into the systemic circulatory system/per unit of time. Skeletal muscle: 4 Large myoglobin stores – more efficient transport of oxygen (from the blood capillaries to the mitochondria). 5 Many mitochondria allows greater use of aerobic respiration/less time spent on anaerobic respiration. 6 High enzyme activity – increases rate of glycogen/fat breakdown (making aerobic system more efficient). 7 Large stores glycogen/fats – more fuel available to break down for ATP/resynthesis/ energy. 8 Large number of SO muscle fibres – more suited to aerobic/endurance work.

3 (Description of PNF) [sub max 3] 1 Form of passive stretching with a partner/apparatus. 2 Joint taken to a position just beyond its point of resistance. 3 Performs an isometric contraction (for 6–10 seconds). 4 Muscle is relaxed and stretched again, repeated 3 times. (Explanation) [sub max 3] 5 (Isometric contraction) inhibits the stretch reflex. 6. Muscle spindle no longer detects a stretch in muscle 7. so message to CNS is stopped allowing muscle to stretch further. 8 Golgi tendon detects increase in muscle tension (during isometric contraction). 9 Message sent to CNS. 10 CNS sends message back causing muscle to relax/tension reduced 11 allowing muscle to stretch further. 12 Message to antagonistic muscle telling it to contract.

Chapter 1.2c

1 [6 marks] 1 Cool-down lasts 20–30 minutes. 2 Gradually decreases in intensity. 3 Has several stages: moderate intensity activity, to maintain HR, aid venous return and remove waste; and stretching exercise to reduce muscle tension and lower temperature. 4 Maintain heart rate – to maintain blood flow and metabloc activity, flushing muscle tissue with oxygenated blood. 5 Aid the removal of lactic acid – enhancing future performances, delaying fatigue and injuries. 6 Aid the healing process.

2 [4 marks from] 1 Increase body temperature. 2 Preparing body physiologically. 3 Increase elasticity of muscles, tendons and ligaments. 4 Improves antagonistic co-ordination. 5 Preparing body psychologically/mentally performers are ready for the task ahead. 6 Minimise the risk of injury.

3 [4 marks from; 1 mark for definition] Definition: rehabilitation is the process of restoring full function after an injury has occurred. 1

Rehabilitation depends on an accurate diagnosis and specialist treatment. 2 Early stage: gentle exercise encouraging damaged tissue to heal. 3 Mid stage: progressive loading of connective tissues and bones to develop strength. 4 Late stage: functional exercises and drills to ensure body is ready to return to training.

Chapter 1.3a

1 Levels mark scheme
At Level 3 [8–10 marks] responses are likely to include: accurate definitions of three of Newton's laws, with detailed explanation linked to tennis serve.
At Level 2 [5–7 marks] responses are likely to include: satisfactory definitions of Newton's laws, with satisfactory application to tennis serve.
At Level 1 [1–4 marks] responses are likely to include: Newton's laws defined with limited success, with limited application to tennis serve.
(Definitions) 1 Newton 1/law of inertia. 2 A body will remain in a state of rest or uniform motion unless an (external) force acts upon it/a body doesn't move unless a force is applied to it/a moving body continues to move with the same velocity or in the same direction at the same speed unless a force is applied to it. 3 Newton 2/ law of acceleration. 4 The acceleration or rate of change of momentum or velocity of a body is proportional to the (size of) the force/the larger the force the greater the acceleration of the body; and takes place in the direction in which the force 5 Newton 3/law of reaction. 6 For every action or force there is an equal and opposite reaction. Newton's laws of motion – explanation applied to tennis serve: (Newton 1 to tennis serve) 7 (ball) the tennis ball remains in the server's hand until s/he applies a force to the ball to toss it. 8 (ball) the tennis ball will continue to travel vertically up or down (from the toss) until the force of the racket head changes its direction. 9 (player) the player needs to apply a force to the ground to allow them to stretch up or jump to hit the ball. (Newton 2 to tennis serve) 10 (ball) the harder the player hits the ball the faster it will travel in the direction it has been hit. 11 (player) the greater the force applied to the ground the faster or further the player will jump into the air. (Newton 3 to tennis serve) 12 (ball) the racket strings apply a force to the ball and the ball applies an equal and opposite force to the strings or vice versa. 13 (ball) when bouncing the ball before the serve the ball exerts a downwards force on

the ground and the ground exerts an equal and opposite force on the ball. 14 (player) to jump to hit the ball, the player applies a (downward or action) force on the ground

2 [5 marks from; sub max 4 with no example] 1 (height of CofM) The lower the centre of mass or gravity the more stable or balanced/ the higher the centre of mass or gravity the less stable or balanced/(low CofM) performer has higher inertia or can resist external forces 2 (e.g.) a (rugby) player lowers their centre of mass or gravity to prepare for a tackle. 3 (line of gravity) Line of gravity or centre of mass within base of support creates a balanced or stable position/line of gravity or centre of mass moving away from centre of base of support reduces balance/line of gravity or centre of mass outside base of support creates an unbalanced or unstable position 4 (e.g.) a gymnast performing a handstand keeps line of gravity or centre of mass within base of support to remain balanced or stable/sprinter moves their centre of mass or gravity in front of the body/ close to hands in the set position to enable a faster start. 5 (base of support) A wide(r) base of support allows greater movement of centre of mass or gravity giving better stability or balance/allows greater margin for error before unstable position reached/or vice versa 6 (e.g.) in a headstand a gymnast will be able to remain stable (or not overbalance) for longer (than a gymnast in a handstand). 7 (angular motion) By moving the centre of mass or gravity outside line of action of force a performer can create an eccentric force or rotation or spin or angular motion 8 (e.g.) a gymnast leans forward before applying force at feet (that travels outside centre of mass) to perform forward roll. 9 (linear motion) By moving the centre of mass or gravity inside line of action of force a performer can create a linear or direct force or linear motion 10 (e.g.) a performer will apply force that travels through centre of mass to perform a vertical jump. 11 (take-off) By raising the centre of mass or gravity at take off a body can remain in the air longer or gain more height 12 (e.g.) a high jumper raises arms at take-off to raise the centre of mass or gravity to gain more height/a long jumper raises their arms to raise the centre of mass or gravity to remain in flight for longer.

Chapter 1.3b

1 Levels mark scheme
At Level 3 [10–8 marks] responses will show understanding of the concepts involved in the law of conservation of angular momentum and correctly identify the axis of rotation. There will be a full, coherent explanation of the changes that take place during both phases of the throw using the correct technical language. Responses at the lower end of this level may not demonstrate the link with the analogue of Newton's first law of motion.
At Level 2 [5–7 marks] responses should identify correct axis of rotation and show some understanding of the concepts involved. Explanation should be coherent but points will be missed and phases of the throw may not be fully related.
At Level 1 [1–4 marks] responses will be limited and explanation lack clarity. For the top of this level the correct axis of rotation should be identified and phases of the throw should be referred to.

Indicative content
1 (Axis of rotation) Longitudinal. 2 (Concept 1) Analogue of Newton 1 states that an athlete will continue to rotate with constant angular momentum 3 unless acted upon by an unbalanced/net/external torque/moment of force. 4 (Concept 2) MI/ Moment of inertia is the body's resistance to rotate/ change angular motion. 5 (Concept 3) Angular velocity/speed/is the rate of spin of a body. ω (Start of rotation). 6 Generate angular momentum. 7 By applying moment of force/torque to athlete. 8 Friction/force at feet being applied outside axis of rotation/longitudinal axis. 9 Large MI/body parts/ arms and leg a long way from axis of rotation. 10 Small ω/angular velocity/rate of spin. (During throw) 11 Reduce MI/bring body parts/arm and leg/towards axis of rotation. 12 Increases ω/angular velocity/rate of spin. 13 Release speed of discus is greater/discus is thrown further.

2 [2 marks in total] 1 (Action) force/F (from edge of ball). 2 Weight/W/mg (from CM).

3 [4 marks in total from] [1 mark max for identifying two of Newton's laws] (Points must relate to correct law) 1 (Newton 1) The ball remains stationary until it is kicked/force applied. 2 (Newton 2) –The ball's acceleration/rate of change in momentum is proportional to the size of the (resultant) force acting upon it/larger the force the further/faster it will go. 3 The ball will accelerate in the direction at the

(resultant) force. 4 (Newton 3) The foot applies a force to the ball, therefore 5 the ball applies an equal and opposite force to the foot.

4 [3 marks for 3 from] (must have sporting example to gain mark) 1 Longitudinal (top to bottom) e.g. spinning skater or equivalent. 2 Transverse (side to side) e.g. somersault or equivalent. 3 Frontal (front to back) e.g. cartwheel or equivalent.

5 [4 marks for 4 from; (sub max of 2 marks from centre of mass)] 1 CM is the point at which a body is balanced in all directions. 2 It is the point at which weight appears to act. 3 Its position depends on the distribution of mass/can change position when body shape changes. 4 It follows a predetermined flight path/height that CM reaches is predetermined at take-off.
[(sub max of 3 marks from (Fosbury Flop)] 5 Due to arching/hyperextension of back/shape of FF 6 CM can be positioned outside the body. 7 Therefore, CM can pass underneath the bar as body goes over it 8 whereas in other techniques/straddle/western roll 9 where CM stays within body 10 CM has to pass over the bar.

6 [4 marks for 4 from] 1 Discus is an aerofoil shape. 2 Takes on an appropriate angle of attack to the direction of motion. 3 Air has to travel further over the top of the discus. 4 Air travels faster over the top of the discus. 5 This creates a low pressure area on top of the discus 6 called the Bernoulli principle. 7 Air tries to move from high to low pressure (creating the lift force). 8 Makes flight path non parabolic/asymmetrical. 9 Lengthens flight path/discus travels further/is in air for longer.

7 [5 marks for 5 from] 1 Friction (between wheels and track) acts against cyclist. 2 Air resistance/fluid friction (acting against cyclist moving through air). 3 Acts in opposite direction of motion. 4 Increases as cyclist's speed increases. 5 Cyclist needs to reduce forces to achieve a higher speed/velocity. 6 Reduce friction by using thin/high pressured tyres. 7 Reduce friction by streamlining. 8 Creating smooth flow around cyclist/reducing turbulent flow/drag reducing profile drag/turbulence behind. 9 Reduce frontal/forward cross-sectional area. 10 Reduce surface friction of air on cyclist/specialist smooth clothing/helmet. 11 Reduce turbulence behind cyclist/change body shape to smooth air flow behind cyclist.

8 [6 marks for 6 from] 1 Body forms an aerofoil shape. 2 Creating angle of attack. 3 Air travels further under cyclist. 4 Air travels faster under cyclist. 5 Creates low pressure under cyclist.

6 Bernoulli force formed from high to low pressure. 7 Bernoulli force downwards/down force.

9 [5 marks in total from]

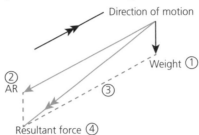

[Diagram, see above – sub max 4] 1 Weight acting downwards. 2 Air resistance acting opposite to the direction of motion and significantly larger than weight. 3 Use of parallelogram Law. 4 Resultant force. [Explanation – sub max 4] 5 RF shows the direction of acceleration. 6 Acceleration is (almost) in the opposite direction to motion therefore shuttle will decelerate/slow down (rapidly). 7 Makes flight path asymmetrical/non parabolic. 8 Shortens flight path.

10 [5 marks in total from] [Generation of spin – sub max 3] 1 Eccentric/off centre/moment of force must be applied. 2 Force applied outside CM of the ball. 3 Gives ball angular momentum/motion. (Effect of spin on bounce – sub max 3] 4 Topspin makes ball shoot forward/accelerate off surface/move at a smaller angle to the surface. 5 Backspin makes ball sit up/decelerate off surface/move at a greater angle to the surface 6 Sidespin has little or no effect on bounce of the ball/allows ball to keep on swerving in same direction.

Chapter 2.1

1 1 (Simple skill explanation) [1 mark] One or few stimuli to process/limited information to process/one or few decisions to make/skill with few sub-routines/limited cognitive demand/limited perceptual requirements/less feedback/limited decision making. 2 (Example of simple skill) [1 mark] swimming/running/sprinting/sprint start; (closed skills e.g.) throwing/kicking/jumping (in a closed situation). 3 (Complex skill explanation) [1 mark] Many stimuli to process/lots of information to process/many decisions to make/increased perceptual requirements/more feedback/skill with more or many sub-routines. 4 (Example of complex skill) [1 mark] Batting or bowling in cricket/basketball dribble/tennis serve/hitting a ball/gymnastics routine/somersault/high jump/triple jump/golf swing; (open skills e.g.) receiving a ball/delivering a pass (in an open situation).

2 Description and suitable practical example needed for each mark. [4 marks for 4 from] 1 (Part) Practise by splitting or breaking down skill into sub-routines or sections, e.g. practice the tennis serve by doing the toss up first/triple jump or other suitable example. 2 (Whole) Practise by doing the total or complete or entire movement/not breaking skill into sub-routines or parts, e.g. tennis serve/penalty kick in football or other suitable example. 3 (Progressive part) Practise in stages that are linked or chained/e.g. gymnastics or trampoline routine/triple jump/ gymnast learning a roll then a jump, then roll and jump together/athlete practises the hop, then step, then hop and step, etc., or other suitable example. 4 (Whole–part–whole) Practise the complete skill, then split it into sub-routines and then practise complete skill again/e.g. practise the tennis serve completely to start then concentrate on the toss up of the ball and then integrate this back into a practice of the complete skill/for teaching front crawl, or other suitable example.

3 [sub max 4 for any one phase; at least one mark from each phase needed for max marks] (Cognitive/first/beginner phase) 1 Visual – demonstration/video/poster (of a movement)/ gives mental picture/gives idea of what skill should look like. 2 Verbal – giving (basic) information of what needs to be done/ positive feedback/positive reinforcement/to correct errors/keep verbal guidance simple/ to focus on key points. 3 Manual – (physically) supporting movements to increase safety or confidence or timing/to reduce risk/to learn basic body position/to get feel of movement/ to develop kinaesthesis. 4 Mechanical – using a mechanical aid/stabilisers on a bike/swimming float/to increase safety or confidence/to reduce risk/to learn basic body position/to get feel of movement/to develop kinaesthesis/helps understanding/helps you understand what you need to do. (Associative/second/intermediate phase) 5 Visual – demonstration of more difficult or new movements or skills. 6 Verbal – feedback to refine or correct or develop skills/to introduce tactics or strategies. 7 Manual – for more specific or more advanced body position or movement/ for safety or confidence/should be gradually or completely removed. 8 Mechanical – twisting belt in trampolining or bowling machine in cricket (or equivalent) to practise more complex actions or to groove skill.

(Autonomous/third/advanced phase) 9 Visual – demonstration of difficult moves/as reminder of basic moves/show video of a top class performer/ video analysis/allows analysis. 10 Verbal – (advanced) tactics or strategies/technical detail/ discussing outcomes/negative feedback as well as positive/predominant or best method (at this stage). 11 Manual – for highly complex or difficult moves/limit manual at this stage to encourage kinaesthesia or kinaesthetic awareness/ used less in this stage. 12 Mechanical – a bowling machine set at a difficult setting (to stretch and challenge).

4 [1 mark only for each numbered point] 1 (Short-term sensory store/STSS) STSS is where: info enters (from senses or display)/selective attention happens/important information filtered in/ irrelevant info filtered out/capacity limitless/ duration < 1 second. 2 (Example for STSS) concentrating on the ball when hitting or catching/blocking out crowd noise/position of team mates or opponents, etc./other suitable examples showing contribution of STSS. 3 (Short-term memory/STM).
STM is where: information is perceived or understood or judged or interpreted/incoming information compared to learned information/ initiates movement/retrieves information (from LTM)/information organised or chunked or encoded/rehearsal helps transition to LTM/ capacity 5–9 items/7+ or –2/duration < 30 seconds/duration increased if info rehearsed. 4 (Example for STM) judging the speed of the ball/ grouping information relating to skill or situation/ other suitable example showing contribution of STM. 5 (Long-term memory/LTM)
LTM is where: information or motor programmes or patterns of movement or schema are stored/ information decoded/information sent back (to STM)/(current) performance associated with previous performances (to recognise strengths and weaknesses)/capacity limitless/duration permanent. 6 (Example for LTM) having or remembering technique of netball shooting/ storage of named MP or sporting technique/other suitable example showing contribution of LTM.

Chapter 2.2

1 [2 marks each from] Extrovert: seeks social situations, likes excitement, lacks concentration, confident. Introvert: does not seek social situations, likes peace and quiet, good at concentrating. [2 marks from] Coaching

consideration: consider arousal levels, consider type of feedback, and consider environmental conditions (crowd, noise levels).

2 [1 mark for] 1 Attitude is a pre-disposition (mixture) of beliefs or feelings or behaviours towards an (attitude) object/something/someone (e.g. training or participation in sport). [3 marks for] Cognitive element which is a belief about training/playing well/participation/health. Affective element which is an emotional aspect such as enjoyment/positive feelings/hostility/ negative feelings towards training/playing well/participation/health. Behavioural element which is behaviour towards training/playing/ health/shows commitment/persistence/sticking to the task/trying hard/avoidance behaviours/ giving up.

3 [1 mark for each] Type A: Practical example showing high personal stress levels/anxious/high arousal/apprehensive/intolerant/impatient/works fast/ambitious/aggressive/highly competitive, for example, football player being very anxious and wound-up about playing. Type B: Practical example showing low personal stress/low arousal/ cool under pressure/confident/tolerant/relaxed/ passive/less competitive (than Type A), for example, an athlete being very confident or calm when preparing for a race.

4 (4 marks total) (2 marks for aggression) 1 Definition/explanation – aggression is intent to harm or injure outside the rules of the game. 2 Practical example e.g. throwing a punch at the opposition in a rugby match. Any other suitable example acceptable. (2 marks for assertion) 3 Definition/explanation – assertion is forceful behaviour within the laws of the event. 4 Practical example – e.g. an athlete shoulder-pushing another on the final bend in a 1500 metre race. Any other suitable example acceptable.

5 (4 marks total) (2 marks for trait anxiety) 1 Definition/explanation – trait anxiety is a trait that is enduring in an individual. A performer with high trait anxiety has the predisposition or the potential to react to situations with apprehension. 2. Practical example – e.g. a person who is often anxious in most situations, will be anxious before their first swimming competition. Any other suitable example acceptable. (2 marks for state anxiety) 3 Definition/explanation – state anxiety: an athlete's emotional state at any given time is variable from situation to situation. 4 Practical example – e.g. if a swimmer is experienced and has any competed in many races they may no longer be anxious at the start of a race. Any other suitable example acceptable.

6 Levels mark scheme
At Level 3 [8–10 marks] the candidate explains fully the positive and negative influences of an audience on performance. There is very good use of psychological theories and terminology. Many relevant practical examples are used.
At Level 2 [5–7 marks] the candidate explains, but is at times descriptive. There are few psychological theories and psychological terminology is rarely used. There are few relevant practical examples.
At Level 1 [1–4 marks] the candidate is mostly descriptive with little or no psychological theories. Very few or no practical examples are used.
Indicative content
1 (Drive) Arousal/drive/anxiety increased (drive theory/dominant response/Zajonc's theory. 2 (Drive) Dominant response/habit more likely to occur/learned responses automatic/ motor programmes are run. 3 (Zajonc/inverted U) Weaker players'/novices' performance deteriorates/incorrect dominant response. 4 (Drive/inverted U) Good performances from well learned/stronger/elite/correct dominant response produced. 5 Extroverts likely to perform better with an audience/reticular activating system (RAS) favours extroverts when audience present. 6 Introverts likely to perform worse with an audience/reticular activating system (RAS) does not favour introverts when audience present. 7 (Home/away) If audience in familiar setting performance helped/advantage/disadvantage if away/unfamiliar/hostile environment. 8 (Evaluation apprehension) Anxiety raised by being judged/perceived judgement of others/ evaluation apprehension/the nature of the audience/who is in the audience. 9 (Proximity) Proximity of the audience/how close the crowd is to the player. 10 Distractions/widening of attentional focus/utilisation of too many cues. 11 Attention narrows for those who are used to audiences/high levels of ability/optimum cue utilisation. 12 Gross skills are helped by high arousal, therefore an audience can facilitate performance. 13 Fine or complex skills are more desirable at lower levels of arousal so an audience could inhibit performance.

7 [4 marks from] 1 Can give focus/target that gives sense of direction. 2 Lowers arousal/calms you down. 3 Sharing goal setting can give shared responsibility/can lower anxiety. 4 Goal setting can include goals that are attainable/success more likely and therefore lower anxiety. 5 Measured goals can give evidence of improvement/gives reward/positive reinforcement that can improve

confidence/lower anxiety. 6 Goal setting that is timed correctly or appropriately can give sense of control/steps towards success that can control anxiety. 7 Exciting/inspiring goal setting can motivate and enthuse/encourage/be enjoyable which may control anxiety. 8 Recorded goals attained gives sense of achievement/progress which controls anxiety. 9 (Negative view) poor/irrelevant/inappropriate goal setting can lead to high anxiety.

8 [6 marks from] 1 (Situational characteristics) Effective leadership will take into account the situation. Or the environmental circumstances may dictate a certain strategy of leadership to encourage participation. Or, for example, dangerous environment so autocratic style needed. 2 (Leader characteristics) Effective leadership is related to the personality of the leader. Or the personality/experience/ability of the leader will influence whether a person participates or not. 3 (Member characteristics) Effective leadership is related to the nature/type/motivation of group members. Or they may be friendly and therefore encouraging. 4 (Required behaviour) The style of leadership that is suitable/appropriate will either motivate or demotivation to participate. 5 (Actual behaviour) The leader's behaviour can have a direct impact on participation. 6 (Preferred behaviour) What is wanted from group members. Or if you lead the way/style that the group members want you to then you may motivate/win hearts and minds and increase participation. 7 Consequences are good/more participation/more satisfaction/enjoyment if the needs of the group match the leader's behaviour. 8 Consequences are good/more participation/more satisfaction/enjoyment if the situational demands are met by the leader's behaviour. 9 Leaders should be flexible/can change/can adapt to differing styles (to accommodate the differing needs to improve participation and enjoyment). 10 You are more likely to participate if you are satisfied/pleased/see the value with the leader/see leader as a role model.

9 [6 marks from] 1 Objective sport situation is, for example, a penalty kick in football. 2 Trait sport confidence (SC-trait) is innate/born with it, underlying potential, stable, for example, the football player might have an in-built high level of confidence. 3 SC-trait affects state sports confidence (SC-state)/self-efficacy, for example, the football player's confidence in taking the kick depends on SC-trait levels. 4 Competitive orientation is the level of competitiveness that the performer may have, set challenging goals, for example, the football player is naturally

very competitive and really wants to score the penalty. 5 State sports confidence (SC-state) is the confidence you have in an actual/specific situation or environment. It is changeable, for example, the football player has high confidence in scoring the penalty kick. 6 Behavioural responses are the actions or performance outcomes, for example, the football player kicks the ball at the goal. 7 The subjective outcomes are how the performer judges or interprets the outcomes/performance, for example, the football player interprets that a good goal has been scored from the penalty and the goalkeeper was well beaten. 8 The subjective outcomes affect future SC-trait/future competitiveness, for example, the football player's view of the goal may make him more confident generally and more competitive. 9 The subjective outcomes therefore eventually affect state sports confidence (SC-state); how you interpret your actions affects your confidence in the future. SC-trait and competitiveness and SC-state all affect confidence/self-efficacy.

10 [4 marks from] 1 (Attribution) Encourage attribution of any previous failure or learned helplessness to controllable/internal factors or unstable factors or don't blame yourself/give other reasons for past failures, for example lack of effort/inappropriate goals in netball. 2 (Reinforcement) Give verbal persuasion, encouragement/praise/reward, positive reinforcement, for example, the coach praises a young volleyball player's serve to raise confidence. 3 (Control arousal/stress management) Control arousal, give them anxiety or stress management strategies, emotional control or control arousal, imagery or mental practice/rehearsal or visualisation, positive thinking/self-talk or negative thought stopping, somatic strategies to calm down, e.g. biofeedback or PMR, for example, encourage the sprinter to imagine winning the race. 4 (Vicarious) Vicarious experience/see others achieve/show others of similar ability succeeding/show role models to inspire, for example, the diver lacked confidence but saw another diver of a similar ability dive off the top board and this raised her confidence. 5 (Success) Performance accomplishments/give early success to raise confidence/encourage small achievable goals at first/goal setting, highlight previous success/practice/train hard/learn skills/strategies, for example, remind the discus thrower that he has reached a certain distance before. 6 (Educate) Educate or inspire or teach appropriate skills or tactics, show what the player can do to enhance performance, for example, the coach teaches the hockey player new stick skills to beat an opponent. 7 (Others) Show others who are less good or who are less able or who also lack confidence/show them that they are not abnormal or that lack of confidence is not to be ashamed of, for example, show a tennis player a video of other players who have been successful but who show low confidence levels.

Chapter 3.1

1 [4 marks from] 1 Upper class were aristocracy/gentry/were hereditary landowners. 2 Lower/peasant class were peasants who worked manually/mainly on the land. 3 (Upper class took part in) Real tennis/fox hunting: these were sophisticated activities with complex rules or required money to participate. 4 Pedestrianism as patrons (sponsors) of lower class competitors. 5 Cricket as 'gentleman' amateurs. 6 (Lower class took part in) Mob football/dog fighting/prize fighting: these were simple activities/often violent/with few rules. 7 Pedestrianism as competitors, racing and beating others. 8 Cricket as professional/'player'.

2 [4 marks from] 1 Amateurs were not paid. 2 Cricket: Amateurs and professionals played in the same team. 3 Social distinction was preserved through different changing rooms. 4 The lower class professionals bowled and cleaned the kit. 5 Soccer and rugby: The growth of social mixed northern teams led to broken-time payments, where lower classes were paid in order to miss a day's work to play. 6 These payments were against the amateur principles of the upper classes. 7 Golf: Before 1861 there were separate Open Championships for amateurs and professionals. 8 The professionals did not fit in with the image of the gentlemanly game.

3 [2 marks from] [1] Athleticism is a combination of physical endeavour/trying hard and [2] moral integrity/being honourable/truthful/showing good sportsmanship.

4 [3 marks from] 1 Participation of women in physical recreation had dropped dramatically in 1900. 2 Crowds at professional soccer and rugby league became male dominated. 3 Professional sport was mainly watched by male skilled workers, with only a few women. 4 Working-class women were excluded from professional sport by the constraints of time and money.

5 Levels mark scheme
At Level 3 [8–10 marks] responses are likely to show: detailed discussion of political, sporting, social and economic factors of hosting a global sporting event; detailed explanations of advantages and disadvantages of hosting a global sporting event; include a number of relevant sporting examples.
At Level 2 [5–7 marks] responses are likely to show: satisfactory discussion of political, sporting, social and economic factors of hosting a global sporting event; satisfactory explanations of advantages and disadvantages of hosting a global sporting event; include a few relevant sporting examples.
At Level 1 [1–4 marks] responses are likely to show: basic discussion of political, sporting, social and economic factors of hosting a global sporting event; basic explanations of advantages and disadvantages of hosting a global sporting event; include little or no relevant sporting examples.
Indicative content
(Sporting impacts – advantages) 1 Raises the profile of the sport; may lead to increased participation. 2 New or upgraded venues are built. 3 Event can focus on minority sports, which may inspire participation. 4 Increase in funding for sports involved. (Sporting impacts – disadvantages) 5 Events lead to bursts of increased participation, but general current trend is a gradual decline in participation. 6 New facilities can end up not being used after the event. 7 Lesser known non-global sports can suffer. 8 Sports deviance is likely to be highlighted by media at global events. (Social impacts – advantages) 9 More money brought into city or country, which can be used to benefit local population. 10 Events can give pride to the host nation or city and help with 'nation-building'. 11 Improved use of sport facilities by local communities. 12 Can improve transport systems. 13 Accommodation built for the event can be used by the community (Social impacts – disadvantages) 14 Some areas of the country may not get the same benefits as the host city. 15 Some areas of the host country do not benefit from improved infrastructure and transport. 16 Local inhabitants may have to vacate land being used for sport venues. (Economic impacts – advantages) 17 Increased income leads to positive economic impact. More money is bought to host city by those who participate or spectate. 18 More jobs created through building of facilities, transport infrastructure and support for the event. 19 Increase in tourism and related economic benefits during and after the event. 20 Commercial benefits rated to goods sold in the area of the event and also in the sale

of event-related goods. (Economic impacts – disadvantages) 21 Bidding to host an event can be expensive. 22 Events can cause an overall economic loss. 23 Benefits to employment and long-term jobs are often exaggerated. 24 If events or participants are linked with failure, can lead to loss of revenue in merchandising sales. (Political impacts – advantages) 22 Individual political parties and their leaders can gain credit and therefore more votes and reflect well if a bid is successful. 23 Staging an event can bring unity to a country and a sense of purpose. 24 The country or city can be used as a 'shop window' for its culture and commerce and therefore raise the status in the eyes of the world. (Political impacts – disadvantages) 25 If the cost is too high or over budget, it can be a political disadvantage, losing votes and decrease in economic resources. 26 If something goes wrong, e.g. a terrorist attack, politicians have to shoulder responsibility. 27 If host nation does poorly it can reflect badly on the political party. 28 Negative environmental impacts can decrease political popularity. 29 If legacy of event is negative, this can be politically damaging. 30 Protest by athletes or spectators can be embarrassing.

Chapter 3.2

1 [2 marks from] 1 Sports performers are high profile/role models so behaviour might be copied. 2 Sport reflects society, so if there is violence in sport it is because that is what some people 'want'/because society is violent/has violence. 3 Violence in sport by performers can lead to violence among spectators. 4 Violence may put parents off letting their children participate in sports.

2 [sub max 4 from] (Positive) 1 It can improve sports performance. 2 It can make sports safer for performers or spectators/fewer injuries. 3 Sports can be more exciting/entertaining/enjoyable with technology advances. 4 Can help make fairer decision/a fairer contest. 5 Can help spectators see/experience more when watching sport. 6 Can make sports more accessible.
[sub max 4 from] (Negative) 7 But can take away the personal effect/more about the technology than the individual. 8 Technology gives those with money an advantage in performance. 9 Can increase the chance of injury/harm. 10 Can take away the element of chance. 11 Can make some sport less of a spectacle/more predictable.

3 [5 marks from] 1 Growing public interest and spectatorship. 2 More people now play sport at least once a week. 3 There has also been growth in the numbers that spectate. 4 More money is attracted to sports – the greater their spectatorship. 5 More media interest/leading to companies wanting to sponsor events and their participants. 6 Increased professionalism/sporting professionals are now likely to attract sponsorship from commercial organisations. 7 Increased advertising. 8 Opportunities to sell more goods and use sports as a 'billboard'. 9 Increased sponsorship/support of events or performers by providing money or goods.

4 Levels mark scheme
At Level 3 [8–10 marks] responses are likely to include: detailed understanding of the effect of the media on sport (including both advantages and disadvantages), supported by appropriate examples.
At Level 2 [5–7 marks] responses are likely to include: satisfactory understanding of the effect of the media on sport; discussion of the some aspects attempted with some success supported by some examples.
At Level 1 [0–4 marks] responses are likely to include: basic understanding of the effect of the media on sport; a focus on a few aspects; a limited attempt at discussion.

Indicative content
(Performer – positive) 1 Can raise the profile of a performer. 2 Can help develop their career. (Performer – negative) 3 Media can highlight and promote sensational news, which can increase pressure to perform. (Individual sports – positive) 4 Can raise the profile of a sport. 5 Can boost participation numbers, e.g. Wimbledon. 6 Increase financial revenues, in terms of sponsorship and funding for sports events and facilities. 7 Attract more funds for international teams. 8 More minority sports and more coverage of disability sports, e.g. Paralympics. (Individual sports – negative) 9 Media can highlight negative aspects of sport, e.g. hooliganism in football. (Spectator – positive) 10 Increase number of people watching. 11 Rules have been influenced to make sports more accessible to a wider audience. 12 Different types of media are available 24/7, sport is broadcast live all over the world. (Spectator – negative) 13 Through negative coverage – possible promoted hooliganism and unrest among some countries, e.g. England v Germany (football). 14 The cost of subscriptions to satellite TV can be prohibitive.